Introducing Neuropsychology

Introducing Neuropsychology investigates the functions of the brain and explores the relationships between brain systems and human behaviour. It draws on both established findings and cutting edge research. The material is presented in a jargon-free, easy to understand manner and aims to guide students new to the field through current areas of research. John Stirling's *Introducing Neuropsychology* not only covers brain function but gives clinical examples of what happens when different brain regions are damaged.

The text deals first with the basics of neuropsychology, discussing the structures of the central nervous system and methods of research used in neuropsychology. The book covers sensory function, the lateralised nature of the brain and motor control and movement disorders. The author then looks at higher order cortical functions, with chapters on language, memory and amnesia, visual object recognition and spatial processing and attention. A further chapter covers executive functions and describes some psychiatric disorders resulting from dysfunction.

With over 80 illustrations, John Stirling has provided a user-friendly text-book that will be essential reading for those studying neuropsychology within the disciplines of psychology, medicine, clinical psychology and neuroscience.

John Stirling is a Reader in Psychology at Manchester Metropolitan University. He specialises in neuropsychology. He is the author of two previous books, *Psychopathology* (1999), co-written with Jonathan Hellewell, and *Cortical Functions* (1999), both published in the *Routledge Modular Psychology* series, and has also written/co-written numerous journal articles in the areas of neuropsychology, clinical psychology and psychiatry.

Psychology Focus

Series editor: Perry Hinton, University of Luton

The Psychology Focus series provides students with a new focus on key topic areas in psychology. It supports students taking modules in psychology, whether for a psychology degree or a combined programme, and those renewing their qualification in a related discipline. Each short book:

- presents clear, in-depth coverage of a discrete area with many applied examples
- assumes no prior knowledge of psychology
- has been written by an experienced teacher
- has chapter summaries, annotated further reading and a glossary of key terms.

Also available in this series:

Friendship in Childhood and Adolescence
Phil Erwin

Gender and Social Psychology
Vivien Burr

Jobs, Technology and People
Nik Chmiel

Learning and Studying
James Hartley

Personality: A Cognitive Approach
Jo Brunas-Wagstaff

Intelligence and Abilities
Colin Cooper

Stress, Cognition and Health
Tony Cassidy

Types of Thinking
S. Ian Robertson

Psychobiology of Human Motivation
Hugh Wagner

Stereotypes, Cognition and Culture
Perry R. Hinton

Psychology and 'Human Nature'
Peter Ashworth

Abnormal Psychology
Alan Carr

Attitudes and Persuasion
Phil Erwin

The Person in Social Psychology
Vivien Burr

Introducing Neuropsychology

- John Stirling

First published 2002
by Psychology Press
27 Church Road, Hove,
East Sussex, BN3 2FA
www.psypress.co.uk

Simultaneously published in the USA and
Canada
by Taylor & Francis Inc.
29 West 35th Street, New York, NY 10001

*Psychology Press is a member of the Taylor
& Francis Group*

© 2002 John Stirling

Typeset in Sabon by Florence Production Ltd,
Stoodleigh, Devon

Printed and bound in Great Britain
by TJ International Ltd, Padstow, Cornwall

Cover design and illustration by Terry Foley

*British Library Cataloguing in Publication
Data*
A catalogue record for this book is available
from the British Library

*Library of Congress Cataloging-in-
Publication Data*
A catalogue record for this book is available
from the Library of Congress

ISBN 0–415–22759–3 (pbk)
ISBN 0–415–22758–5 (hbk)

'Into the highlands of the mind let me go'

(Adapted from a poem entitled 'Shakespeare' from *A Hundred Poems by Sir William Watson, Selected From His Various Volumes*, NY: Dodd Mead & Co., 1923.)

Contents

List of illustrations   ix
Series preface   xiii
Preface   xv
Acknowledgements   xvii

1 The beginnings of
   neuropsychology   1

2 Methods in neuropsychology   13

3 Lateralisation   31

4 Somatosensation   53

5 Motor control and movement
   disorders   73

6 Language and the brain   103

7 Memory and amnesia   129

8 Visual object recognition and spatial processing   153

9 Attention   181

10 Executive functions   207

11 Summary and concluding thoughts   227

Appendix   235
Further reading   253
Selected neuropsychology web sites   257
Glossary   259
References   265
Index   283

Illustrations

Figures

1.1 A phrenology skull   5
1.2 Some language areas in the brain   8
2.1 Brodmann's cortical areas   16
2.2 Recording of EEG and ERPs   19
2.3 Diagram of CT, MRI and PET   21
2.4 A fMRI scan   22
2.5 (a) Corsi's block-tapping test and
     (b) the Wisconsin card sort test   26
3.1 Externally visible structural asymmetries
     of the human brain   34
3.2 The corpus callosum   35
3.3 Visual pathway from eye to brain   36
3.4 A typical split-brain experiment with objects
     and words   38
3.5 Summary of Levy et al.'s (1972) split-brain
     study   40
3.6 Figures similar to those used by Delis et al.
     (1986)   44
4.1 The process of sensory transduction   56
4.2 The somatosensory pathways   58
4.3 The somatosensory cortex and sensory
     homunculus   60

4.4   A detailed view of the primary somatosensory strip (S1)   61
4.5   Woolsey's whisker barrel study   63
4.6   Summary of Mogilner et al.'s (1993) study   64
4.7   Referred phantom experiences from facial stimulation   66
4.8   Ramachandran's explanation of phantom limb experiences   67
4.9   Basbaum and Fields' (1984) model of pain modulation   70
5.1   Descending 'movement' control pathways   76
5.2   The cerebellum and its connections   80
5.3   Components and connections of the basal ganglia   82
5.4   Direct and indirect basal ganglia pathways   83
5.5   The basal ganglia as a facilitator/inhibitor of action plans   84
5.6   Hierarchical organisation of movement in the frontal lobes   87
5.7   Ideational apraxia   90
6.1   Connectionist models of language   106
6.2   Lichtheim's model of connectivity serving language functions   111
6.3   Left hemisphere areas involved in syntactic processing   119
6.4   The location of the superior tip of the insula (on the left)   124
7.1   Psychological models of memory   132
7.2   The key components in Baddeley's model of working memory   134
7.3   The subdivisions of long-term memory   136
7.4   HM's retrograde and anterograde amnesia   138
7.5   Goldman-Rakic's study of spatial working memory in monkeys   145
7.6   Subdivisions of long-term memory indicating possible anatomical
      substrates of different components   150
8.1   The 'what' and 'where' streams of visual perception   155
8.2   Pohl's double-dissociation study of landmark and object
      discrimination in macaques   156
8.3   Cortical regions typically damaged in apperceptive and associative
      agnosia   161
8.4   Unusual views of objects, and items from the Gollin test   163
8.5   Ellis and Young's model of visual object recognition   165
8.6   A view of ventral regions involved in object and face recognition 171
8.7   Rey-Osterreith figure and WAIS blocks test, and patients' attempts
      to complete these tests   176
9.1   A typical dichotic listening experiment   184
9.2   Two filtering models of attention   185
9.3   The type of array used in visual search studies   186
9.4   An illustration of Posner's (1980) study   187
9.5   Auditory ERPs to attended and non-attended stimuli   190
9.6   Early and late components of an auditory ERP   191
9.7   Brain structures and attention   195
9.8   Typical responses of hemineglect patients in drawing tasks   198

9.9   An illustration of the effects of hemineglect on spatial attention   200
9.10 The sort of picture/story stimulus used by Farah   201
9.11 LaBerge's triangular circuit of attention   204
10.1 A control subject's and frontal patient's attempts at the
      memory for designs test   210
10.2 Typical responses in the WCST   212
10.3 The 'Tower of London' test   215
10.4 Norman and Shallice's supervisory attentional system   220
A1   The lobes of the cortex   236
A2   A neuron (a) and glia (b)   238
A3   A neuron conveying a volley of nerve impulses, and a schematic
      synapse   239
A4   The convergence of an excitatory and inhibitory input on to a
      receiving neuron   242
A5   A medial sagittal view of the adult human brain   245
A6   The corpus callosum   247
A7   The layers of the cortex and a pyramidal neuron   248

Tables

2.1   A single and a double dissociation experiment   28
3.1   Anatomical hemispheric asymmetries   33
6.1   The underlying difficulties of five anomic patients   116
8.1   The results of Farah's meta-analysis of the co-occurrence of
      prosopagnosia, visual agnosia and alexia   170

Series preface

The Psychology Focus series provides short, up-to-date accounts of key areas in psychology without assuming the reader's prior knowledge in the subject. Psychology is often a favoured subject area for study, because it is relevant to a wide range of disciplines such as sociology, education, nursing and business studies. These relatively inexpensive but focused short texts combine sufficient detail for psychology specialists with sufficient clarity for non-specialists.

The series authors are academics experienced in undergraduate teaching as well as research. Each takes a topic within their area of psychological expertise and presents a short review, highlighting important themes and including both theory and research findings. Each aspect of the topic is clearly explained with supporting glossaries to elucidate technical terms.

The series has been conceived within the context of the increasing modularisation which has been developed in higher education over the last decade and fulfils the consequent need for clear, focused, topic-based course material. Instead of following one course of study, students on a modularisation programme are often able to choose modules from a wide range of disciplines to complement the modules they are required to study for a specific degree. It can no longer be assumed that students studying a particular module will necessarily have the same background knowledge (or lack of it!) in that subject. But they will need to familiarise themselves with a particular topic rapidly because a single module in a single topic may be only 15 weeks long, with assessments arising during that period. They may have to combine eight or more modules in a single year to obtain a degree at the end of their programme of study.

One possible problem with studying a range of separate modules is that the relevance of a particular topic or the relationship between topics may not always be apparent. In the Psychology Focus series, authors have drawn where possible on practical and applied examples to support the points being made so that readers can see the wider relevance of the topic under study. Also, the study of psychology is usually broken up into separate areas, such as social psychology, developmental psychology and cognitive psychology, to take three examples. While the books in the Psychology Focus series will provide excellent coverage of certain key topics within these 'traditional' areas, the authors have not been constrained in their examples and explanations and may draw on material across the whole field of psychology to help explain the topic under study more fully.

Each text in the series provides the reader with a range of important material on a specific topic. They are suitably comprehensive and give a clear account of the important issues involved. The authors analyse and interpret the material as well as present, an up-to-date and detailed review of key work. Recent references are provided along with suggested further reading to allow readers to investigate the topic in more depth. It is hoped, therefore, that after following the informative review of a key topic in a Psychology Focus text, readers not only will have a clear understanding of the issues in question but will be intrigued and challenged to investigate the topic further.

Preface

Just over 18 months ago I completed the first draft of an introductory book about the brain entitled *Cortical Functions*, subsequently published by Routledge in the *Modular Psychology* series in 1999. While researching the material for that book, I accumulated more information than could be shoe-horned into the *Modular* series format, and in discussing the fate of my surplus chapters/material with the editors at Routledge the idea of writing a concise up-to-date introductory text in the area of neuropsychology slowly took shape. *Introducing Neuropsychology* is, somewhat belatedly, the result.

As with other books in the 'Psychology Focus' series, this one is intended as an accompanying text for courses in neuropsychology for students new to the subject area. I have written the book in such a way that a detailed understanding of neurophysiology (neurons, action potentials, synapses and so on) is not a necessary prerequisite to getting something out of it, so the book should also be accessible to non-psychology students too. However, to be on the safe side, I have included an appendix to which the reader may want to refer for a quick reminder of the basic layout of the nervous system, the structure and function of neurons, and the ways we might usefully wish to divide up the central nervous system in order to make more sense of it. Complete novices may prefer to read the entire appendix before tackling the rest of the book. This is allowed!

Mindful of the difficulties students sometimes have with the subject matter of neuropsychology, I have tried to write *Introducing Neuropsychology* in a jargon-free style (insofar as this is possible). However, a glossary is included to cover highlighted first use terms that may be new to the reader. I have also provided a large number of figures and diagrams to illustrate key points, and I have included several boxes dotted throughout the book encompassing key research findings or, in some cases, the results of neuropsychological case studies. Shaded 'interim comment' sections can also be found at regular intervals in every chapter. As their name suggests, these summaries are intended to allow the reader to make sense of particular passages of material in manageable chunks, before progressing further.

Although *Introducing Neuropsychology* aims to do what the title says – with coverage of the core ideas, concepts and research findings in each of the substantive chapters – I have also tried to add a flavour of recent/current research in each area, but particularly, in the later chapters. The recommended reading for each chapter (set out in the 'Further reading' section) also reflects my wish to encourage readers to seek out up-to-date research reports if they want to take their studies of a topic further. There are several excellent texts with a broader and deeper coverage of the material than can be achieved in *Introducing Neuropsychology*, and I would urge enthusiastic readers to research these resources too. I have listed some of my preferred texts in the 'Further reading' section. Similarly, there is some valuable material available on the Internet. The sites listed in the 'Selected neuropsychology web sites' section provide an entry point to this material, and links will soon take you to 3D images of the brain, lists of gory neurological disorders and the web pages of research institutions and even individual neuroscientists and neuropsychologists. Happy surfing!

For me, neuropsychology represents a confluence of most of the things I am interested in as a psychologist: normal and particularly abnormal behaviour, the workings of the brain, lifespan changes, the common ground between neurology, psychology and psychiatry, and even the concept of 'consciousness'. The more we learn about neuropsychology the more amazed I am about how a structure weighing as little as an adult human brain (about 1500 grams) can do everything it does, often faultlessly, for 70, 80 or even more years! I hope that as you read this book, you come to share my wonder about this rather insignificant-looking lump of tissue, and that *Introducing Neuropsychology* whets your appetite to learn more about it.

John Stirling
Manchester
July 2001

Acknowledgements

I would like to thank my MMU colleagues John Cavill, Gary Munley and Emma Creighton, for their general support and for their helpful comments in respect of earlier drafts of particular chapters of this book. I would also like to thank the external reviewers for their extremely useful comments and suggestions, almost all of which I have woven into the final version of the text. Ian Reid from MMU is responsible for much of the artwork, and Marilyn Barnett for various secretarial services. My thanks and appreciation go to both of them. The series editor Perry Hinton has prodded, directed, encouraged and cajoled me in good measure, and at just the right time. Thanks Perry.

I also want to express my gratitude to Rebecca Elliott and her research colleagues Ray Dolan and Geraint Rees for allowing me to use their superb fMRI images as cover plates, and to my friends and colleagues in the functional neuro-imaging and neuropsychiatry research group at the medical school, Manchester University, for inviting me to join their meetings and learn about up-to-the-minute research presented by a raft of internal and external speakers, often before it is published.

Thanks finally to students at MMU who, over the years, and through their own manifest enthusiasm for neuropsychology, have sustained my interest to learn more about the field; not least so that I can answer all the ingenious questions that come my way at the end of my lectures. I take heart from the fact that my classes actually prompt my students to think critically about brain-behaviour relationships, and I hope this book is of use to their successors in coming years.

John Stirling

Chapter 1

The beginnings
of neuropsychology

■ Introduction   2

■ Neuropsychology as a distinct discipline   2
  The origins of the brain hypothesis   3

■ Localisation of function   4
  The rise and fall of phrenology   4
  Interest in aphasia   6

■ Mass-action and equipotentiality   8

■ The (re)emergence of neuropsychology   10

■ Summary   12

Introduction

IN THIS CHAPTER I PROVIDE a brief history of the beginnings of scientific research into the brain, and I introduce some of the theories (and debates) that have surfaced as our understanding of the relationship between structure and functions has developed. I describe some discoveries that led to the development of the so-called 'brain hypothesis', a concept that is central to neuropsychology (if not to psychology as a whole). I then introduce the 'localisation of function' debate, which has rumbled on from its origins in the work of the 19th century neuroanatomists, and which continues to influence the distinct approaches and methodologies of clinical and cognitive neuropsychologists that I describe towards the end of the chapter. The background provided is intended to help the reader better understand the context in which neuropsychologists and other scientists have set about doing brain research in this rapidly evolving area.

Neuropsychology as a distinct discipline

Kolb and Whishaw (1996) define neuropsychology as the study of the relation between brain function and behaviour. However, to most neuropsychologists the term has come to mean something more specific than this: Were we to stick with Kolb and Whishaw's definition, we would need to include in our enterprise material that (by common consent) is not usually considered to fall within neuropsychology's ambit. Psychopharmacology (the study of drug action on behaviour), endocrinology (hormones and behaviour) and behavioural genetics are three examples. Kolb and Whishaw's definition is much better suited to the more general area of 'physiological psychology', or 'biopsychology', from which neuropsychology developed. Neuropsychology is a bridging discipline that draws on material from neurology, experimental psychology and even psychiatry. However, its principal aim is to try to understand the operation of human *psychological* processes in relation to brain structures and systems.

The term 'neuropsychology' was used as a subtitle in Hebb's influential book, *The Organisation of Behaviour: A Neuropsychological Theory*, published in 1949, although the term itself was not defined. With the demise of **behaviourism** (terms in bold type in the text indicate that the term is included in the Glossary section at the end of the book) and renewed interest in cognitive processes in the 1950s and 1960s, the term appeared with increasing frequency, although its definition remained vague, being used in different senses by different people. It was arguably sometime after this period that neuropsychology began to emerge as a distinct discipline, and its parameters were further clarified by the publication of the first edition of Kolb and Whishaw's *Fundamentals of Human Neuropsychology* and Lezak's *Neuropsychological Assessment* in 1980 and 1983 respectively.

It would be misleading of me to suggest that, following its protracted birth, neuropsychology has emerged as an entirely unified discipline. In reality there remain different emphases among practitioners and researchers, which broadly divide into two domains; those of clinical and cognitive neuropsychology. At the risk of oversimplifying the distinction, the former tends to focus on the effects of brain damage/disease on psychological processes (such as memory, language and attention), while the latter tries to understand impairments to psychological processes in terms of disruptions to the information-processing elements involved. In other words, the clinical approach goes from the damaged brain to psycho-logical dysfunction, whereas the cognitive approach goes from psychological dysfunction to hypothetical models about the individual stages of information processing that could explain such dysfunctions, which may (or may not) then be tied to the brain. A glimpse at the chapter titles in this book might suggest to the reader that I too have chosen to take a cognitive approach towards neuropsychology. However, this is not the case, and it is my hope that you will see that both approaches have much to offer in our quest to understand the relationship(s) between psychological processes and brain functioning.

The origins of the brain hypothesis

Historical records from the Middle East suggest that the importance of the brain as a 'behaviour control centre' (what we might now call the brain hypothesis) was first considered at least 5000 years ago, although the predominant view then, and for many centuries thereafter, was that the heart was the organ of thinking and other mental processes. The ancient Greeks debated the relative merits of heart and brain, and Aristotle, noting that the brain was relatively cool in comparison with the heart, came down in support of the heart as the seat of mental processes, arguing that the brain's principal role was to cool blood. Hippocrates and Plato both had some understanding of brain structure, and attributed various aspects of behaviour to it: Hippocrates warned against probing a wound in the brain in case it might lead to **paralysis** in the opposite side of the body.

In first century (AD) Rome, the physician Galen spent some time working as a surgeon to gladiators, and was well aware of the effects that brain damage could have on behaviour. The 'heart hypothesis' was fundamentally undermined

3

by Galen's descriptions of his clinical observations: he showed that **sensory nerves** project to the brain rather than the heart, and he also knew that physical distortion of the brain could affect movement whereas similar manipulation of the heart, though painful, did not directly affect behaviour.

For reasons that are never entirely clear, the knowledge and understanding of these early writers was lost or forgotten for the next 1500 years or so of European history. Those with any interest in the brain concentrated on misguided attempts to find the location of the soul. Their search focused on easily identifiable brain structures including the pineal gland and the corpus callosum. Today, these same structures are known to be involved in the control of bodily rhythms and communication between the two sides of the brain respectively.

Localisation of function

The renewed interest in rationalism and science that accompanied the Renaissance in Europe in the 15th and 16th centuries prompted scientists of the day to revisit the brain and to try to establish the functions of particular brain structures. Because a lot of brain tissue appears undifferentiated to the naked eye, these researchers also concentrated their efforts on the same easily identified structures as the earlier 'soul-searchers'. They explored the functions of the fluid cavities of the brain (the ventricles), the pineal and pituitary glands and corpus callosum. However, their ideas about the functions of these structures were usually well wide of the mark: **Descartes** (1664), for example, argued that the pineal gland was the point of interaction of the mind and body.

Implicit in this early work was the core idea of 'localisation of function'; that different regions of the brain are involved in specific and separate aspects of (psychological) functioning. This idea later intrigued both Gall, the German physician, and his student Spurzheim, whose work represents the starting point of what we might call the modern era of brain-behaviour research. Gall (1785–1828) readily accepted that the brain rather than the heart was the control centre for mental function, and, with Spurzheim, the two made many important discoveries about the anatomy of the brain, its connections with the spinal cord, and its ability to control muscles.

The rise and fall of phrenology

Both Gall and Spurzheim are primarily remembered for their ideas about 'strict' localisation of function in the brain, although they came to this area only after extensive research on other aspects of brain functioning. Gall thought that the **cortex** of the brain consisted of 27 compartments or regional faculties. These ranged from common sense (or recognisable) ones such as language and

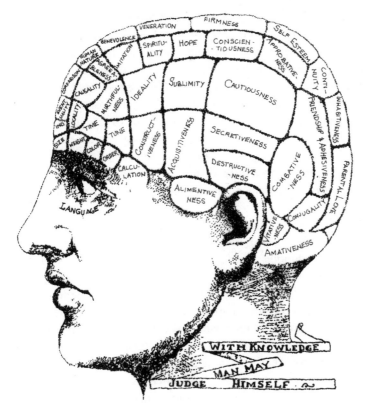

FIGURE 1.1 A phrenology skull

The concept of phrenology was developed by Gall and Spurzheim. By the mid-1800s it had become a respectable pseudo-science gaining royal patronage in the UK and spawning a mini-industry in charts, journals and consultants.

perception to ambiguous and obscure ones including hope and self-esteem. According to Gall, the more a person used their faculties, the bigger the brain in that region grew, causing the shape of the skull to be distorted. Thus was born the 'science' of phrenology, which claimed to be able to describe an individual's personality and other 'faculties' on the basis of the physical size and shape of the skull (see Fig. 1.1). Interest in phrenology gradually spread widely, receiving royal support when Queen Victoria had her children's heads measured and analysed.

Gall and Spurzheim collected thousands of phrenology measurements, including a series taken from the skulls of 25 murderers, and even from an amorous widow who was described as having prominent features (bumps) behind her ears! Each observation was simply taken as confirmation of the general theory, except that the number of faculties crept up to 35.

However, doubts about phrenology first arose when it became apparent that the shape of the skull bore little relationship to the shape of the underlying brain. Obviously, at the time, Gall and Spurzheim had no way of measuring internal brain structure in living people, save for those rare instances of individuals surviving (and often not for very long) **open head injuries**. Actually, records show that Gall had access to a small number of such cases, and he is credited with providing the first full account of loss of language (**aphasia**) linked to brain damage. Unfortunately, he seemed to regard these cases as being of only anecdotal interest, failing to realise that brain-injured people could offer an important test of his theory. Instead, he and Spurzheim continued to accumulate more and more measurements from members of the general population that 'confirmed' their ideas.

The French scientist Pierre Flourens provided the first scientific evidence that led people to question the value of phrenology. Working mainly with birds, he developed the technique of surgically removing small areas of brain tissue, and, after a period of recovery, observing the effects of the surgery on behaviour. (We now refer to these procedures as **lesion** and **ablation**, and they are described more extensively in Chapter 2.) Flourens' research led him to argue that the degree of behavioural impairment was more closely linked to the *amount* of damage than to its *location*; a finding that runs counter to the principle of localisation of function that Gall and Spurzheim had so vigorously promoted. Flourens believed that the entire brain operated as 'an aggregate field' or single faculty to serve the functions of perception, memory, volition and so on, as required. He also believed that undamaged regions could take over the responsibilities of damaged ones; an idea giving rise to the popular (but mistaken) belief that people only use a small proportion of their brains, keeping other areas in reserve for learning new skills or replacing damaged areas.

Although at the time, Flourens' findings dealt something of a blow to Gall and Spurzheim's ideas about localisation (and by implication; phrenology), hindsight suggests that his conclusions were probably wrong. First, Flourens worked with pigeons and chickens, which are now known to have almost no cortex. Secondly, his behavioural measures assessed activities (such as eating, movement and so on) unrelated to Gall and Spurzheim's faculties. Thirdly, his surgical procedure was imprecise, leaving open the possibility that behavioural changes were caused by damage or lesions to brain structures beyond the cortex.

Interest in aphasia

Despite Flourens' lack of enthusiasm for localisation of function, interest in it grew following a series of case studies of aphasia. French physicians Bouillaud and Dax independently described patients they had seen who had lost the use of language after brain damage to the left side. These patients often became paralysed in the right side of their bodies too, despite no apparent loss in intelligence. Bouillaud's work was reported in 1825, and Dax's in 1836, yet little interest was shown until Auburtin (who happened to be Bouillaud's son-in-law) described the same work at a conference in 1861 also attended by Paul Broca. A few days later, Broca met Monsieur LeBorgne, a patient who became known as Tan because this was almost the only sound he could utter. However, Tan could understand speech well and could, for example, follow quite complicated instructions, although he was also paralysed on his right side. Broca proposed that Tan had suffered damage to the same area of cortex (the left frontal region) earlier identified as crucial for language production by Gall. When Tan died from an unrelated disease later that year, Broca conducted a superficial post-mortem on his brain and confirmed that he had indeed incurred damage to the left frontal cortical region of his brain from a **stroke**.

Within two years, Broca had collected post-mortem data on eight similar cases. This research led him to conclude that language production depended on intact left frontal function, and that, in more general terms, the two sides of the brain controlled the opposite sides of the body. (In fact, neither of these ideas was new: the relationship of one side of the brain to the opposite side of the body had been described by Galen at the beginning of the first millennium, and the link between left-sided damage and aphasia had first been proposed by both Dax and Bouillaud in the 1830s.) Nevertheless, Broca seemed to gain the credit, and the region of brain (part of the left frontal cortex) he described is now known as Broca's area.

Soon, other regions of the cortex were identified as being important for various aspects of language. In 1874 Carl Wernicke described two additional forms of aphasia that were distinct from Broca's type. In **fluent aphasia** the patient could speak at a normal rate but what was said usually made little sense. In **conduction aphasia** the patient seemed able to understand what was said to them but was unable to repeat it. Wernicke surmised (on the basis of just one documented post-mortem investigation) that fluent aphasia was caused by damage to the posterior region of the left **temporal lobe**. He speculated that conduction aphasia was caused by a **disconnection** between this region (which we now know as Wernicke's area) and Broca's area.

Interim comment

Two important consequences followed from Wernicke's observations. First, language could no longer be considered a unitary 'faculty' and would have to be subdivided (at least) in terms of receptive and expressive functions. Secondly, it was clear that focal disease could cause specific deficits. The first observation meant that the scientists of the day would have to rethink the

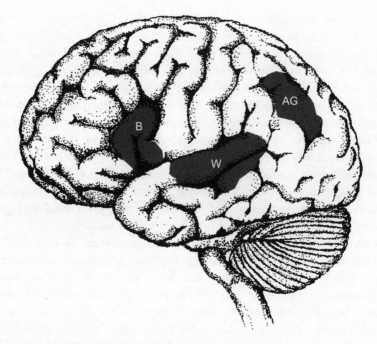

FIGURE 1.2 Some language areas in the brain

Area W is Wernicke's area, conceptualised as the region responsible for linking speech sounds to stored representations of words. Area B is Broca's area, identified as a region involved in the generation of speech. Area AG depicts the angular gyrus, known to be important in understanding visually presented material.

concept of 'faculty'. The second lent considerable weight to the idea of localisation of function. When, in 1892, Dejerine identified the cortical area (these days called the **angular gyrus**) related to the loss of the ability to read (known as **alexia**), three language areas, all on the left side, had been identified, and the localisation of function concept gained considerably in credibility (see Fig. 1.2).

Mass-action and equipotentiality

Despite the evidence presented in the previous section, it would be misleading to suggest that all researchers now accepted the basic principles of cortical localisation. For example, although the renowned physiologist Hughlings-Jackson supported localisation for some cortical functions, he knew that focal damage rarely led to complete loss of the function. As if to underline this point, the German physiologist, Goltz, regularly attended scientific meetings in the 1880s with a dog whose behaviour seemed relatively 'normal' despite Goltz having removed a large chunk of its cortex!

At the beginning of the 20th century European psychology came under the influence of the 'Gestalt' movement, which emphasised the importance of 'the whole as being greater than the sum of its parts'. This view was anathema to localisationists, but it prompted other scientists such as the British neurologist, Henry Head, to describe the brain as a dynamic, interconnected system that should be considered in its own right rather than as a collection of independently functioning units. Head's ideas were shared by Karl Lashley, an American psychologist, whose theories of **mass-action** (that the entire cortex is involved in all functions), and **equipotentiality** (that each cortical region can assume control for any given behaviour) were based on the same 'holistic' principles, and were, for a while, extremely influential, particularly in psychology.

Lashley's ideas can be traced back to the earlier work of Flourens. Like him, Lashley used brain lesions and worked exclusively with animals. Many of his studies measured the effects of lesions (removal of brain tissue) on maze learning in rodents. Initially, there would be a period of orientation during which time an animal learned its way around a maze to locate a food pellet. Then he would remove a small region of cortex, and, following a period of recovery, see how many trials it took the animal to relearn the maze and find the food pellet. On the basis of many such trials, Lashley concluded that the amount of lesioned brain tissue rather than its location best predicted how long it would take the rat to learn the maze, supporting his idea of mass-action.

These findings jibed well with new ideas about **behaviourism** emanating from American experimental psychology at the beginning of the 20th century. This approach stressed the importance of learning and **reinforcement** at the expense of interest in the brain. However (and notwithstanding the difficulties in generalising from rat to human behaviour), there are in fact a number of flaws in Lashley's argument, and his findings could also be used to support localisation of function. Think for a moment about the information a rat might use to find food in a maze: This is likely to include sensory information from the visual, tactile and olfactory modalities, in addition to any more sophisticated conceptual information such as sense of direction, distance travelled and so on. Indeed, effective maze learning probably depends on the integration of all this information. When Lashley lesioned different parts of cortex, he might have interfered with the animal's tactile skills or sense of smell, while leaving other functions intact. The animal could still learn the maze using the 'localised' functions that remained, but perhaps not as quickly as before.

> ## Interim comment
>
> In fact, sound experimental support for Lashley's ideas has been hard to come by, and it is probably helpful to know that most neuropsychologists continue to favour some form of localisation. Indeed, at present the main questions in this area are less to do with *whether or not* the human cortex is organised locally, than the *extent* to which localisation of function applies, and whether it applies equally on both the left and right sides of the brain (an issue I consider in Chapter 3).

The (re)emergence of neuropsychology

Historians seem unsure as to why, after such a promising start in the late 19th century, neuropsychology seemed to go into a form of hibernation until after World War II. In reality a combination of factors was responsible, notably the increased interest shown by mainstream psychology in behaviourism and **psychoanalysis**, both of which could be understood without reference to the brain, coupled with a lack of progress in understanding brain action. However, as I have already suggested, the 1950s and 1960s witnessed a gradual re-emergence of interest in physiological psychology and, *inter alia*, in the subject matter that we now consider to fall within the domain of neuropsychology, although the concepts of mass-action and equipotentiality gained little support from the new wave of brain research, and interest in them dwindled.

New understanding about the connectivity of the brain, on the other hand, prompted a revival of interest in 'connectionist models' of brain function. Such models had first appeared almost a century earlier (Lichtheim, 1885) but then fell into disrepute. In clinical neuropsychology, their re-emergence as 'neural wiring diagrams' has helped to clarify the different cortical regions responsible for particular psychological processes, and most neuropsychologists now think that the human brain coordinates these processes through the collaboration of (and interconnections between) multiple brain regions. Such circuits are sometimes called 'distributed control networks'. Although this sounds rather complicated, think of it as meaning that psychological functions (such as language or movement) depend on the activity of, and connections between, several (many) different but specific locations. Clearly, this is a different idea to the 'strict' localisation of function concept mentioned earlier because it implies that no one region has sole responsibility for particular psychological functions. However, it is also quite distinct from Lashley's ideas of mass-action and equipotentiality because it suggests that some regions of cortex are fundamentally involved in particular psychological processes while others are not.

In a way, the concept of distributed control is a compromise between the two approaches, because it implies cortical specialisation (localisation of function) but also suggests that several interconnected (but anatomically distributed) centres may be involved in the overall process. As Kosslyn and Anderson (1992) have commented, the problem for the strict localisationists was of thinking that psychological processes like memory, attention or language were equivalent to Gall's faculties, and therefore could be localised to one particular brain region. In reality, such processes are complex and multi-tiered, and can only be accomplished through the collaboration of multiple underlying mechanisms. These subsidiary processes may well be 'localised' to very specific cortical regions, but they effectively encompass broad areas of cortex when connected together to serve the particular psychological process. Fodor (1983) has captured the prevailing assumption in both clinical and cognitive neuropsychology by arguing that cognitive processes can be organised into distinct processing units or **modules**, which, in his view, are likely to be hard-wired (immutable), autonomous and localised. Our current understanding of the modular structure of cortical visual processing (described in Chapter 8) is a good example of this thinking.

Cognitive neuropsychologists also make extensive use of diagrams and models to identify both the component processing units (modules) and the way they collaborate to enable psychological processes such as memory, object recognition or attention to operate. In certain respects, however, the cognitive neuropsychology approach and methodology is quite distinct from that of clinical neuropsychology. Whereas clinical neuropsychologists develop models that are anatomically referenced to specific cortical regions, cognitive neuropsychologists generate hypothetical models that more closely resemble flow diagrams. These serve as templates (hypotheses) that attempt to account for *known* cases of brain damage, but which must be amended if other cases come to light that do not fit. Cognitive neuropsychologists therefore put great weight on detailed case study of individuals with very specific brain damage, eschewing research based on groups of individuals on the grounds that brain damage is infinitely variable. Some, such as Caramazza (1984), also take issue with Fodor's assumption of localisation, pointing out that similar lesions do not *always* generate similar deficits. As a consequence, cognitive neuropsychological models may make no reference at all to possible underlying brain regions.

Interim comment

Although the cognitive neuropsychology approach has been especially useful in certain fields such as language (see Chapter 6) and object recognition (see Chapter 8), its reliance on case study rather than group comparisons and its indifference towards brain structures have not been to everyone's taste. The eminent psychologist George Miller (see Gazzaniga et al, 1998) has, for example, championed the cause of what he terms 'cognitive neuroscience' as a distinct discipline that plots a middle course between the clinical and cognitive neuropsychology paths. In any case, the development of **in-vivo techniques** (see Chapter 2) will mean that data about functional activation in the brains of people without damage becomes more readily accessible, so that cognitive neuropsychologists will have to take more notice of the brain.

Summary

Scientific interest in the relationship between brain structure and function can be traced back to the work of the 19th century European neurologists. In the intervening years, researchers have debated the extent to which the brain operates on the basis of localisation of function or according to the principles of equipotentiality and mass-action. Today, the concept of **modularity** (in some form or other) underpins most thinking in modern neuropsychology and best accounts for our understanding of brain-behaviour relationships.

In this chapter I have traced the development of scientific brain research and introduced some of the theories that have surfaced as our understanding of these relationships has developed. A promising start in the 19th century gave way to a period in the first half of the 20th when psychology was dominated by theories and ideas that made only passing reference to the brain. Renewed interest in physiological psychology in the second half of the 20th century along with greater interest in cognitive processes within psychology set the scene for the birth (rebirth?) of the discipline we recognise today as neuropsychology. Although it is not an entirely unified enterprise, its cognitive and clinical strands complement one another in many domains. The arrival of in-vivo imaging procedures (which brings into the equation both clinical and non-brain damaged cases) is likely to lead to greater convergence.

Methods in neuropsychology

■ Introduction   14

■ Techniques for measuring brain structure
    and function   15
    Examining tissue   15
    Lesion and ablation   17
    Electrical stimulation   18
    Electrical recording   18
    In-vivo imaging   19

■ Neuropsychological assessment   24

■ Dissociations and double dissociations   27

■ In-vivo imaging in psychiatry   28

■ Summary   29

chapter 2

Introduction

IN THIS CHAPTER I INTRODUCE some of the methods that researchers use to explore the relationships between brain structure and function. I have already described neuropsychology as a 'bridging' discipline, and the area is served by a diverse collection of investigative measures ranging from neuroanatomical procedures at one end of the spectrum to assessments from experimental psychology at the other. A particularly exciting development over the past 30 years has been the introduction of a raft of in-vivo imaging techniques. The rapid spread in availability of scanning and imaging hardware (particularly during 'the decade of the brain' in the 1990s) has provided neuroscientists with research opportunities that were, until recently, unthinkable. In-vivo imaging has provided independent confirmation of the suspected role(s) of particular brain regions in psychological processing (for example, the role of the **anterior cingulate** in attention: see Chapter 9). In other instances, in-vivo techniques have revealed the true complexity of processes that other procedures had tended to oversimplify. The application of imaging techniques to language, discussed in Chapter 6, is a case in point.

Informative though the various procedures can be, it is also important to realise that most neuropsychological techniques (including in-vivo scanning) have their limitations. So, although the demise of older procedures has frequently been predicted as imminent, many still have an important role to play. In fact, the combination of imaging with traditional techniques can turn out to be a particularly fruitful and informative collaboration. (See Chapter 9 for examples in the field of attention research.)

I start this chapter with a brief review of classic techniques that are, for the most part, neuroanatomical in origin. Next I consider the use of electrical stimulation and electrical recording of the brain. Then I identify some of the in-vivo techniques that allow researchers to visualise the structure and/or functioning of the 'living' brain. I also review neuropsychological procedures, some of which can be used in conjunction with in-vivo imaging. I try, whenever possible, to refer the reader to specific examples of the use of techniques described elsewhere in this book. The chapter concludes with an illustration of an exciting application of in-vivo imaging in psychiatry.

Techniques for measuring brain structure and function

Examining tissue

Until quite recently, the options for measurement of brain structure were, effectively, limited to post-mortem, and on very rare occasions, **biopsy**. The latter is a drastic technique involving the removal and analysis of small (but irreplaceable) samples of brain tissue from the 'appropriate' area of brain. A combination of the 'hit and miss' nature of biopsy and the inevitable damage it causes mean that it is hardly ever used on humans. Post-mortem, on the other hand, has a long and fairly 'colourful' history in medicine, but requires the person to be dead! Thus, early signs of disease are likely to be masked by changes that occur as the disease progresses.

Sometimes, there are obvious signs of damage in **end-stage illness** that may nevertheless be of interest: Broca only conducted a superficial post-mortem investigation of Tan's brain but damage to the left frontal region was clear to see. The brain of a person who has died as a result of **Huntington's disease** or **Alzheimer's disease** will also look abnormal even to the naked eye. It will appear shrunken inwards from the skull; the **gyri** (surface bumps) will look 'deflated' and the **sulci** (surface grooves) will be wider. Usually, however, researchers are less interested in the outward appearance of the brain at death than in the subtle changes that occur during, or even before, the development of overt signs and symptoms. In any case, the external appearance of the brain at post-mortem may be entirely normal, with damage or disease only apparent on closer inspection of internal structures or tissues.

Brain tissue looks solid to the naked eye (it has the consistency of stiff jelly), so 'finer-grain' investigations had to await two technological developments. The first was the gradual refinement over many years of the light microscope, and the second was the discovery of tissue staining techniques that had the effect of 'highlighting' particular component structures of tissue. The combination of these developments enabled researchers to identify small groups of **neurons,** or even individual neurons, using a microscope. Thanks to technological improvements in lens manufacture, microscopy has developed considerably since its first reported use to examine biological tissues (of a cow) by Van Leeuwenhoek in 1674. Light microscopes can now reliably magnify by a factor of several hundred, but electron microscopes can magnify by a factor of several thousand. They can produce images of individual **synapses** (junctions between neurons), or even of **receptor sites** for **neurotransmitters** on the surface of neurons.

New staining techniques have also been developed since the pioneering work of Golgi in the late 19th century, although his silver-staining method (which makes stained material appear dark) is still used to produce images of individual neurons. Other staining techniques, such as horseradish peroxidase (HRP), have

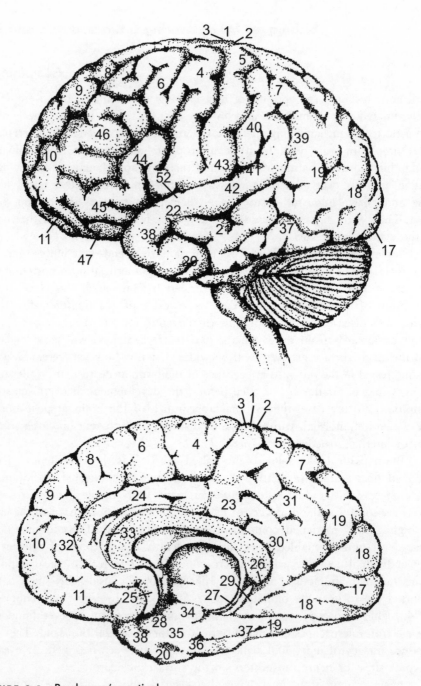

FIGURE 2.1 Brodmann's cortical areas

Brodmann identified 52 cortical areas on the basis of the type and density of neurons present. The identification and demarcation of most of these areas is still of value for neuroanatomists today.

been developed to enable the tracing of connections between neurons. This stain gets absorbed by **distal** (remote) regions of a neuron, but is carried back to the cell body (by retrograde transport within the neuron) to reveal the pathway that the neuron's axon takes. A combination of silver and HRP staining techniques can be used to establish functional connectivity between brain regions, such as the innervation of the **striatum** by the **substantia nigra** (see Chapter 5).

Early last century the neuroanatomist Brodmann used a combination of staining and microscopy to map the cytoarchitecture (cell structure/type) of the human cerebral cortex. His research led him to the realisation that different cortical locations comprised structurally distinct cell types, and his map identified 52 numbered regions, many of which are still used for identification purposes today (Brodmann, 1909). The primary visual cortex is, for example, also known as area 17, and Broca's area straddles Brodmann's areas 44 and 45 in the left hemisphere (see Fig. 2.1).

Lesion and ablation

A long-standing technique in neurology has been to observe the effects on behaviour of lesion (cutting) or ablation (removal) of nerve tissue. Lashley, whose work I introduced in the previous chapter, put forward the theory of mass-action largely on the basis of a series of lesion studies with animals. For obvious reasons these procedures are not used experimentally on humans, but sometimes brain tissue is removed (ablated) for medical reasons such as the excision of a tumour. Occasionally, surgical lesioning is also undertaken. Taylor's (1969) study of the effects of lesions to the left and right sides of the cortex in two patients (described in Chapter 3) is an example of the former. The surgical procedure of lesioning the corpus callosum as a treatment for **epilepsy**, which I also describe in Chapter 3 is an example of the latter. Sometimes, accidents cause lesions (or ablations). The case of Phineas Gage (described in Chapter 10) is one celebrated case in point. The case of NA, who developed amnesia following an accident with a fencing foil, is less well known but equally interesting (see Chapter 7).

It is also possible to induce lesions by the application of chemicals/drugs. The **Wada test** (Wada & Rasmussen, 1960) involves administering a fast acting barbiturate to one hemisphere at a time, via the left or right carotid artery, to induce a temporary lesion lasting a matter of minutes (see Chapter 6 for an illustration of the use of this procedure to determine the dominant language hemisphere in left and right-handed subjects). Other drugs may induce permanent lesions through their toxic influence. The substance MPTP, a toxin which was inadvertently mixed with synthetic heroin by recreational drug users in California in the mid-1980s, irreversibly destroys **dopamine** neurons in the substantia nigra, bringing about a very 'pure' form of induced **Parkinson's disease** in humans and animals (see Chapter 5).

Electrical stimulation

Much of the pioneering work on mapping out the primary somatosensory and motor cortex was done by the neurosurgeon Wilder Penfield (e.g. Penfield & Boldrey, 1958). His participants were also his patients, many of whom required surgery for life-threatening conditions such as removal of brain tumours or blood clots. He asked them whether, in the course of surgery, they would mind if he applied a mild stimulating electrode to the surface of their brains. Partly thanks to the brain's lack of pain receptors and resultant insensitivity to pain, brain surgery is sometimes conducted with the patient awake, so Penfield could talk to his patients as he stimulated different parts of their exposed brains! Using this technique, Penfield was the first researcher to discover the amazing topographic representation of body areas in the primary motor and somatosensory cortex. (I describe this in some detail in Chapters 4 and 5.)

Electrical recording

We can also learn about brain function by recording its electrical activity. In electroencephalography (EEG) and the closely related procedure of event-related potential (ERP) recording, electrodes are attached to the scalp and the amplified electrical activity detected by them is displayed on a chart recorder or computer screen. Surface recording is possible because the electrochemical activity of the brain is conducted passively through the meninges (protective membranes surrounding the brain), and the skull to the scalp. The recorded voltages represent the summed activity of millions of neurons in the area of brain closest to the recording electrode so, in order to get an idea about the spatial distribution of activity, several separate channels of EEG corresponding to electrodes in different positions on the head can be recorded simultaneously. This procedure has proved invaluable in the diagnosis of epilepsy and in the identification of sleep-related disorders (see Fig. 2.2).

In order to record ERPs a series of stimuli such as tones or light flashes are presented to the participant, and the raw EEG for a precise one or two-second period following each stimulus is recorded and fed into a computer where it is summed and averaged. There will be a response (or 'event-related potential') in the brain to each separate stimulus but this will be small (millionths of a volt) in comparison with the background EEG (thousandths of a volt). By summing all the EEGs together and averaging them, the more-or-less random EEG averages to zero, to leave an ERP that has a characteristic waveform when shown on the computer screen. Various abnormalities in this waveform have been linked to predisposition to alcoholism and schizophrenia. The ERP technique has also been useful as a tool to explore the mechanisms of attention and I describe some of this research in Chapter 9.

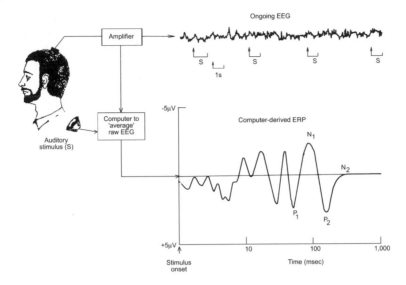

FIGURE 2.2 Recording of EEG and ERPs

Raw EEG can be recorded from surface electrodes on the scalp. If a series of stimuli are presented to the respondent, there will be a small but characteristic response to each stimulus, but this will be 'hidden' in the EEG. ERPs are obtained by feeding brief 'epochs' of the EEG (typically of between 500 to 1000 msec following each stimulus) into a computer that averages them. The random background EEG tends to average to zero, leaving the characteristic ERP waveform.

Recently, a variant of ERP known as magnetoencephalography (MEG) has been developed. (Mogilner et al.'s (1993) study of remapping in the cortex described in Chapter 4 employs this procedure.) MEG, which is still in its infancy, requires upwards of 60 electrodes to be attached to the participant's scalp, and takes advantage of the fact that when neurons are active they generate tiny magnetic fields. Event-related fields (ERFs) can be detected by an MEG analyser in much the same way as ERPs, but they provide a more accurate means of identifying the origin of particular signals. MEG can locate the source of maximum magnetic field activity in response to stimuli, and, if required, map these areas three dimensionally and in real time. This technique has been of use in identifying the precise focal origins of epileptic seizures, and, as I hinted above, it has also been used to map areas of the somatosensory cortex.

In-vivo imaging

The first of the in-vivo imaging techniques, computer tomography (CT) scanning, came on stream in the early 1970s. As technologies developed, and the value of scanning became clearer, it was soon followed by other procedures including PET (positron emission tomography), rCBF (regional cerebral blood flow) and MRI (magnetic resonance imaging). The common feature of these procedures is that researchers can produce images of the structure or functional activity of the brains of *living* people (see Fig. 2.3).

Computerised tomography (CT, but also known as computerised axial tomography, or CAT) provides structural images. To generate brain scans, low levels of X radiation are passed through an individual's head at a series of different angles (through 180°). A computer analyses each 'image' and generates what is, effectively, a compound X-ray. It can produce a 'slice-by-slice' picture of the entire brain, or other parts of the nervous system such as the spinal cord if required. A drawback of CT scanning is that the contrast between more and less dense tissue is not particularly good, although it can be improved by the administration of a dye (injected into the bloodstream just before the scan is taken). CT scans cannot measure functional activity but they have provided valuable information about *structural* changes seen in the brains of some people with dementia, and about the effects and location of brain damage in general (see Fig. 2.3a).

MRI is a more recent development that was initially introduced as a rival to CT. The technique itself is complex, relying on measurement of the response of hydrogen atoms to radio waves in a very strong magnetic field (I did say complex!). The MRI scanner measures the tiny magnetic fields that the spinning hydrogen atoms produce, and since the density of hydrogen atoms varies in different types of (brain) tissue, the scan data can be computer-processed to generate images. The entire brain can be imaged in successive slices, which can be produced in **sagittal** (side), **coronal** (front) or horizontal transverse planes. The high resolution of MR images (in comparison with CT images) is a major plus point. A second advantage is that participants are not exposed to radiation sources (see Fig. 2.3b).

PET scans provide colour-coded images of a person's brain as they undertake different sorts of task, such as reading words, solving mental arithmetic and listening to music (see Fig. 2.3c). The technique relies on the fact that active neurons use more glucose (fuel), so, shortly before the scan, a small amount of radioactively labelled glucose is given to the participant by injection, some of which will be taken up by active neurons. Several different radioactive markers are now available; some have longer or shorter half-lives; others may have specific targets in the brain. A commonly used isotope is oxygen15, which has a half-life of about 2 minutes. This means it can only be used for relatively brief scanning periods so repeated administration will be necessary in complex or lengthy studies. As it decays it gives off gamma rays that are detected by the PET scanner, and the activity level of different regions of the brain can then be assessed.

PET is a powerful means of assessing *functional* brain activity, although it does not directly measure neuronal events. Rather, it indicates relative levels of

(a) Computerised tomography (CT)

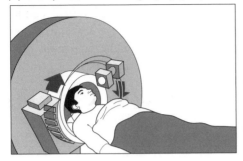 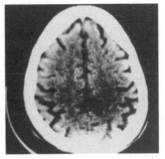

(b) Magnetic resonance imaging (MRI)

 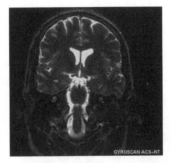

(c) Positron emission tomography (PET)

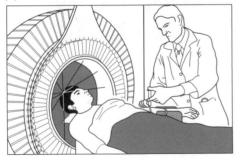 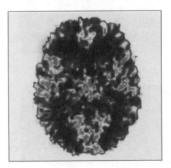

FIGURE 2.3 Diagram of CT, MRI and PET

CT scans provide reasonably well-defined images of brain structure. PET scans generate images of functional activity, though structure is only poorly defined. MRI can generate 'photographic' quality images of brain structure, and functional MRI (see Fig. 2.4) can produce integrated structural and functional images. Source: Rosenzweig et al. (1999). *Biological Psychology*. Sunderland, MA: Sinauer Associates Inc. Reproduced by permission of Sinauer Associates Inc. (Thanks to Bruce Moore from Liverpool University for providing the CT scan shown in (a). Thanks to Richard Hopkins and Richard Drake, respectively, from the University Department of Psychiatry, Manchester, for providing MRI (b) and PET (c) images of their own brains.)

(or changes in) activity under different conditions. To do this, 'image subtraction' is often employed, meaning that activity during a control condition is (literally) subtracted by computer from activity during the active test condition, and the remaining PET activity taken as an index of the activation specific to the test condition. Petersen et al.'s (1988) PET study of language functions (which uses subtraction logic) is described in Chapter 6.

Other in-vivo imaging procedures that you may read about include regional cerebral blood flow (rCBF) and single photon emission computerised tomography (SPECT). Both are variants of PET technology. In rCBF, the participant inhales a small amount of a radioactive gas such as xenon, which is absorbed into the bloodstream and thus transported around the body. The participant sits in a piece of apparatus that looks a little like a dryer seen in hair-salons! This has a series of sensors that detect the radioactivity from the transported xenon, and because more blood is required by 'active' brain regions, a computer can build up an image of areas of greater (and lesser) activity based on the detection rates. SPECT differs from PET in certain technical respects, the upshot of which is that the clarity of the scans is less precise because they take longer to generate.

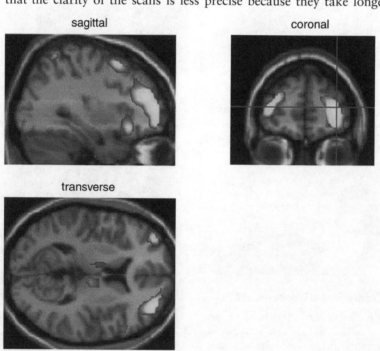

FIGURE 2.4 A fMRI scan

These scans identify brain regions that become active during a gambling decision task. (I am indebted to Rebecca Elliott and her colleagues, Geriant Rees and Ray Dolan from the Psychiatry and Neurosciences Unit at Manchester University and The Wellcome Department of Cognitive Neurology, London, for making these plates available.)

Functional magnetic resonance imaging (fMRI) is a recent development that permits simultaneous measurement of brain structure and function. The technique relies on the same principles and hardware as (structural) MRI described earlier. However, it takes advantage of the fact that active neurons require higher levels of oxygenated haemoglobin. The MRI scanner can be 'tuned' to detect the very subtle disturbances to the magnetic field induced by the different proportions of oxygenated and deoxygenated blood in active and inactive regions. The so-called BOLD (blood oxygen level dependent) signal can be further improved by the use of more powerful magnets in the scanner, and the spatial resolution (which generates the structural scans) is barely compromised (see Fig. 2.4).

Although fMRI has only been available for a few years, it has been adopted enthusiastically by researchers because, like MRI, fMRI scanning does not expose participants to radiation. Among many of its applications, it has recently been used to identify functional changes in frontal brain regions as participants undertake tests of **working memory** (e.g. Wickelgren, 1997). I describe this and other similar work in Chapter 7.

Interim comment

The development of in-vivo scanning marked the beginning of a new era in brain research. For the first time scientists could examine the structure or functioning of *the living brain*. It became possible to see exactly how extensive a patient's internal brain injury or damage was, and researchers could begin to do valuable brain research in individuals with 'intact' brains. By using special 'labelling' techniques it even became possible to observe for the first time where in the brain drugs were acting.

Despite the scientific advances that have been made as a result of the wider availability of CT, PET and MRI, there are drawbacks to each technique. Both PET and CT expose participants to radiation; X-rays in the case of CT and radioactive markers in the case of PET. Although the quantities are small, any exposure probably carries some risk. In the case of PET, the markers are a matter of concern for two practical reasons too. First, they are expensive because they need to be specially prepared 'on-site'. Secondly, they soon leave the body, which constrains temporally the psychological measurements that can be taken. MRI and fMRI do not have these problems, and may soon replace CT and PET as the techniques are further refined. However, even with fMRI, there remains a problem in interpreting the output because it is currently impossible to say whether the hot spots of activity that this technique reveals result from activation in excitatory or inhibitory neurons, or both.

Another problem relates to the temporal resolution of the scans themselves. In the case of PET, a condition may need to be 'current' for 30 or more seconds to produce detectable and reliable activations, so PET studies typically involve 'blocked' presentations of stimuli rather than single stimuli. The temporal resolution of fMRI is much better and it can be used on single trials as well as 'blocked' trials. However, there is still a time lag of several seconds between stimulus presentation and BOLD response.

Lastly, it is worth remembering that all scanning techniques currently require the respondent to lie in a scanner. Not only can this be uncomfortable, and, in the case of MRI – very noisy, but it also places significant constraints on the sorts of psychological investigation that can be conducted.

Neuropsychological assessment

The neuropsychological approach relies on the use of tests in which poor performance may indicate either focal (localised) or diffuse (widespread) brain damage. Neuropsychological assessment serves several purposes. First, it can give a 'neurocognitive' profile of an individual, identifying both strengths and weaknesses. For example, an individual's initial assessment may highlight a specific problem with spatial memory set against a background of above average IQ. Since many tests are 'standardised', a person's performance can be readily compared with scores generated by other age and/or sex matched respondents (a process known as norm referencing). A second advantage is that repeated testing over time can give an insight into changes in cognitive functioning that may relate either to recovery after accident/injury or the progression of a neurological illness.

Usually, a series of tests (called a test battery) will be given. One widely used battery is the Halstead-Reitan, which includes measures of verbal and non-verbal intelligence, language, tactile and manipulative skills, auditory sensitivity, and so on (Reitan & Wolfson, 1993). Some of the tests are very straightforward: The tapping test, which assesses motor function, requires nothing more than for the respondent to tap as quickly as possible with each of his/her fingers for a fixed time period on a touch sensitive pad. The Corsi block-tapping test measures spatial memory using a series of strategically placed wooden blocks on a tray (see Fig. 2.5a). A third test measures memory span for sets of digits. The Luria-Nebraska test battery (Luria, 1966) is an even more exhaustive procedure taking about two to three hours to administer, and including over 250 test items.

The lengthy administration of a test battery may be unsuitable for some individuals (such as demented or psychiatric patients) who simply do not have the requisite attention span. In such instances a customised battery may be more appropriate. Such assessments typically still include some overall index of intelligence: the comprehensively norm-referenced WAISR (the revised Wechsler Adult Intelligence Scale; Wechsler, 1981) is commonly used. In addition, specific measures may be adopted to test particular hypotheses about an individual. For example, if the person has received brain damage to his/her frontal lobes, tests might be selected that are known to be especially sensitive to frontal damage. The Wisconsin card sort test (see Fig. 2.5b), the trails test (in which respondents have to join up numbered dots on a page according to particular rules) and verbal fluency (generating words starting with a particular letter or belonging to a specific category) are cases in point.

Poor performance on one particular test may signal possible localised damage or dysfunction, while poor across-the-board performance may indicate generalised damage. For example, inability to recognise objects by touch (**astereognosis**) may be a sign of damage to the parietal lobes (see Chapter 4). A poor verbal test score (compared with a normal non-verbal test score) may indicate generalised left hemisphere damage (see Chapter 3). The WAISR is particularly useful in this respect because the eleven component tests segregate into six verbal and five performance sub-tests, from which it is possible to derive separate verbal and non-verbal estimates of IQ.

The National Adult Reading Test (NART; Nelson, 1982) allows the researcher to obtain an estimate of an individual's IQ prior to damage or disease onset. This may be useful if a neuropsychologist is making an initial assessment of a person who has been brain-damaged/ill for some time. The NART rather cunningly comprises 50 words that sound different to their spelling (such as yacht, ache and thought). The respondent reads through the list until they begin to make pronunciation errors. Such words were almost certainly learned before the onset of illness or brain damage, and because this test has been referenced against the WAIS, the cut-off point can be used to estimate IQ prior to illness, disease or accident.

Interim comment

Neuropsychological testing has gained considerable respect in recent years. However, it would be wrong to think that a battery of neuropsychological tests alone could somehow provide the researcher or clinician with a complete map of brain functioning. At best they give an indication of underlying problems. Two further concerns also merit consideration. First, an apparently normal performance on neuropsychological tests can be deceptive. We know that as individuals recover from brain damage, they often develop alternative strategies or techniques to overcome their deficits – see, for example, the case study of the brain-damaged architecture student (Clarke, Assal, & DeTribolet, 1993) which I review in Chapter 8.) Secondly, although neuropsychological and

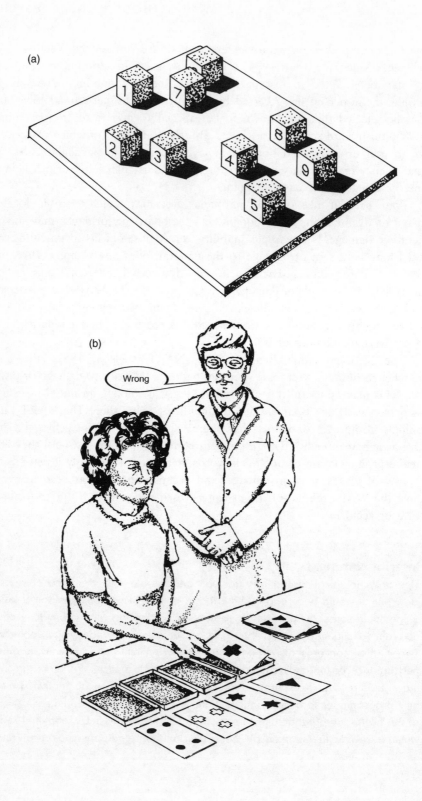

in-vivo assessments usually agree about what regions of brain are dysfunctional or damaged, they do not always, and the reasons for this are unclear.

Despite these concerns, researchers agree that the use of neuropsychological tests in combination with in-vivo techniques is potentially a very informative procedure. If a test is known to draw on the capacity of a particular brain region, it could be given to a subject while he or she is being scanned. This combined technique has been used by Smith and Jonides (1994) to examine the role(s) of the frontal lobes in working memory. They selected various neuropsychological tests of verbal and non-verbal working memory, and recorded PET scans of normal subjects as they completed them. The results showed a clear division of labour: Non-verbal working memory led to increased right frontal activation, whereas verbal working memory caused greater activation in the left frontal (and parietal) regions (see Chapter 7 for a further discussion of Smith and Jonides' findings).

Dissociations and double dissociations

Neuropsychologists typically try to design studies that provide evidence of the differential performance of brain-damaged and control subjects because such studies can inform structure–function relationships. Consider the following example: The right frontal lobe is thought to be important for memorising designs. To test this hypothesis, a researcher assesses memory for designs (MemD) and memory for words (MemW) in a group of people with known right frontal damage and a second group of non brain-damaged controls.

Hypothetical results from this study are shown in Table 2.1a. At first glance they seem to support the hypothesis because the right frontal subjects appear to be selectively impaired on the MemD condition. Many neuropsychological investigations employ this sort of design, and use the evidence of a (*single*) *dissociation* between groups in the MemD but not the MemW as support for the hypothesis. There is, however, a design problem with single dissociation studies stemming

---

FIGURE 2.5 (a) Corsi's block-tapping test and (b) the Wisconsin card sort test

Corsi's test assesses spatial memory. The tester taps out progressively longer sequences of blocks to establish spatial memory 'span'. The patient does not have the advantage of being able to see the numbers, so must memorise the correct sequence using spatial memory. In the Wisconsin card sort test, the patient sorts cards into four piles according to an 'unspoken' rule (sort by colour, shape or number). The only feedback the patient receives from the tester is an indication as to whether or not a particular card has been correctly sorted. The patient must use this feedback to guide future card sorts. Every so often the tester changes the sorting rule and the patient must try to adjust to it. Source (2.5(b)): Gazzaniga et al. (1998). *Cognitive Neuroscience: The Biology of the Mind.* Copyright © 1998 by W.W. Norton & Company, Inc. Reproduced by permission of W.W. Norton & Company, Inc.

TABLE 2.1 A single and a double dissociation experiment

| | Group | Tasks (% correct) | |
		MemD	MemW
(a)	**Single dissociation experiment**		
	Right frontal	70%	90%
	Control	90%	95%
(b)	**A double dissociation experiment**		
	Right frontal	66%	90%
	Left frontal	93%	60%
	Control	95%	95%

Note: In the single dissociation experiment, frontal patients appear worse on the MemD task than controls, and about the same on the MemW task. However, this result might be due to poor attention (or some other extraneous variable) which happens to affect the patients on this test. In the double dissociation experiment, the 'opposite' performance of right and left frontal patients suggests that damage to the different brain regions has a specific and selective effect on the two memory tests.

from the assumption that the two conditions are equally 'sensitive' to differences between the two groups of participants (which may or may not be the case). For example, it could be that right frontal subjects have poor attention, which happens to effect the MemD task more than the MemW task.

A much 'stronger' design is one with the potential to show a double dissociation. For example, if we also thought that left frontal damage impaired MemW but not MemD, we could recruit two groups of patients – one group with left and the other with right frontal damage, plus a control group – and test all participants on both measures. Hypothetical results from this design are shown in Table 2.1b. They indicate that one group of patients is good at one test but not the other, and the reverse pattern is true for the second group of patients. In other words, we have evidence of a double dissociation (similar to the one described in the previous interim comment), which suggests to neuropsychologists that the two tasks involve non-overlapping component operations that may be anatomically separable too.

In-vivo imaging in psychiatry

To conclude this chapter, and to illustrate the ingenious applications to which in-vivo imaging can be put, consider the use of PET in the study of **hallucinations** by Frith and colleagues in London (see Silbersweig et al., 1995), and a similar application of fMRI by Woodruff's group (Woodruff et al., 1997). Silbersweig and colleagues used PET to measure brain activity in a group of mentally ill patients who were experiencing hallucinations *at the time* of scanning. Preliminary results indicated that auditory hallucinations were linked to cortical activation in the left temporal lobe and parts of the left orbital region of the frontal lobe. Woodruff et al. (1997) examined seven schizophrenic subjects on two occasions. First, during a period of severe ongoing verbal hallucinations and secondly after these had diminished. External speech was found to activate the temporal cortex significantly more powerfully and extensively in the hallucinations-absent condition than in the hallucinations-present condition. The greatest difference was found in the right mid-temporal gyrus (MTG). This finding suggests that auditory hallucinations compete with external stimulation for temporal cortex processing capacity.

A recent update of Woodruff's study has been reported by Shergill et al. (2000). The researchers recorded fMRI activity in six regularly hallucinating schizophrenic patients. Approximately every 60 seconds respondents had to indicate whether (or not) they had 'experienced' an auditory hallucination during the last time epoch. In comparison with non-hallucinating epochs, the presence of hallucinations was associated with widespread activation, which was especially pronounced in bilateral inferior frontal and temporal regions, the left hippocampus and adjacent cortex (para-hippocampal gyrus). Although it is still too early to say precisely where, how, or why hallucinations form, the use of in-vivo imaging shows beyond doubt that the *experience* of hallucinations is related to changes in activity in various regions of cortex.

Summary

Researchers interested in understanding brain function and its relations to psychological function can now draw on a wide range of investigative techniques. In this chapter I have introduced lesion and ablation, electrical stimulation and recording, and the structural and functional in-vivo imaging procedures. Consideration is also given to the burgeoning use of neuropsychological testing. Researchers have moved rapidly from an era in which analysis of brain structure could usually only be assessed after the person had died to an era in which the various in-vivo imaging techniques are quickly becoming almost as commonplace as X-radiography: their use in combination with neuropsychological procedures is a particularly promising research area. Although we have not yet reached the point where in-vivo imaging can be used to establish *what* people are thinking, the applications of PET and fMRI to psychiatry are bringing us close to identifying brain areas that may contribute to the types of disordered thinking so characteristic of mental illnesses.

Chapter 3

Lateralisation

■ Introduction   32
■ Structural differences   32
■ Unilateral neurological damage   32
■ The split-brain syndrome   34
  Experimental studies   36
  The split-brain syndrome and language   37
  The split-brain syndrome and other
    psychological functions   39
■ Callosal agenesis   41
■ Asymmetries in normal individuals   43
  What is lateralised?   44
  Inter-hemispheric transfer via the corpus
    callosum   46
  Developmental aspects   46
■ Individual differences in brain
    organisation   47
  Handedness   47
  Handedness and cognitive function   49
  Sex differences   49
■ Laterality: A footnote on the evolutionary
    perspective   51
■ Summary   52

Introduction

AT FIRST GLANCE, THE TWO cortical **hemispheres** look rather like mirror images of each other. The brain, like other components of the nervous system, is superficially symmetrical along the **midline**, but closer inspection reveals many differences in structure, and behavioural studies suggest differences in function too. The reason for these so-called asymmetries is unclear, although they are widely assumed to depend on the action of genes. Some writers have suggested that they are particularly linked to the development in humans of a sophisticated language system (Crow, 1998). Others have argued that the asymmetries predated the appearance of language and are related to tool use and hand preference. Language is, after all, a relatively recent development having probably arisen no more than 100,000 years ago, and Corballis (1991), among others, has suggested that language skills, being analytical and sequential in nature, gravitated naturally to the left hemisphere, which already operated preferentially in this way. Whatever the cause or causes of asymmetry, hemispheric differences in psychological functions certainly encompass many areas in addition to language. In this chapter I consider the various ways that scientists have examined lateralisation, and the conclusions that they have drawn from their research.

Structural differences

Despite their superficial similarity, the two hemispheres of the human brain consistently differ in a number of characteristic ways that are summarised in Table 3.1. Even at this relatively coarse level of analysis we begin to see a pattern suggesting links between structure and function, with the left hemisphere being concerned with linguistic skills and the right hemisphere spatial skills. (Externally visible asymmetries are also shown in Fig. 3.1.)

Unilateral neurological damage

We cannot manipulate brain damage experimentally in humans but we can assess function in individuals whose brains have been damaged or have become diseased. In general terms, damage to the left hemisphere seems to result in a greater impairment to language-related skills than to spatial (or non-linguistic)

TABLE 3.1 Anatomical hemispheric asymmetries

- Viewed from the top of the head, the right frontal lobe extends further forward, and the left occipital lobe further back.

- The Sylvian fissure, which is the dividing line between the frontal and temporal lobes, is longer and less sloped on the left side than the right.

- A region of the temporal lobe known as the planum temporale, which is adjacent to the Sylvian fissure and encompasses Wernicke's area, is significantly larger on the left than the right.

- Cells in the region of the left frontal lobe, which we now call Broca's area, have many more synapses (contacts with other neurons) than the equivalent region on the right side.

- The angular gyrus (located in the posterior parietal lobe), which may be important in reading and semantic aspects of language, is larger on the left than the right side.

- The parietal area on the right side (just behind the location of the angular gyrus on the left) is larger and has more synaptic contacts. This region is linked with visual perception and spatial processing.

---

skills, whereas the reverse is true for right hemisphere damage. However, it is important to bear in mind that the degree and extent of damage is variable and idiosyncratic, and it is difficult to generalise on the basis of case studies alone.

More control is possible when tissue must be surgically removed for medical reasons. Taylor (1969) reported two case studies of patients who underwent temporal lobectomies (ablation of temporal lobe) to remove brain tumours. Each patient completed a battery of neuropsychological and IQ tests both before and after surgery. For the patient whose left temporal lobe was removed, a significant decline in performance on tasks with a verbal component was noted, but there was little change in non-verbal function. For the patient who underwent a right temporal **lobectomy**, the exact reverse pattern of outcome was observed. Verbal skills were preserved, but spatial performance dipped markedly.

You may recall from Chapter 2 that this pattern of distinct/opposite impairment is referred to by neuropsychologists as a double dissociation, and it is also observed in patients with left and right frontal, temporal and parietal lesions. Once again (in general terms) left-sided damage tends to impact more on verbally based skills, and right-sided damage on non-verbally based skills. For example, damage to the left frontal lobe usually leads to a decline in verbal fluency (*'Think of as many words beginning with the letter S as possible'*), but not to design fluency (*'Draw as many patterns made of four lines as possible'*), and vice versa. Right-sided damage is linked to impairments in a wide range of psychological

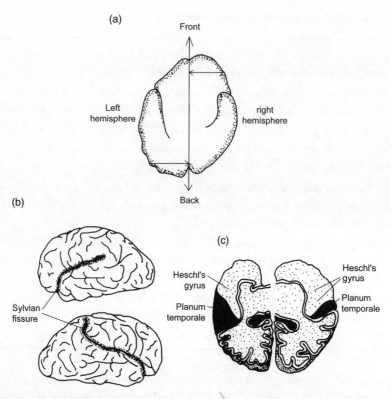

FIGURE 3.1 **Externally visible structural asymmetries of the human brain**

(a) The right frontal region typically projects further forward and is wider than the left frontal region. The reverse pattern is seen in the occipital lobes. (Adapted from Hellige, 1990.)

(b) The Sylvian fissure extends further back horizontally on the left side than the right (where it takes a more upward course). (Adapted from Kolb & Whishaw, 1996.)

(c) The planum temporale is larger on the left side than the right.

skills, including spatial orientation, discrimination of auditory tones and face recognition (see also Chapter 8). Left-sided damage is more likely to be associated with some loss of language function. This demarcation is not, however, complete because certain forms of **apraxia** (a disorder of purposeful movement introduced in Chapter 5) are linked to left parietal damage, and failure to detect emotional intonation in verbal messages (a quasi-linguistic skill) is associated with right temporal damage (see Chapter 6).

The split-brain syndrome

Fifty years ago, anti-epilepsy drugs were not as effective as those available today, and for some people even the highest safe levels of medication could not prevent regular seizures. As these could occur 10 or 15 fifteen times per day, normal life could be profoundly compromised. Yet scientists were beginning to understand that the seizures themselves could cause progressive damage to the brain so there was an urgent need for new treatments to reduce or prevent their potentially damaging effects.

Seizures usually originate in a particular location known as the **ictal focus,** but then spread (rather like ink on a blotter) to affect adjacent cortical regions. Sometimes, they pass via the corpus callosum to the opposite hemisphere to bring about a bi-lateral seizure. Having exhausted other treatments, two Californian surgeons, Bogen and Vogel, decided to try to contain seizure activity to just one hemisphere by lesioning the corpus callosa of their patients. Although this sounds drastic, remember that, at the time (in the 1940s and 1950s), scientists did not fully understand what the corpus callosum did, and they knew that animals given this surgical procedure seemed to suffer no lasting ill effects (see Fig. 3.2).

Over a period of several years about 100 people underwent 'sectioning' of the corpus callosum. In some cases the lesion was partial; just the anterior (front) or posterior (rear) region would be cut. For most patients, however, complete

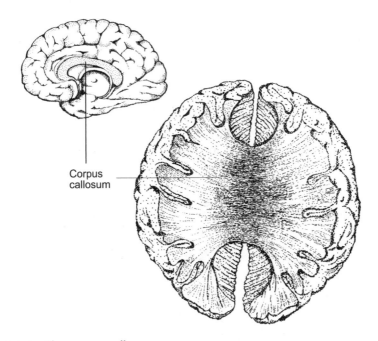

Corpus callosum

FIGURE 3.2 The corpus callosum

The corpus callosum is (by far) the largest pathway linking the two sides of the brain. In adult humans it comprises at least 200 million myelinated axons carrying information from the left to the right hemisphere and vice versa.

35

sectioning was performed, rendering the two hemispheres anatomically isolated from one another. Individuals were assessed on batteries of psychological tests both before and after their operations, and at first glance the procedure appeared remarkably effective. After a period of recovery, both the intensity and frequency of epileptic activity was almost always reduced, and some patients no longer experienced major seizures at all. Moreover, patients' IQ scores and scores on many other tests often improved, and, perhaps because of reduced seizure activity, most people claimed to feel better too. These preliminary data presented a paradox: How could a surgical procedure that involved lesioning the major inter-hemispheric pathway not have a significant effect on psychological functioning? To address this question, a group of psychologists led by Sperry and Gazzaniga developed a series of tests that were designed to shed more light on the true nature of the split-brain syndrome.

Experimental studies

To fully understand the experimental procedures that Sperry, Gazzaniga and others developed it is important to realise that in higher mammals, including

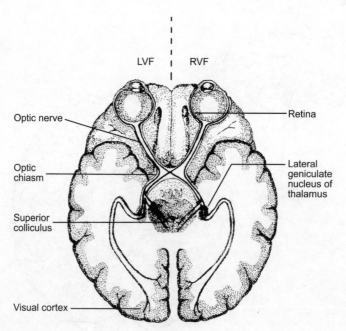

FIGURE 3.3 Visual pathway from eye to brain

The route from retina to occipital cortex via the lateral geniculate nuclei of the thalamus. Note that information from the right visual field (everything to the right as you look straight ahead) entering *both* eyes will be fed back to the left occipital lobe. Visual input from the left visual field will be fed to the right occipital lobe.

humans, most visual information from the right visual field (that is everything to your right if you look straight ahead) travels from both eyes, via the visual pathways, to the left occipital lobe. Similarly, most information from the left visual field travels to the right hemisphere. Auditory and somatosensory input is also predominantly, though not completely 'crossed', so the left ear sends most of its sensory input to the right auditory cortex, and the left hand is controlled by, and sends sensory information back to the right hemisphere, and vice versa for the left hand (see Fig. 3.3).

Sperry and colleagues were interested to know what would happen if information was presented to the split-brain patient one hemisphere at a time. Using a **tachistoscope**, they presented visual stimuli very briefly to either the left or right of a central fixation point on a screen in front of the patient. (A presentation duration of under 200 msec allowed for accurate recognition while ensuring that the participant did not have time to move their eyes towards the stimulus, which would have meant that the image went to both hemispheres.) After each presentation, the participant had to say what (if anything) they had seen. Sometimes, they were also given the opportunity to reach behind a screen to feel items with either their left or right hand that might be related to the stimuli presented via the tachistoscope. On other occasions, they were invited to draw (with their left or right hand) images of the presented material.

With these procedures the true nature of the split-brain syndrome was revealed. Consider, for example, the results of an early study reported by Sperry (1968). If a picture of a car was flashed to the right of the fixation point, the patient reported seeing a car. This would be expected because the image travelled to the left (talking) hemisphere so the patient could say what they saw. If the same picture was flashed to the left of the fixation point, the patient usually reported seeing nothing: now the image went to the non-verbal right hemisphere. However, if the patient was allowed to reach behind a screen with their left hand, they could usually select a model car from among other out-of-sight objects. (Remember that the left hand connects to the right hemisphere.) Similarly, if the patient was allowed to 'doodle' with their left hand, a drawing of a car often appeared! Even more amazingly, when asked why they had drawn a car, patients usually expressed surprise and were unable to give the right answer (see Fig. 3.4a).

The split-brain syndrome and language

The results of the early split-brain studies supported the view that for almost all right-handers, and the majority of left-handers, control of speech was localised to the left hemisphere. Did this mean that the right hemisphere was devoid of language? How, for example, would spilt-brain patients deal with letters or words presented to the right hemisphere? The results of such studies are not quite as clear-cut as we might expect. Gazzaniga and Hillyard (1971) reported that when

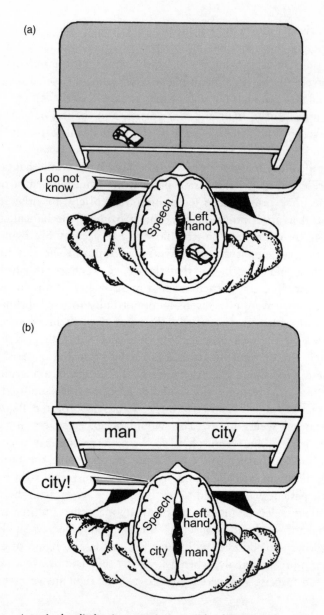

FIGURE 3.4 A typical split-brain experiment with objects and words

In the first figure (a) the respondent is unable to 'say' what image has been briefly projected to the non-speaking right hemisphere. In the second figure (b) the respondent reports only the word appearing in the right visual field, which projects to the 'speaking' left hemisphere. (Adapted from Temple, 1993.)

words were briefly presented to the left visual field (right hemisphere) they could not be read aloud, but split-brain patients could often select related items with their left hand from behind a screen. This and other similar observations soon led to the claim that the right hemisphere also possessed language skills but was simply mute (see Fig. 3.4b).

This view was supported by Zaidel (1978) who developed a lens system (as an alternative to the tachistoscope) as a means of selectively presenting visual input to just one hemisphere. Because Zaidel's system was not restricted to brief presentations he could present longer words. Alternatively, he could present linguistic material aurally (and thus bi-laterally), but require participants to make response selections uni-laterally from a choice of alternatives presented to just one or other visual field via his lens. Using this method, and working in depth with two spilt-brain patients, Zaidel reported that the right hemisphere had an extensive 'lexicon' (vocabulary) equivalent to that of a normal 10-year-old. However, evidence of a marked receptive language deficit was apparent from his subjects' difficulties in completing the Token Test (DeRenzi & Vignolo, 1962). In this test respondents have to follow a set of simple verbal instructions, such as, 'Place the yellow circle above the blue square'. Zaidel's subjects performed at a level no better than that seen in patients with severe aphasia. In other words, despite an extensive vocabulary, the right hemisphere's ability to extract meaning from sentences was clearly very limited.

The debate about the extent of right hemisphere language function has rumbled on. Critics have pointed out that only a small proportion of the split-brain cohort (possibly no more than six cases) have shown any notable right hemisphere linguistic skills, and that even for these individuals there was no evidence of right hemisphere syntax (grammar) (see Springer & Deutsch, 1993). On the other hand, one of the most staunch supporters of the 'left hemisphere–language hemisphere' viewpoint has recently acknowledged that, on rare occasions, right-handed split-brain patients may develop the ability to speak single words with their right hemisphere (Gazzaniga, Ivry, & Mangun, 1998)! In one case, speech only developed 13 years after surgery. This is an astonishing finding, although there are parallels in the neurology literature, which contains several anecdotal reports of individuals who, having lost their left hemisphere (through accident or surgery), subsequently developed rudimentary right hemisphere language skills.

The split-brain syndrome and other psychological functions

The split-brain studies support the idea of a key role for the left hemisphere in linguistic skills, but do they tell us anything about the particular roles and responsibilities of the right hemisphere? Franco and Sperry (1977) reported a study in which right-handed split-brain patients were tested using both their right and left hands on a range of visuo-spatial tasks including route finding and solving jigsaw puzzles. These patients consistently performed better with their non-preferred left hand than their right hand. This finding is similar to that reported by Sperry, Gazzaniga, and Bogen (1969) in which split-brain patients were tested using a version of the block design test (see Chapter 8 for an example). In this test, geometric visual patterns must be 'built' using individual coloured blocks. Right-handed split-brain patients could do this spatial construction test much more effectively with their non-preferred left hand (which is connected to the right hemisphere) than with their dominant hand.

Levy, Trevarthen, and Sperry (1972) presented data consistent with the view that face-processing may also be dealt with preferentially in the right hemisphere. Patients were shown images of pairs of half-faces via a tachistoscope. These 'chimeric' images might, for example, comprise half the face of a girl on the left side, and half the face of an elderly man on the right. The fixation point was exactly on the joint at the bridge of the nose. When the participant was asked to say what they had seen, they usually reported seeing an intact (i.e. complete) picture of a man. We might have predicted this because this half image went to the left/talking hemisphere. However, when asked to select what they had seen from a set of complete pictures, split-brain patients invariably chose the picture of the girl, which had gone to their right hemisphere (see Fig. 3.5).

The surgery that brings about the split-brain syndrome effectively disconnects the two hemispheres. The amazing thing is that it has so little effect on

FIGURE 3.5 Summary of Levy et al.'s (1972) split-brain study

The split-brain patient views chimeric figures. When she is asked to 'say' what she saw, she describes the whole image of the half chimeric figure from her right visual field (the child). When asked to 'select' what she saw, the right hemisphere tends to dominate and she chooses the whole image of the half chimeric figure from her left visual field that projected to her right hemisphere (the woman wearing glasses). Source: Levy, J., Trevarthen, C.W., & Sperry, R.W. (1972). Perception of bilateral chimeric figures following hemispheric deconnection. *Brain, 95,* 61–78. Reproduced by permission.

routine daily activities for the patients themselves. Just occasionally, however, anecdotal accounts from individuals suggest that in particular situations there may be some disagreement between hemispheres (a phenomenon known as hemispheric rivalry). One woman complained that as she went to select a dress from her wardrobe with her right hand, she found her left hand reaching for a different one! On another occasion, the right hand turned the heating up, only for the left hand to turn it down again!

That these events are few and far between is probably because in ordinary day-to-day activities, visual, auditory and most other sensory information actually finds its way into both hemispheres. (It takes a group of cunning psychologists to think of situations in which input is restricted to just one!) Patients additionally develop strategies to try to ensure that sensory information gets to both hemispheres. The use of exaggerated head movements is one trick. Another is to make more use of 'cross-cueing'. This is best illustrated by the following example: a split-brain patient trying to identify a comb by touch alone might tweak the teeth, which will make sounds that travel to both ears, and hence to both hemispheres.

Interim comment

Despite the wealth of findings to have emerged from more than 40 years of research into the split-brain syndrome, caution is required in evaluating it. First, the individuals who underwent the surgery could not be regarded as a normal or random sample. They were, in reality, a small group of individuals who had suffered from intractable epilepsy, and, in the process, had usually been treated with a range of powerful drugs for many years. Secondly, it is likely that the cumulative effects of seizure activity will have led to discrete areas of damage. Thirdly, background information about IQ or other basic cognitive abilities such as memory or attention is missing from some split-brain cases. Overall, it is probably best to regard the evidence from individuals who have had spilt-brain surgery as just one strand of a comprehensive research quest to establish the true nature of the different psychological specialisms of the cerebral hemispheres.

Callosal agenesis

The split-brain procedure was, of course, usually carried out on adults who had been born with an intact corpus callosum. However, a small number of people are born with a grossly malformed or entirely missing corpus callosum. Callosal agenesis, as the condition is known, is a very rare disorder of unknown cause, and is often associated with other structural anomalies. In particular, there are more pathways linking the front and back of each hemisphere, and pathways between the hemispheres other than the corpus callosum (notably the **anterior commissure** and/or the **hippocampal commissure**) are sometimes more fully developed. In view of these structural alterations we might expect acallosal children to have multiple handicaps, and in reality many do. But some do not, and these children are of particular interest because, in principle, they offer an opportunity to examine the role of the corpus callosum during development. If these individuals show the 'usual' pattern of asymmetry, this would suggest that lateralisation is determined very early on in life and that the corpus callosum is not necessary for its development. If, on the other hand, lateralisation is partly a developmental process that depends on the corpus callosum, we should find abnormalities of lateralisation in acallosal cases. It is also of interest to compare such individuals with split-brain cases (Geffen & Butterworth, 1992).

In general, research on acallosal children has indicated that they too have language skills lateralised to the left hemisphere, and spatial skills lateralised to the right; findings that tend to support the first hypothesis that lateralisation is not gradually acquired during childhood. However, people with callosal agenesis do have certain difficulties with aspects of *both* language *and* spatial processing. In language tasks, difficulties are frequently reported when the 'sound' of a word is important. This becomes apparent in rhyming tasks or when the subject is asked to generate words beginning with a particular letter (Jeeves & Temple, 1987). Adding to this picture, acallosals also have difficulties with spatial tasks such as jigsaws, copying drawings, puzzles, depth perception and so on (Temple & Ilsley, 1993). The reasons for these deficits are not known but it may be that, as with other tasks, these are best dealt with by a collaborative brain effort, which is compromised in acallosals. We should also remember that it would be inaccurate to describe the brains of people with callosal agenesis as 'normal apart from missing the corpus callosum'.

The most consistent deficits seen in callosal agenesis relate to the general problem of inter-hemispheric transfer. Indeed, a strong hint about the role of the corpus callosum in cortical functioning comes from the observation that acallosal children and adults are very clumsy in tasks that require bi-manual cooperation. Examples include playing a musical instrument, doing certain sports or even tying shoelaces. In certain respects, acallosal adults are rather like normal young children whose corpus callosum is immature. Its presence seems less involved in the process of shaping asymmetry than in promoting collaboration between the hemispheres.

Interim comment

In many cases of callosal agenesis other brain abnormalities are also apparent so it is difficult for neuropsychologists to identify with any confidence those behavioural disturbances that have resulted specifically from the absence of a corpus callosum. In cases where meaningful data have been collected, asymmetries occur regardless, indicating that the corpus callosum is not necessary for lateralisation to develop. Although inter-hemispheric transfer is still apparent in acallosals, presumably occurring via one or more of the other remaining intact pathways, response speeds on tasks requiring bi-manual comparisons are invariably slower. Moreover, the general clumsiness and lack of two-handed coordination seen in acallosal individuals are reminders of the importance of rapid inter-hemispheric communication (via the corpus callosum) for normal behaviour.

Asymmetries in normal individuals

A variety of experimental procedures permit investigation of lateralisation in normal individuals. Dichotic listening tasks take advantage of the fact that most auditory input to the right ear is relayed to the opposite auditory cortex for detailed processing, and vice versa for the left ear. Different auditory stimuli can thus be presented simultaneously to both ears (via stereo headphones) and participants can be asked to report what is heard. Most research of this kind shows a small but consistent right ear advantage for linguistic material (Kimura, 1973). This is thought to occur because words heard by the right ear are processed directly by the left hemisphere, whereas words heard by the left ear are initially processed by the right hemisphere, before being relayed to the left hemisphere for fuller analysis.

The same general pattern of right side advantage for verbal material and left side advantage for non-verbal material appears to hold in the visual and tactile modalities too. Normal subjects can recognise words more quickly when they are presented briefly (using a tachistoscope or computer) to the right visual field, and faces more efficiently when presented to the left visual field (Levine, Banich, & Koch-Weser, 1988). Asymmetry can also be seen in relation to movement. While most humans are right-handed, a motor skill performed with the right hand is more likely to be interfered with by a concurrent language task than the same skill performed by the left hand. You can illustrate this in a very simple experiment. Ask a friend to balance a wooden dowel on the end of the first finger of either their left or right hand. When they have mastered this task, ask them to shadow (i.e. repeat as soon as they hear it) a paragraph of text that you read aloud. The concurrent verbal task will usually affect right-hand balance sooner than left-hand balance.

What is lateralised?

The evidence from brain-damaged, split-brain, acallosal and normal individuals reviewed so far points to a division of labour along the lines of language – left hemisphere and spatial skills – right hemisphere, and this model has been the dominant one until quite recently. Yet a moment's thought suggests that if this were the entire story, our brains would be working in a very inefficient way! As we tried to solve a jigsaw puzzle our left hemispheres could take a nap, and as we worked at a crossword puzzle, our right hemispheres could do likewise. In recent years, a somewhat different explanation of laterality effects has grown in popularity. The 'processing styles' approach (Levy & Trevarthen, 1976) suggests that the main functional difference between the hemispheres is not so much 'what' they process, but 'how' they process it. According to this view, the left hemisphere is specialised to process information in an 'analytical-sequential' way, whereas the right hemisphere adopts a more 'holistic-parallel' mode of processing. In other words, the left hemisphere's modus operandi is to break tasks down into smaller elements that are dealt with one by one, whereas the right hemisphere tends to ignore the fine detail, paying more attention to the 'whole image'.

One advantage of this approach is that it allows for the possibility that *both* hemispheres will be involved in linguistic and spatial tasks, but that they will differ in the type of processing that is undertaken. For example, the right hemisphere is better at judging whether two photographs are of the same person. Face recognition is a holistic skill in the sense that it involves putting together 'the facial image' from its individual elements. However, the left hemisphere is better at identifying individual facial features that may distinguish between two

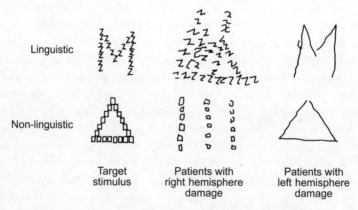

FIGURE 3.6 Figures similar to those used by Delis et al. (1986)

These figures comprise large images made up of smaller, different components. Patients with left-sided damage tend to make identification or memory errors relating to the fine detail. Those with right-sided damage are more likely to make 'holistic' errors.

otherwise identical faces. This is an analytic skill, because it requires the 'whole' to be broken down into its constituent parts. Language is both sequential and analytical – sequential because word order is critical for meaning and analytical because the meaning of language depends on analysis of the verbal message. It is thus dealt with mainly by the left hemisphere, whereas spatial skills including face recognition require holistic analysis and are thus dealt with by the right hemisphere.

The different processing styles of the two hemispheres were very clearly illustrated in a study by Sergent (1982). She developed a set of visual stimuli that were large capital letters, made up of small letters that were either the same as, or different to the capital letter. The stimuli were shown briefly via a tachistoscope to either the left or right visual fields of normal participants. Their task was to indicate whether or not particular target letters were present. On some trials subjects were directed to attend to the large capital letters and at other times to the small letters (that made up the capitals). Sergent found that the left hemisphere (right visual field presentation) was better at detecting the small letters, and the right hemisphere (left visual field presentation) was better for the large letters. The left hemisphere focused on the fine detail, while the right hemisphere attended to the 'big picture'. Similar findings have been reported by Delis, Robertson, and Efron (1986) in their study of memory impairment in uni-laterally damaged individuals (see Fig. 3.6).

Interim comment

These studies show us that rather than having a division of labour, the hemispheres may have complementary processing roles: The right hemisphere sees (so to speak) the forest, while the left hemisphere sees the trees. The right hemisphere processes information at a coarser level than the left, which deals with information at a more detailed and local level. As an analytical and sequential skill, language is dealt with predominantly (but not exclusively) by the left hemisphere. Spatial tasks, which usually involve integrative rather than analytic skills, are handled primarily by the right hemisphere. This model of hemispheric specialisation, with its emphasis on processing style rather than psychological function, arguably makes better sense of the laterality research data than the traditional left brain–language, right brain–spatial skills model, and is becoming widely accepted by neuropsychologists.

Inter-hemispheric transfer via the corpus callosum

Despite its heuristic appeal, the processing styles approach still doesn't entirely explain the 'seamless' nature of psychological functioning. People do not generally feel that they have two separate processors in their heads set to operate at different levels of analysis. On the contrary, we feel that we have one brain, and we also tend to respond serially (one thing at a time). Remember that despite our otherwise remarkable psychological skills, humans actually have difficulty doing two different things at once. Think, for example, of the playground prank in which a child tries to pat their head and rub their stomach at the same time!

In a study by Sergent (1990), split-brain patients had difficulty deciding whether (or not) pairs of photographs presented briefly and simultaneously to right and left visual fields were of the same or different people. As I mentioned earlier, normal people can usually complete this task without error, even when the photographs are taken from a variety of different angles and perspectives. These observations illustrate the importance of the corpus callosum for integrating the activity of the two hemispheres. Although other pathways connecting the two sides of the brain clearly exist, the corpus callosum is the largest commissure, and it enables the two hemispheres of the cortex to relay information backwards and forwards almost instantaneously: ERP recording has shown that inter-hemispheric transfer takes no more than 20 msec. Each hemisphere is thus constantly updated about the other's 'experiences', and together they can collaborate to coordinate joint processing. When this pathway is absent from the outset (as in callosal agenesis) other pathways may take on some of the work normally done by the corpus callosum, but they generally fail to work as efficiently or as quickly in the cause of inter-hemispheric transfer, and hence the slower response speeds seen on tasks requiring inter-hemispheric comparisons.

Developmental aspects

The adult human corpus callosum is made up almost entirely of myelinated axons. These are axons (of neurons) that have an insulated wrapping formed from tissue known as a **myelin sheath**. However, it is important to realise that 'myelination' is a slow developmental process that continues throughout childhood (as more myelin is deposited) to be completed only in late adolescence. In fact, the corpus callosum is one of the last brain structures to reach full maturity. Yet we know that hemispheric specialisation is apparent even in very young children, and it is also apparent in the acallosal individuals we discussed earlier. These findings indicate that the corpus callosum is probably not critical in determining hemispheric specialisation; or even in its development. In fact, the available evidence suggests that lateralisation is essentially a feature of basic nervous system development, and probably under genetic control. For example, in babies only one week old brain activity was greater on the left side to verbal nonsense stimuli ('Pa' or 'Ba') and greater on the right side to non-verbal auditory stimuli such as musical chords or bells (Best, Hoffman, & Glanville, 1982).

If the characteristic pattern of specialisation is apparent so early on, what happens if the normal developmental process is interrupted or disabled in some way? We can partly answer this question by considering what happens to children who are born with one malformed or very small hemisphere. Such instances are rare, but when they occur the preferred course of action is to remove the hemisphere altogether to eliminate it as a potential source of epileptic activity in later life. Following surgery, language and spatial skills usually both develop to some degree, but children with only a left hemisphere outperform those with only a right hemisphere on linguistic tasks, while the opposite is found for spatial tasks (Dennis & Kohn, 1975). However, it is important to note that such children are usually not as proficient at either sort of task as normal children, and this is equally true for children who have 'lost' a hemisphere due to accident early in life. Nevertheless, these observations serve as a reminder that when the normal pattern of development is not possible, the cortex is sufficiently adaptable ('plastic') to facilitate *some* transfer of function to the other hemisphere.

Individual differences in brain organisation

The evidence that I have considered thus far indicates that both structural and functional asymmetries are intrinsic features of nervous system development. However, it is also of interest to know whether (or not) the degree of lateralisation described above varies between people. Two areas where this question seems particularly relevant (and controversial) are handedness and gender.

Handedness

Neuropsychologists are now sure that handedness is something you are born with rather than something you acquire with experience, although researchers continue to debate whether it is genetic in origin as Annett (1985) has argued, or related to intrauterine factors such as the position of the foetus in the womb (Previc, 1991). In fact, the two accounts may not be mutually exclusive, and it is interesting to note that researchers using **ultra-sound** have reported that hand preference is actually apparent in unborn babies, judging by their preference for sucking either left or right hand digits (Hepper, Shalidullah, & White, 1991)! Hepper, McCartney, and Alyson (1998) also reported a strong preference for right (over left) arm movements in 10-week-old foetuses. This is an interesting finding because this laterality preference predates, by six to eight weeks, any overt indications of asymmetry in the developing brain. This may indicate that genetic factors operate to predispose preferential one-sided movements, which, in turn, influence subsequent asymmetries in the developing brain.

About one-in-ten humans is left-handed according to Annett (1985), although *degree* of left or right-handedness certainly varies. Left-handedness has, historically, been frowned on and, at one time, it was common practice for 'natural' left-handers to be forced to use their non-dominant right hands both at school and at home. Interestingly, as this practice has faded, the proportion of left-handers has increased, but only to the figure cited above.

For many years it was more or less assumed by psychologists that the organisation of the left-hander's brain was the mirror image of that of the right-hander. However, data from the Wada test (see Chapter 2) put paid to this myth. Results indicated that the pattern of lateralisation already described above was found in almost all right-handed individuals. For left-handers a different result emerged. About 70% have the same arrangement as right-handers. Of the remainder, half (that is, 15%) show the opposite pattern (reversed asymmetry) and half (the other 15%) show language and spatial skills both distributed in each hemisphere (bi-lateral distribution).

What, if any, are the psychological consequences of left or right-handedness? Researchers have tried to answer this question by examining psychological deficits in right and left-handed individuals who have incurred brain damage. In one of the most comprehensive reviews of such cases, Hardyck and Petrinovich (1977) found that, on average, left-handers with damage to the right hemisphere were more likely to experience language problems than right-handers with similar damage (14% versus 7%). The incidence of aphasia following left-sided damage was the same for right and left-handers. Similarly, spatial skills were more likely to be affected after right hemisphere damage in right-handers than in left-handers. These findings suggest that left-handers as a group may be less 'lateralised' than right-handers. Research on normal left-handers using tests of both dichotic listening and divided visual attention has also led to the suggestion that left-handers show less functional asymmetry than right-handers (Springer & Deutsch, 1993). However, are these results so surprising? Remember that some left-handers show left hemisphere dominance, some show right hemisphere dominance and some show mixed patterns. So as a group, we might expect to find that left-handers were less lateralised, on average, than right-handers. The more interesting question would be to compare test performance between left-handers with left, right and mixed dominance patterns, but at present large-scale studies of this type have yet to be undertaken.

Handedness and cognitive function

It has long been known that left-handedness is more common among mentally handicapped and reading-delayed individuals. Is there any evidence that this relationship generalises to the 'normal' population? Several research projects have set out to compare performances of normal left and right-handers on measures that tap higher mental functions, and the results could best be described as inconsistent. In Hardyck and Petrinovich's (1977) **meta-analysis** of 14 studies, left-handers did marginally worse than right-handers on some tests, and better than right-handers on others. In one particular study by Levy (1969) left-handers were found to have a small but consistent generalised non-verbal IQ deficit as measured by the WAIS: left-handed readers might begin to feel especially indignant at this point! However, her data were based on scores from just 10 left-handers and 15 right-handers. Moreover, all participants were graduate students; a fairly unrepresentative sample to say the least! Levy's research findings have not been well supported in follow-up studies, and where differences have been reported, they have usually been very small (Ratcliff & Newcombe, 1973).

Sex differences

One of the most contentious areas of research has been the question of psychological differences between the sexes, and, among other things, their relation to brain organisation. There are good reasons for thinking that there might be differences in brain organisation (or at least function) between the sexes: Boys are known to be about twice as likely to be born with a range of central nervous system developmental disorders as girls. It has been estimated that at birth the general level of tissue development in boys is between four and six weeks behind that of girls. It is also well documented that cognitive developmental disorders including **autism**, **hyperactivity**, stutter, aphasia and **dyslexia** are all four to six times more common in boys than girls.

MacCoby and Jacklin's (1974) text remains one of the most comprehensive reviews of sex differences and behaviour. Although their research also encompassed the study of social play and aggression, critical attention has focused on their conclusion that girls tend to do better than boys (more or less from the word go) at language-related tasks, and that boys tend to do better at visuospatial tasks. Consider, for example, language: girls begin to talk earlier, they learn to read earlier and they develop a greater vocabulary. These differences begin to emerge almost as soon as it is possible to measure them, and they increase through childhood and adolescence: teenage girls have consistently higher scores for comprehension, fluency and translation. Boys, on the other hand, are better at tasks of visual tracking, aiming, maze-learning, mental rotation and map-reading. Clearly, we cannot rule out the possibility that some of these differences are acquired through experience: for example, male advantage at mathematics becomes more pronounced in adolescence (Hyde, Fennema, & Lamon, 1990) but boys are more likely to be studying maths courses at this stage of schooling. However, the appearance of at least some differences so early in development suggests that they are, in part, a consequence of differential brain organisation.

The work of Kimura and her colleagues has helped to clarify some of the differences first described by MacCoby and Jacklin. As with the earlier debate about the functions of the left and right hemispheres, the rather simplistic conclusions drawn by early researchers (that boys are better at visuo-spatial skills and girls are better at linguistic skills) has been revised. Take, for example, the skill of route-learning. In one variant of this visuo-spatial task, participants were required to learn a route from point A to B depicted on a map. Boys as young as three years old found this task easier to do than age-matched girls (Kimura, 1992). However, once learned, girls remembered more landmarks along the route than boys. As with the earlier laterality research, these findings raise again the possibility that boys and girls employ somewhat different strategies to complete the task. Perhaps boys form an abstract plan of the relationship between points A and B, whereas girls negotiate the route via a series of landmarks. In support of this hypothesis Kimura (1992) reported that girls are consistently better at the party game in which they are allowed to look around a room, then blindfolded and then, when the blindfold is later removed, asked to identify objects in the room that have been moved or taken away. Boys, on the other hand, having seen a particular room layout, are better at avoiding bumping into things when blindfolded.

The neurological literature has been cited as supporting the view that women's brains are functionally less lateralised than men's. McGlone (1980) reported on a large number of case studies of people who had suffered damage to just one side of their brain. Left-sided damage was more likely to result in impaired language function in men than women. Right-sided damage was more likely to impair visuo-spatial function in men than women. Although these data suggest that both language and spatial abilities are more bi-laterally controlled (i.e. less lateralised) in women than men, an alternative explanation is that women tend to use verbally mediated strategies to solve *both* linguistic and visuo-spatial problems. At present it is not possible to say which of these is more likely, but the second explanation tallies well with Kimura's theory of strategy differences between the sexes. However, in two recent reviews of tachisto-scopic and dichotic listening studies of sex/laterality differences, Hiscock et al. (1994; 1995) concluded that the evidence in support of sex differences in degree of lateralisation was inconsistent, and at best indicative of only very small differences.

An interesting footnote to this debate comes from research that considers within subject variability rather than differences between sexes. Although this work takes us some way from the central issue of lateralisation, it has nevertheless become apparent that cortical functioning is influenced by hormonal factors, and this in turn may affect measures of lateralisation. Kimura and Hampson (1994) have studied differences in psychological function in relation to the menstrual cycle. Immediately after ovulation (when levels of oestrogen and progesterone are relatively high) women tend to perform better at tasks involving fine motor control, thought to depend on left hemisphere function, and worse on spatial tasks that tap right hemisphere function. The opposite pattern is seen at menstruation when levels of these hormones are low.

Interim comment

The study of sex and handedness differences in relation to lateralisation has arguably generated as much heat as light! In each domain, the results of countless investigations have been pored over in order to establish the presence/absence of meaningful group differences, and their consequences for ideas about lateralisation. In the case of handedness, we know that at least a proportion of left-handers (perhaps one in three) have a functional asymmetry that differs from the 'right-hander' asymmetry, but we have no reliable data to judge whether (or not) this has any 'knock-on' effects in terms of basic psychological functioning. As for the question about general cognitive skills in left and right-handers the evidence is equivocal, and a prudent interpretation would have to be that if we steer clear of the extremes of the ability range, left and right-handers do not differ.

In the case of sex differences, this author's reading of the available literature leads to the conclusion that the reported differences in the performance of males and females on certain psychological tests (which may, in turn, be related to greater or lesser degrees of lateralisation) are modest, accounting for only a small proportion of the overall variability in the data.

Laterality: A footnote on the evolutionary perspective

According to Corballis (1991), who has developed an evolutionary explanation for the asymmetries in cortical function seen in humans, the key asymmetry concerns the left hemisphere's ability to plan and execute behaviour sequentially. Corballis argues that although the overall blueprint for nervous system structure is symmetry, not asymmetry, the presence of what he calls a 'generative assembly device' (GAD) in the left hemisphere allows us to think and act in a 'generative' manner. Not only does this mechanism enable us to generate almost endless utterances from a pool (in English at least) of less than 50 phonemes (the sounds that make up spoken words), it also explains why humans generally favour their right hand, especially when skilled actions (such as those linked to tool use) are required. Of course, it is probable that the GAD first evolved for tool use, and only later contributed to the development of language. In this context, recall that apraxia (see Chapter 5) is usually associated with left and not right hemisphere damage

Summary

The research that I have reviewed in this chapter supports a model of hemispheric specialisation in humans. While it would be an oversimplification to call the left hemisphere the language hemisphere and the right hemisphere the spatial (or non-language) hemisphere, it is easy to see why earlier researchers jumped to this conclusion. Research conducted on people with brain damage, with surgically lesioned or absent corpus callosa, and on normal people all points to a 'primary' responsibility in the left hemisphere for language. This does not mean that all language skills are, somehow, contained within this hemisphere. Rather that, on balance, this hemisphere 'has the final say' when it comes to language. Whether this is because the left hemisphere is preordained for language, or because it is innately better at analytic and sequential processing, is currently a matter of debate. Certainly, right hemisphere processing seems to be more holistic and integrative, although Corballis has suggested that this happens by default rather than because of any non-verbal equivalent to the GAD mechanism in the right hemisphere. Finally, we have seen that lateralisation can, to some extent, be modified by both handedness and sex differences.

Chapter 4

Somatosensation

■ Introduction   54

■ General features of sensory systems   55

■ The somatosensory system   56
Somatosensory pathways   57
The somatosensory cortex   59
Secondary and tertiary somatosensory
    cortex   61

■ Plasticity in the somatosensory
    cortex   62
The phantom limb syndrome   65

■ The paradox of pain   68

■ Summary   71

Introduction

IT HAS BECOME SOMETHING OF a mantra to refer to *Homo sapiens*' five senses: vision, hearing, touch, smell and taste. Yet most neuropsychologists will quickly seek to qualify this list, which trivialises our true sensory capacities. To start with, what about balance? As bipeds, humans, above most other animals, rely on their sense of balance to teeter around on two legs, sacrificing stability for the opportunity to use their hands and arms for other purposes. How about our sensitivity to temperature? Humans might be able to survive extremes of both high and low temperature, but they are exquisitely sensitive to temperature changes of very small increments. Next, consider pain. Humans (like other mammals) have a highly evolved pain sensitivity system, and are able to differentiate between many types of pain induced by a wide range of focal or diffuse stimuli, including heat, pressure, chemical irritant and injury. Finally, what about the experience of sensory input when clearly there should be none? We need to have a model of sensory processing that can accommodate the phantom limb experiences of amputees too.

Our list is clearly in need of revision, but instead of extending it (which would presumably mean that our 'sixth' sense becomes our 'tenth' or 'eleventh'), the solution has been to replace 'touch' with 'somatosensation'. In this chapter, rather than offering a brief synopsis of each sense system, I have chosen to describe this multi-faceted sensory system in detail. This is not altogether an accident. First, in certain respects, somatosensation relies on the same sort of neural wiring as other senses, so it may serve as an approximate model for them too. Secondly, we know quite a lot about the neural wiring itself, which is somewhat less complex than the wiring of the visual system, for example. Moreover, we are beginning to realise that an understanding of how the brain responds to damage in this system may give an insight into the recuperative functions of the brain in other domains. Lastly, as we learn more about this system, psychological phenomena that we may, at one time, have attributed to our sixth sense or the power of mind-over-matter are finally yielding their secrets. Pain sensitivity and the phantom limb phenomenon are considered later in this chapter.

To set us on our way, however, we need to review some general features of sensory systems, and familiarise ourselves with some of the confusing terminology.

General features of sensory systems

Sensory information travels from sensory receptors along afferent pathways towards the central nervous system. Some of this information gets no further than the spinal cord, where, at the same segment at which it enters, there is a synapse, and output leaves the cord via motor neurons to innervate the appropriate muscles to complete what is known as the reflex arc. Most, however, reaches the brain by a series of relays where it is interpreted in the processes of perception.

Sensory receptors may either be modified nerve endings, as is the case with pressure receptors, or separate cellular structures such as rod or cone cells in the retina. In either case, their job is to respond to particular stimulus parameters (distortion of the skin in the case of Pacinian corpuscles; light in the case of rods and cones) by producing nerve impulses (action potentials, or other graded potentials) that can then travel along the sensory neurons towards the central nervous system.

Most receptors demonstrate three further critical features. First, even within a sensory modality, they are 'tuned' to be selectively most sensitive to a particular limited range of sensory input (certain cones in the retina respond maximally only to green-red colours, others to blue-yellow for example). Secondly, they quickly adapt, meaning they produce fewer and fewer nerve impulses the longer the stimulus continues. A consequence of adaptation is that sensory systems are more responsive to changes in stimulation than constant stimulation. Thirdly, there is a physical limit to their excitability, and therefore an upper limit to the number of nerve impulses that can be generated and conveyed from the receptor to other regions of the nervous system (between 100 and 200 per second).

In the nervous system information is 'conveyed' from point to point in the form of nerve impulses so all receptors must be able to convert external energy (be it light, pressure, temperature, etc.) into nerve impulses: this process is referred to as transduction. (The pick-up on an electric guitar does more or less the same job, converting vibration into electric current.) If the receptor is just a modified nerve ending, as is the case for most touch receptors, we refer to this transducing process as giving rise to a receptor potential. If the receptor is a separate cell such as a rod or cone, a receptor potential (in it) gives rise to a generator potential in the sensory neuron. In either case, these potentials are graded, meaning that they are roughly proportionate to the intensity of the applied stimulus, allowing, of course, for adaptation, and a maximal rate of firing (see Fig. 4.1). Thus the intensity, duration, location, variability (or other quality) of a stimulus will be relayed to the spinal cord and brain in the form of volleys of nerve impulses. As these always have the same amplitude in a given neuron (sometimes known as the all or none principle), their frequency rather than any

Environment	Sense organ	Nerve	CNS
External energy	Accessory structures receptor cell	Sensory neuron	Spinal cord/brain
	Modification/ formation of nerve impulses	Frequency coded nerve impulses	

FIGURE 4.1 The process of sensory transduction

Transduction involves the conversion of one form of energy into another. In the nervous system this job is performed by sensory receptors, or by separate receptor cells. In either case they must respond to (i.e. be activated by) external stimuli (light, temperature, sounds, etc.) and convert this energy into nerve impulses. Within limits a frequency coding rule usually operates in which more intense stimuli lead to the generation of more nerve impulses.

other characteristic enables us to distinguish quiet from loud, dim from bright, or bearable from noxious.

The somatosensory system

As I hinted earlier, the somatosensory system is a poly-modal system, meaning it accommodates a variety of sensory inputs. First, it provides us with a constantly updated picture of tactile (touch, pressure, vibration) input on the body surface (called 'exteroceptive information', because it originates outside the body). Secondly, it provides the central nervous system (CNS) with information about the relative position of body parts, and the position of the body in space (so-called 'interoceptive information', from within the body). Thirdly, it processes information about heat and cold, and pain too.

Transduction is performed by a matrix of receptors in the skin, joints, muscles or tendons. In humans and other mammals there are at least 20 different types of receptor dealing with information about touch, temperature, stretch, pain and so on. In common with receptors in other sensory modalities, somatosensory receptors generate action potentials when stimulated. They also tend to be individually 'tuned' to be most 'responsive' to different intensities of stimulation. For example, some of the touch receptors are particularly sensitive to light touch, others to tickle, and still others to vibration, stretch or pressure. Finally, many receptors adapt extremely quickly: hair follicle receptors only respond to movement (of the hair), and not at all even if the hair is held 'out of position'. Try this on a friend . . . it can bring hours of fun!

Somatosensory pathways

In the somatosensory system, receptors are modified nerve endings of sensory neurons, whose axons run from the point of stimulation towards the spinal cord. In some cases (e.g. pain receptors) the receptor is, literally, just a bare nerve ending. In other cases, the nerve ending is modified or even enveloped by an accessory structure such as a hair follicle, or a Pacinian corpuscle (a sort of multi-layered structure that resembles a spring onion when viewed through a microscope, and which responds to pressure and vibration). The accessory structure simply aids in the transduction process.

Once transduction has occurred, the volleys of nerve impulses must be relayed from the receptors to the CNS. (How else would the brain get to know about somatosensory stimulation?) the majority of sensory neurons carrying these impulses are myelinated, which improves the speed of conduction of action potentials dramatically: sensory neurons can convey impulses at up to 100 metres per second.

On entering the spinal cord, many sensory neurons continue uninterrupted up to the brainstem along pathways forming the dorsal column medial lemniscal system (so-called because they are located medially at the back of the cord). Neurons in this pathway are all myelinated. In other cases, sensory neurons synapse as they enter the spinal cord, in a region known as the substantia gelatinosa, on to spinal neurons that then convey the information along their axons to the brain rather like a relay race. This second set of pathways are known as the spino-thalamic (or antero-lateral) tracts (actually comprising three separate pathways) and many axons in this pathway are unmyelinated (see Fig. 4.2). The pathways can also be distinguished in terms of the information they convey. The former carries precise 'fine-grained' localised information such as touch, pressure and **kinaesthetic** information from joints: the latter carries coarser less precisely localised information to do with pain and temperature. A third important distinction between these two pathways is that in the former there is relatively little **convergence**, whereas in the latter there is a considerable amount. One obvious effect of this is that information about 'localisation' is more easily retained in the dorsal column pathways than in the spino-thalamic tracts.

Most somatosensory input crosses on its way to the brain from one side of the body to the other. In the dorsal columns, this occurs in the medulla, whereas in the spino-thalamic tracts, it occurs at the segment of entry in the spinal cord after the synapse in the substantia gelatinosa. In each case, however, information from the left side of the body mostly finds its way to the right thalamus in the brain, from where it is relayed on to the cortex. In the spino-thalamic system, some neurons send out collateral branches that terminate in the ascending reticular activating system (see Chapter 9) and are involved in brain arousal, and others that terminate in the tectum and are concerned with

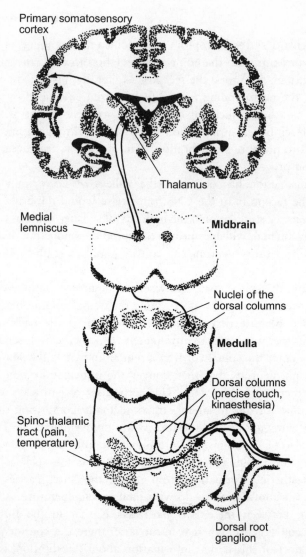

Primary somatosensory
cortex

Thalamus

Medial
lemniscus

Midbrain

Nuclei of the
dorsal columns

Medulla

Dorsal columns
(precise touch,
kinaesthesia)

Spino-thalamic
tract (pain,
temperature)

Dorsal root
ganglion

FIGURE 4.2 The somatosensory pathways

There are two principal sets of spinal pathways carrying somatosensory input. The dorsal
columns (found at the back of the spinal cord) convey precise 'fine-grain' somatosensory
information. The spino-thalamic tracts (at the side of the spinal cord) convey less anatomically precise somatosensory information. In each case the final destination for most of
this input is the primary somatosensory cortex on the opposite side.

Box 4.1

Sensory neurons carrying fine-touch information from your toes are the longest neurons in your body at up to 2 metres. Assuming conduction speed of 100 metres per second, how long would it take for nerve impulses to get to your brain from your toe? (Answer (a) below.)

In some notable cases, speed of conduction is significantly slower. Pain information is predominantly carried along narrow unmyelinated neurons, and travels as slowly as 1 metre per second. This explains why there is sometimes a significant delay between incurring injury (say a burn to the skin) and feeling pain. How long might it take to 'register' the fact that someone has trodden (painfully) on one of your toes? (Answer (b) below.)

Answers: (a) 20 msec assuming typical height. (b) 2 sec assuming typical height.

low-level (unconscious) sensory processing (see Chapter 9). The route from receptor to cortex has involved relays of just two or three neurons (and one or two synapses) and the time it takes to convey information along the pathways is, typically, measured in fractions of a second (see Box 4.1 and Fig. 4.2).

The somatosensory cortex

Like other sensory systems the somatosensory cortex has a primary area for stimulus registration, and other areas (known as secondary and tertiary regions) for further processing, perception and sensory integration. In humans, the primary area (known as S1) occupies a strip of cortex that runs approximately from ear to ear across the top of the brain. Strictly speaking, it is the most anterior (forward) gyrus (bump) of the parietal lobe and comprises Brodmann's areas 3 (a and b), 1 and 2. (See Figs. 4.3a and 4.4.)

A truly remarkable feature of this band of cortex is that the entire body is, in effect, mapped or 'topographically represented' upside-down and left–right reversed along its length. To illustrate this, imagine you could record the activity of neurons in this band starting in the region of cortex located roughly behind the left ear: you would find that these neurons would only become active if there was stimulation to the right side of the tongue or jaw. A little further up you would find neurons that were activated only to stimulation of the right cheek and forehead. Still further up, you would find neurons that respond to tactile stimulation of different parts of the right hand (with each part of each finger, and the palm, and the back of the hand represented separately), and so

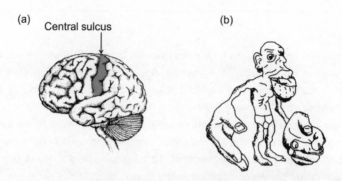

FIGURE 4.3 The somatosensory cortex and sensory homunculus

(a) The primary somatosensory strip (S1) actually comprises three or more parallel bands of cortical neurons responsive to sensory inputs from particular body regions on the opposite side.

(b) The topographic representation is precise but not proportionate with some body regions (notably the lower face and hands) having a disproportionately large S1 representation. This disproportionate allocation is represented in the relative size of body regions in the homunculus ('little man').

on. Towards the top of the left side of the brain you would find neurons that respond to tactile input from the right side of the body, the right leg, right ankle and foot. The identical mirror image pattern would be found on the right side of the somatosensory cortex. As methods of investigation have improved, it has become clear that S1 comprises not one but at least three parallel strips of neurons, each receiving distinct combinations of somatosensory input, while retaining the general pattern of topographic representation mentioned above (Kaas, 1983). The pattern of input to these parallel strips is specified in Fig. 4.4.

Topographic representation in S1 is, however, distorted. Body areas that are more sensitive, such as the hands and lips, have proportionately very much larger areas of somatosensory cortex to project to than body regions that are less sensitive, such as the upper limbs or the back of the head. The evidence suggests that for primates, including humans, about half the total number of neurons in this region receive input from either the face or hands. Researchers have illustrated this disproportionate relationship by drawing or modelling so-called homunculi (little men) whose bodies are proportionate to the area of cortex sensitive to the various body regions (see Fig. 4.3b). The same relationship (of sensitivity and dedicated cortex) is also seen in other species. Mice, for example, have disproportionately large regions of somatosensory cortex dedicated to snout and whiskers, while monkeys have distinct regions dedicated to receiving input from their tails!

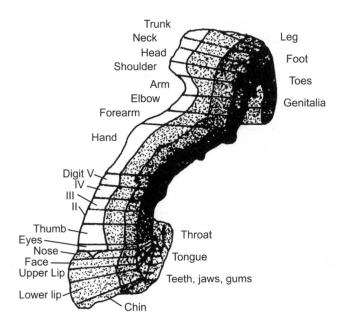

FIGURE 4.4 A detailed view of the primary somatosensory strip (S1)

The figure shows how different body regions (and component parts within those regions) are 'mapped' in S1. Note the disproportionate allocation (in humans) of 'cortical space' to dealing with input from the hands and face. Source: Rosenzweig et al. (1999). *Biological Psychology*. Sunderland, MA: Sinauer Associates Inc. Reproduced by permission of Sinauer Associates Inc.

Secondary and tertiary somatosensory cortex

S1 is only the initial point of processing of somatosensation. While damage to it leads to reduced sensitivity for the particular body region sending inputs to it, identification of objects by touch depends on other regions of cortex. S1 projects (sends outputs) to a secondary area (S2), the role of which is to integrate input from the three (or more) independent primary cortical strips, but now from both sides (i.e. bi-laterally). Both of these areas project to other areas (the tertiary or association areas) of the parietal lobes behind (posterior to) the primary somatosensory strip. In fact, a significant amount of input via the antero-lateral tract goes directly to S2 and tertiary regions including Brodmann's areas 5 and 7.

We can get an idea of the sort of processing that takes place in the secondary and tertiary regions by considering the effects of localised damage here. As a general rule, damage to more posterior regions affects higher order perceptual processing, while leaving basic sensitivity unimpaired. Parietal damage often leads to one of the so-called agnosias, a curious and perplexing cluster of disorders that are described in more detail in Chapter 8. To give just one example here, damage to tertiary somatosensory regions can lead to a condition known as astereognosis, in which blindfolded subjects can describe accurately the main physical features of objects that they feel, yet are unable to match them with other similar objects, or identify them by name.

Interim comment

Somatosensory input from all over the body is relayed via the spinal cord into the brain and eventually to S1. This strip of cortex comprises neurons waiting (in effect) for input from just one partic- ular body region. The strip maps out the entire body contralaterally and upside down, and we refer to this relationship between body region and cortical space as topographic representation. From here, secondary and tertiary regions in the parietal lobe process the sensory input further, to enable perception and integration with other sensory modalities.

Plasticity in the somatosensory cortex

The topographic representation I described in the previous section is very consis- tent from one person to another, which suggests that the basic wiring diagram for neurons here is probably genetically determined. However, psychologists have known since the mid-1960s that the structural integrity of the cortex, at least in rodents, can be affected by experiential factors (Bennett et al., 1964).

Bennett's group showed that adult brain structure depended on the environ- ment in which animals were raised from shortly after birth to maturity, a period of about 60 days. In a typical study there would be a standard (control) condi- tion in an animal laboratory, in which several animals were housed in a cage together. There would be an impoverished condition, which was the same except animals were caged alone, and an enriched condition in which animals had larger cages, lived in bigger social groups and had plentiful play opportunities. In a series of experiments the group found that rats in the enriched environment not only developed heavier brains, but that these had more connections between neurons (synapses) (Turner & Greenhough, 1985), and more neurotransmitter substance (Chang & Greenhough, 1982). The enriched environment rats were also quicker at problem solving and learning (Renner & Rosensweig, 1987). Subsequent research has confirmed that these changes are seen in other species, that they are not restricted to young immature animals and that they can be observed after only short training periods. Although these findings were not directly related to the somatosensory cortex, they were important because they

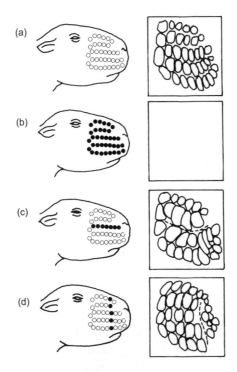

FIGURE 4.5 Woolsey's whisker barrel study

(a) The usual topographic representation of snout whiskers and cortical barrels. If all the whiskers are removed (see b) from one side of the snout of a new-born mouse the entire cortex that would have received sensory input from these whiskers remains silent (i.e. unused). On the other hand, if only a row (see c) or column (see d) of whiskers is removed, the whisker barrels (areas of S1) receiving inputs from adjacent whiskers grow, effectively absorbing much of the 'silent' cortex, which now responds to the remaining adjacent whiskers.

provided experimental evidence that challenged the then-current view that cortical connectivity was fixed (hard-wired) early on in development, and could not be affected by experiential factors.

The first indications that these data may be generalisable to somatosensation came with the findings from Woolsey and Wann (1976). In mice, there is precise topographic representation of snout whiskers contralaterally in sensory cortex. The cortical region can be mapped with each whisker sending sensory input primarily to just one cell cluster (known as a barrel). Woolsey knew that if all whiskers (on one side) were removed in infancy, the area of cortex that would normally receive input from them fell silent. However, if a row or column of whiskers was removed, neurons in the whisker barrels that would otherwise have responded to input from these whiskers begin to respond to adjacent intact whiskers. In effect, the barrels for remaining whiskers absorb the cells from the

63

'silent' barrels, and become larger than normal, so that cortical space is not wasted (see Fig. 4.5).

Merzenich and Kaas (1980) extended Woolsey's paradigm to primates. In the macaque monkey there is topographic representation of the hand area contralaterally in the monkey equivalent of S1 that is very similar to that in humans. In one study, Merzenich and his colleagues removed a digit from a monkey early in infancy, and later on when the monkey had matured, examined the topographic representation in S1. Like Woolsey, they found that the cortical area that would have received input from the amputated digit had, in effect, been absorbed into adjacent regions responding to other digits. In fact the cortical areas for adjacent digits were now bigger than would normally have been expected.

In subsequent research the group has shown that simply preventing or encouraging use of digits, even in mature monkeys can influence cortical maps. In one study by Merzenich and Jenkins (1995), animals were trained to receive food only if they used particular digits to rotate a wheel, which they had to do for several hours each day. After just a few weeks of training, these monkeys

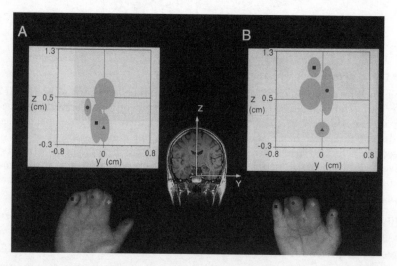

FIGURE 4.6 Summary of Mogilner et al.'s (1993) study

The representation of the hand in the somatosensory cortex changes following surgical correction for syndactyly of digits two to five. (A) A pre-operative map shows that the cortical representation of the thumb, index, middle and little fingers is abnormal and lacks any somatopic organisation. For example, the distance between sites of representation of the thumb and little finger is significantly smaller than normal. (B) Twenty-six days after surgical separation of the digits the organisation of the hand area is somatopic, and the distance between the sites of representation of the thumb and little finger has increased to 1.06 cm. Source: Mogilner et al. (1993). Somatosensory cortical plasticity in adult humans revealed by magnetoencephalography. *Proceedings of the National Academy of Sciences, 90*, 3593–3597. Copyright (1993) National Academy of Sciences, U.S.A.

were found to have significantly larger cortical representation areas in S1 for the trained digits than for the inactive ones.

Can similar effects be seen in humans? Obviously, scientists cannot go around removing babies' fingers and waiting to see how this will influence adult cortical representations! However, Mogilner et al. (1993) have reported on a small number of individuals with syndactyly; a congenital disorder in which the fingers are malformed and fused together. Such individuals can have their fingers surgically separated. The researchers used magnetoencephalography (MEG) (see Chapter 2) to record activity in the 'hand' region of the primary somatosensory cortex of these subjects before, and again after surgery to 'free' their fused fingers. Prior to surgery, the cortical mapping of the hand region in two syndactyly cases was quite distinct and unusual in comparison with the controls. Yet examination of pre and post-operative MEG maps indicated marked reorganisation in the cortical hand area in these cases. In each the result of reorganisation now more closely resembled the cortical maps of controls. The changes were apparent within one week, and further MEGs recorded three and six weeks later indicated relatively little additional change. The remapping occurred over distances of between 5 and 10 mm (see Fig. 4.6).

Interim comment

Mogilner et al.'s (1993) study is the first to illustrate that functional mapping in the human adult somatosensory cortex is not, as was once believed, 'hardwired'. On the contrary, areas of cortex responsive to input from individual fingers 'appear' to move within a few days of surgery. Clearly, the cortex does not actually move, but new regions up to 10 mm away from the original site now respond to sensory input from the newly freed fingers. It is important to remember that Mogilner et al.'s study is based on just two individuals who had the abnormality from birth. However, in certain respects this makes the speed of change all the more remarkable, and scientists are now trying to identify the mechanisms that permit such remapping to occur.

The phantom limb syndrome

A sense of residual (and often painful) feeling emanating from an amputated body region (referred to as phantom limb experience) is felt, at least intermittently, by almost all amputees. The experience is graded, usually being most pronounced soon after surgery, and becoming less marked (or somehow 'shrunken') over time (Melzak, 1992). However, some phantom limb feelings can persist for many years. It is important to emphasise that phantom limb experiences are not 'made-up'. Indeed, a remarkable feature of them for the amputee is their realistic nature. Sometimes, the experience will be so real that the individual might forget that their leg has been amputated, and try to stand up, or may start to reach for something with their 'amputated' arm.

Until recently, little was known about the physiology of the phantom limb phenomenon, and it was generally assumed that phantom experiences were caused by residual neuronal activity from nerves in the stump. At least 50% of amputees have painful phantom limb experiences, and these can sometimes be so severe that further surgery is conducted (often at the behest of the amputee) to try to eliminate the pain. Unfortunately, this is rarely very effective and scientists now think that the phantom limb experience is somehow 'recreated' in the brain.

An insight into the possible mechanisms that are involved has recently been offered by Ramachandran (1994). He reported the case of a young man who had lost his lower left arm in a traffic accident. Four weeks later, the subject reported a series of sensations in his (amputated) arm and hand whenever Ramachandran gently touched the left side of his face. In fact, different regions of the face elicited 'sensations' in different parts of the phantom hand! Touching his cheek evoked feelings in his first finger, whereas touching his lower jaw evoked sensations in his little finger, and so on (see Fig. 4.7).

Ramachandran collected several similar anecdotal reports of phantom experiences being evoked during stimulation of intact body regions. For example, in another case, a woman who had had her foot amputated experienced phantom feelings in it whenever she had sexual intercourse! Ramachandran explained these observations by proposing that the cortical region that should have received input

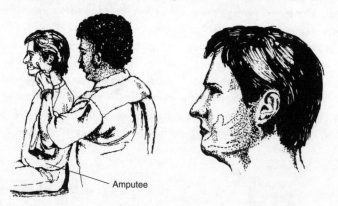

Amputee

FIGURE 4.7 Referred phantom experiences from facial stimulation

The amputee experienced phantom limb 'sensations' when his cheek was gently touched. Ramachandran (1994) observed that different regions of the face evoked 'sensations' in different parts of the amputated limb in a quite precisely mapped way: brushing the lower jaw evoked feelings in his little finger and brushing his cheek evoked feelings in his thumb. Source: Gazzaniga et al. (1998). *Cognitive Neuroscience: The Biology of the Mind.* Copyright © 1998 by W.W. Norton & Company, Inc. Reproduced by permission of W.W. Norton & Company, Inc.

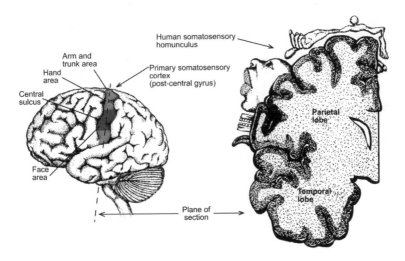

FIGURE 4.8 Ramachandran's explanation of phantom limb experiences

Sensory input from the face region now begins to stimulate adjacent hand regions of S1. This could be due to the growth of new axon branches (offshoots from the inputs to the face region) but the speed of the effect is too quick to be accounted for by the relatively slow growth of new axons. A more likely explanation is that previously inhibited (silent) inputs to the hand region become active, because they are no longer inhibited by the missing input from the hand itself!

from the missing limb was now receiving stimulation from the region that evoked the phantom experience – i.e. the face in the case of the traffic accident victim and the genitals in the case of the woman.

Ramachandran put forward his theory after studying the somatosensory homunculus. He knew that this was very consistent from one person to another, and he also knew that the evocation of the phantom experience could only be achieved by stimulating body regions whose cortical receptive fields were close to the region attendant on input from the amputated limb. You may recall that the hand area is adjacent to the face area, and reference to Fig. 4.4 will show that the genital region is immediately adjacent to the foot region. (Perhaps there is more to reflexology than meets the eye!)

To explain this effect, the growth of new axons from adjacent inputs has been suggested. However, this can be discounted because of the speed with which the effect is observed: axons just do not grow this quickly! Ramachandran's explanation invoked the activation of previously silent synapses. He argued that, ordinarily, sensory input travels both to target and adjacent cortical regions, but that the adjacent input is normally inhibited by the direct inputs to that cortical region. Loss of this input (after amputation) means loss of **lateral inhibition**, so that neighbouring regions' inputs now get through, evoking the phantom experience (see Fig. 4.8).

Interim comment

Actually, Ramachandran's explanation of the phantom limb phenomenon is unlikely to account for all aspects of it. For example, touching the stump itself does usually evoke some feelings, suggesting that peripheral input is still involved. Moreover, phantom limb sensations are also often evoked when an amputee tries to move his amputated limb, suggesting that reafference or feed-forward of motor output directly into somatosensory cortex is probably also involved. Nevertheless, these are important findings because they may lead to the development of new strategies to help people recover lost function after nerve damage. They also serve as a reminder of the potential for 'plastic' change present even in the mature cortex.

The paradox of pain

Pain is not cortically represented in the topographic pattern seen for non-noxious stimuli. In fact, the only region of cortex that can be reliably activated by noxious input is the anterior cingulate (Craig et al., 1996), and even this activation is thought to be associated with an 'emotional' rather than sensory response. Moreover, pain is an experience that may be elicited by excessive stimulation of any type, and, under certain circumstances, by innocuous stimulation too. A moment's introspection may illustrate a further paradox of pain: why, for example, should rubbing or blowing on a painful body part lessen or even eliminate the pain? Why should an injury incurred in the heat of battle go unnoticed until many hours after the event? Why might a gentle touch be excruciatingly painful to someone with sunburn?

Clearly, the experience of pain can be influenced by a raft of other circumstances or stimuli. In 1965 Melzak and Wall put forward their 'gate control theory' to explain how pain could be moderated by other innocuous events, or even by the psychological circumstances that prevailed. In the intervening years the theory has been modified several times as new research has come to light. However, the basic features have survived intact, and merit consideration now.

Melzak and Wall argued that a full understanding of pain 'modulation' must take into account the observation that counter stimuli (such as rubbing an injured area) and cognitive factors (such as analgesia during the heat of battle) can both 'shape' the experience of pain. They suggested that two separate mechanisms act to influence the pain signals on route to the brain. Peripheral gating explains the effects of counter stimuli, and this takes place in the substantia gelatinosa region of the spinal cord. Psychological factors can influence the perception of pain via a central gating mechanism involving neurons whose cell bodies originate in the brain and whose axons terminate in the same substantia gelatinosa.

Peripheral gating was thought to work like this: when pain receptors are stimulated, they generate action potentials that travel along A-delta and C fibres (specialised pain message-bearing pathways) into the spinal cord where they synapse in the substantia gelatinosa region. The messages are then relayed to the brain via the spino-thalamic tracts. However, if an innocuous counter stimulus such as rubbing or gentle pressure is applied to the injured area, this stimulates sensory input via the major A-beta fibres. When these enter the spinal cord, the main fibres ascend to the brain, but branches (collaterals in the jargon) influence synaptic activity in the substantia gelatinosa by inducing **interneurons** in this area to release endogenous opioids. These are neurotransmitter substances with opiate-like effects that reduce the overall activity of the pain synapse, so the experience of pain is reduced.

Appealing though this peripheral gating mechanism is, evidence of the existence of the neural hardware for it has been difficult to come by, although there is ample evidence for the existence of opioid interneurons in the substantia gelatinosa. There has been more support for the central gating arm of the theory. The periaqueductal grey area (PAG) in the midbrain receives inputs from the cortex and limbic system. It contains inhibitory neurons which themselves can be inhibited by opioids. When this happens, the PAG is 'freed' to send nerve impulses to the Raphe nucleus in the brain stem, from which major descending neurons plunge into the spinal cord, terminating in the substantia gelatinosa where they release serotonin. Serotonin causes local interneurons to block incoming pain signals via the release of endogenous opioids. (See Fig. 4.9, which illustrates the major elements of Basbaum and Fields' interpretation of spinal pain modulation: Basbaum & Fields, 1984.)

The model provides a ready explanation for the analgesic effects of opiates, which are thought to act by imitating or supplementing the role of endogenous opioids in the PAG and/or the substantia gelatinosa. Opioids (and opiates as well) have also been found to act directly on peripheral pain receptors (Taddese, Nah, & McClesky, 1995). The observation that **analgesia** induced by transcutaneous electrical nerve stimulation (TENS) is partly reversed by the drug naloxone also provides an indication of how the system brings about analgesia in the first place. Naloxone is a powerful inhibitor (blocker) of opioid action, so its use renders the opioid system inert. The fact that naloxone also reduces the effect of TENS is strong evidence that the TENS analgesia ordinarily relies on the actions of opioids. There is even evidence that acupuncture and placebo analgesia may be mediated by similar mechanisms, for each is partly reversed by naloxone (Tang et al., 1997). However, naloxone does not entirely eliminate their analgesic effects, suggesting that non-opiate mechanisms, largely ignored in Melzak and Wall's model, must also be involved.

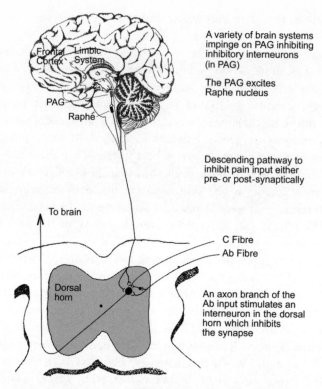

FIGURE 4.9 Basbaum and Fields' (1984) model of pain modulation

The model allows for both ascending and descending modulatory influences on pain input, although experimental support for the former is hard to come by. The ascending component is similar to the idea of peripheral gating in Melzak and Wall's (1965) original theory. Axon branches from A-beta fibres stimulate interneurons in the dorsal horn of the spinal cord which inhibit the pain information-bearing C fibres. The descending central modulation involves the PAG, which contains neurons that normally inhibit the Raphe nucleus. When the PAG neurons are themselves inhibited (by other brain inputs from the frontal lobes or limbic system) the Raphe neurons become disinhibited. Their axons descend the cord and release serotonin in the dorsal horn. This neurotransmitter inhibits the C fibres from relaying their inputs on to the brain.

Interim comment

For fairly obvious reasons, most pain research has focused on mechanisms of pain reduction. However, under certain circumstances pain sensitivity may be modulated upwards too. Consider for instance the excruciating pain that may be induced by gentlest touch to an area of sunburn. These effects are thought to be mediated by the heightened sensitivity of pain receptors following the release of chemicals such as substance P, serotonin, histamine, and other algogens (pain inducing chemicals) in the tissue adjacent to injury. There is also evidence of a long-term increased synaptic activity in the spinal cord related to enduring pain, which may involve a form of **long-term potentiation** of spinal synapses.

Summary

Somatosensation depends on a poly-modal sensory system handling exteroceptive information about touch, pressure and vibration, and interoceptive information from muscles and joints. It also deals with temperature and pain. The sensory input is garnered from at least 20 different types of receptor located predominantly in the skin or muscles, and each relays sensory information in the form of frequency coded volleys of action potentials via one of two major afferent pathways – the dorsal columns and the spino-thalamic tracts – towards the brain.

Much of this sensory input is received by S1, which is a topographically organised gyrus at the front of the parietal lobe, along which the entire body is, in effect, mapped contralaterally and upside-down. Further bi-lateral and higher order perceptual processing is undertaken in S2 and posterior regions of parietal cortex.

Despite its highly consistent topography, S1 can, under certain circumstances, undergo quite marked functional changes. Initially it was thought that this capacity was only present in the immature nervous system, but further investigation has confirmed that plasticity can also be observed in 'adult' mammalian nervous systems under certain circumstances, even after relatively short periods of 'changed' input.

One particular example of functional plasticity is thought to be responsible for some of the features of the phantom limb phenomenon. After injury, it appears that input from body regions mapped cortically adjacent to the missing limb can invade and 'innervate' the cortex attendant to the missing limb and evoke phantom limb experiences. However, other mechanisms probably contribute to the overall experience too.

Mammals have evolved a sophisticated pain perception system, which, although superficially similar to other components of the somatosensory system, presents a number of paradoxes. Pain input can be modulated by circuits in the brain stem and the substantia gelatinosa of the spinal cord. Endogenous opioids seem to be involved at each site. A number of well-established analgesic procedures, including acupuncture and TENS seem, in part, to depend on this system in order to be effective, as their analgesic effect is lessened or abolished by prior administration of the opioid blocker naloxone. Chemicals released in the skin close to pain receptors and/or functional synaptic changes in the substantia gelatinosa are responsible for the increased sensitivity to pain observed in certain conditions, such as burns, where there has been tissue damage.

Chapter 5

Motor control and movement disorders

■ **Introduction**   **74**

■ **Brain–spinal cord pathways**   **75**
  The cortico–spinal tract   75
  The cortico–bulbar pathway   78
  The ventro–medial pathway   78
  The rubro–spinal pathway   78

■ **The cerebellum**   **79**
  Cerebellar structure   79
  Cerebellar functions in humans   80

■ **The basal ganglia**   **81**
  Basal ganglia components   81
  Basal ganglia functions   82

■ **The cortex**   **85**
  The motor strip   85
  The SMA and pre-motor cortex   86
  Other frontal regions involved in movement   88
  Parietal involvement in movement   89

■ **Peripheral and spinal movement**
  disorders   **91**
  Myasthenia gravis   91

Diseases associated with neuronal
   damage/loss   92
Spinal damage   93

■ **Cortical movement disorders**   **93**
Hemiplegia   93
Cerebral palsy   94

■ **Subcortical movement disorders**   **94**
Parkinson's disease (PD)   94
Huntington's disease   97
Tics, Tourette's syndrome and obsessive-
   compulsive disorder   98

■ **Summary**   **99**

Introduction

THE PSYCHOLOGICAL STUDY OF BEHAVIOUR is, substantially, the study of movement. True, humans *can* engage in psychological processes (such as imagining or planning) in the absence of movement but these are exceptions rather than the rule. For the most part, 'behaviour' is fundamentally and inextricably linked to action, whether of discrete muscles in our mouth and throat to bring about spoken language, or of massive muscle systems in our trunk and limbs giving rise to the movements required to approach and hit a tennis ball.

The nervous system's control of movement is phenomenally complex: it has to be in order for individuals to engage in behaviours requiring precise muscle coordination. Think, for example, of the skill of a trained acrobat or the dexterity of a concert pianist. But skilled movement is something that most of us can develop with a little practice. When considered objectively, riding a bicycle is quite clever, so too is touch-typing, and even tying a shoelace calls on temporally coordinated bi-manual skilled movement.

Although muscles can obviously stretch, this is a passive process: movement only occurs when muscles are made to contract. The contraction results from the release of neurotransmitters from the terminals of motor neurons, although there will, of course, be passive expansion of any oppposor muscles. The cell bodies of motor neurons are to be found in the spinal cord. They are controlled by a variety of descending (and some ascending) neurons in the cord itself, and whether or not they fire will depend on the summed influence of inputs (both excitatory and inhibitory) on them. But to understand the control of movement we need to work backwards; to examine the origin of the inputs that can influence motor neurons.

For many years it was thought that 'deliberate' movement was under the direct control of the motor cortex via the so-called pyramidal system, and that all other movement was controlled by a separate so-called extra-pyramidal system and/or the spinal cord itself. But, as usual, the true picture turns out to be rather more complicated. First, there are not one but several pathways from different parts of the cortex to the spinal cord, and thus to the cell bodies of motor neurons. Secondly, in the brain itself there are several regions that are involved in the control of movement: the frontal lobes of the cortex, the subcortical structures of the basal ganglia, and the cerebellum, to name but three. Finally, there is good evidence that the parietal lobes, which hitherto have been associated with various sensory and perceptual functions, may also be important in certain kinds of motor function. Our review of the nervous system's control of movement must give due consideration to all these components, and should also take into account certain characteristic movement disorders linked to nervous system damage or disease.

Brain–spinal cord pathways

Although neurons in the cortex do not make direct contact with muscles, it has been known since the pioneering work of Fritsch and Hitzig (1870) that electrical stimulation of the brain can bring about movement. In fact, there are at least four major tracts from the brain that can convey nerve impulses about movement (see Fig. 5.1), and we need to consider the specialised roles of each in turn.

The cortico–spinal tract

As the name suggests, this pathway comprises neurons whose cell bodies are found in the cortex (mainly the primary motor strip). This strip is the most posterior gyrus of the frontal lobes, and is located immediately forward of the primary somatosensory cortex (S1) on the other side of the central sulcus. Like S1, the motor strip is topographically organised. The axons of pyramidal neurons in this region descend within the brain to the medulla, where most cross (decussate) to the opposite side, before continuing into the spinal cord to synapse with motor neurons. These then relay the impulses to the muscles themselves. Actually, this pathway comprises two functionally distinct tracts; the 'lateral' tract helps to control distal muscles (in the forearm, lower limb, hand and fingers) mainly

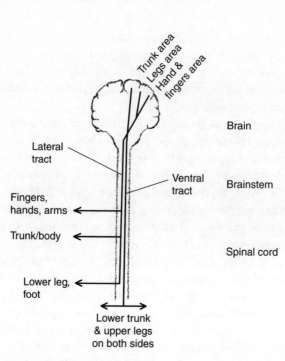

(a) The cortico–spinal tract

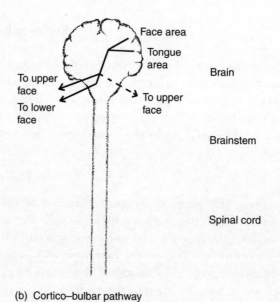

(b) Cortico–bulbar pathway

FIGURE 5.1 Descending 'movement' control pathways

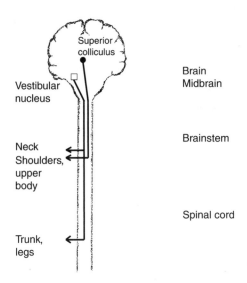

(c) Ventro–medial pathway

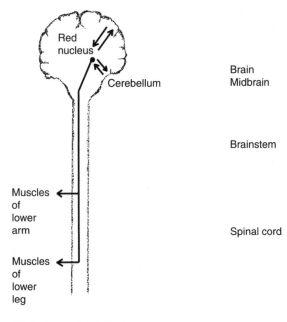

(d) Rubro–spinal pathway

on the opposite side of the body, while the 'ventral tract' controls more medial muscles (in the trunk, upper limbs and so on) on both sides. Damage to the former will compromise skilled movement involving hands or fingers; damage to the latter will affect posture and ambulation.

The cortico–bulbar pathway

This pathway also has its origins in the primary motor strip, although the axons descend no further than the pons, where they innervate some of the cranial nerves to control facial, mouth and tongue muscles. Projections to the upper part of the face tend to be bi-lateral, whereas those to the lower face and mouth regions tend to be contralateral: you can, for example, easily raise one side of your mouth, but it is harder to raise one side of your forehead.

The ventro–medial pathway

Once again, this pathway actually comprises several interlinked tracts, but unlike the cortico–spinal tract and cortico–bulbar pathways, the point of origin of each component is in the brainstem or midbrain rather than the cortex, and projections terminate in proximal (i.e. close to midline) muscles in the trunk, shoulders and neck. One component whose cells originate in the superior colliculus is important for coordinating eye movements in relation to body posture. A second component whose cell bodies reside in the vestibular nuclei of the brainstem help to coordinate balance. Other brainstem components coordinate relatively automatic processes such as sneezing, breathing and so on.

The rubro–spinal pathway

The point of origin of this pathway is the red nucleus of the midbrain, which receives inputs from both the motor cortex and the cerebellum (with which it has reciprocal connections). The main projections, however, are to distal limb parts (excluding fingers), and the primary function of the tract is thought to be the movement of limbs independent of movements of trunk. The importance of this pathway in humans has come into question because, in comparison with other primates, and especially other mammals, the size of the red nucleus is small, and the axons of the pathway are unmyelinated.

Interim comment

Earlier I introduced the terms 'pyramidal' and 'extra-pyramidal' to delineate two separate systems of motor control. Although these terms have, to some extent, fallen into disuse (because they oversimplify the organisation of motor control both in the brain and the spinal cord) it is easy to see how the distinction came about in the first place. Two major descending pathways link the motor cortex to muscles in different body regions in a fairly direct way, and two other pathways (which in the case of the ventro–medial system may be further subdivided) act on muscles in an indirect or more automatic way. Incidentally, the pyramidal tract got its name from the 'wedge-shaped' structures that are visible in the brainstem at the point where the axons decussate to the contralateral side. Fibres that did not form part of this pathway were 'extra-pyramidal'. Today, a more useful distinction (supported by lesion studies) is that between lateral and medial pathways. Animals with lesions to lateral pathways lose the ability to engage in skilled digit coordination (such as reaching for food, or releasing food once in the mouth), whereas animals with ventro–medial lesions manifest enduring postural and whole body movement abnormalities (Kuypers, 1981).

The cerebellum

This structure accounts for at least 10% of the brain's complement of neurons yet, perhaps because it lies outside the cortex, it has received relatively little attention until recently. Two vital observations should be noted at the outset. First, although it is now thought that this structure may be involved in a range of psychological phenomena (in addition to movement), its pivotal role in movement coordination is unquestioned. In the higher mammals at least, the cerebellum is fundamentally involved in the modulation of motor coordination and the acquisition of motor skills. This is made possible by the large number of reciprocal connections between the cortex and parts of the cerebellum. Secondly, a quirk in the nervous system's wiring diagram means that the cerebellum influences motor control on the **ipsilateral** side (right-sided damage affects movement on the right side of the body). We consider some of the deficits associated with cerebellar damage in due course. First, we need to summarise the key anatomical regions and functional components of the structure.

Cerebellar structure

The cerebellum vaguely resembles two walnuts connected to each other, and, via two short stalks, to the brainstem in the pons region. The structure is bilaterally symmetrical, and each hemisphere comprises a highly regular neuronal structure. In fact, the cerebellum contains just four different neuron types.

The inner-most (medial) regions of each hemisphere comprise the vermis. This region receives somatosensory and kinaesthetic information from the spinal

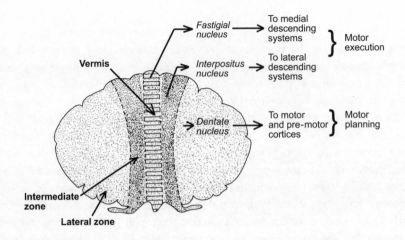

FIGURE 5.2 The cerebellum and its connections

Output from the vermis influences medial descending systems to affect motor execution. In similar vein, output from the intermediate zone affects more lateral descending systems. Output from the lateral zone is primarily to the frontal lobes. The lateral zone is thought to be involved in motor planning, particularly in relation to responding to external stimuli. (Adapted from Kandel et al., 1991.)

cord. The next region (moving outwards) is the intermediate zone. This region receives information from the red nucleus, and returns output to it. The most lateral regions are, unsurprisingly, known as the lateral regions! They receive information from motor and association cortex. Embedded deep within the cerebellum on each side are three nuclei. The vermis projects to the fastigial nuclei, which in turn influence medial descending motor systems. The intermediate zones project to the interpositus nuclei, which influence lateral descending motor systems. The lateral zones project to the dentate nuclei, which in turn project to motor and pre-motor cortex, and these regions are thought to be involved in motor planning (see Fig. 5.2).

Cerebellar functions in humans

In view of its somatosensory inputs and its descending medial outputs, we should not be surprised to learn that damage to the vermis is likely to affect balance and posture, and may lead to a person staggering or even falling over as they try to carry out some simple movement such as bending to pick up an object. Damage to the intermediate zone gives rise to a phenomenon known as 'intentional tremor': an action can still occur, but the execution of it is jerky or staggered. This observation reinforces the view that a normal function of the intermediate zone is to 'smooth out' otherwise poorly coordinated actions, especially of the distal regions of limbs.

Damage to the lateral zones also affects movement of limbs, especially for tasks that require complex muscle coordination (sometimes called 'ballistic' movements) over a short period of time. This type of skilled movement requires the concerted and temporally organised action of many muscles, but in a particular sequence which is too quick for the action to be modified by feedback. An excellent example would be a well-practised tennis serve, or playing a scale on the piano. After lateral damage the movement may still be attempted, and even completed, but instead of being smooth and well rehearsed, it is tentative and often inaccurate. The more joints involved in the action, the worse the deficit seems to be. Moreover, it will probably not improve much with practice because people with this type of brain damage are not only clumsy, but they also find it difficult to learn new motor skills.

Interim comment

The cerebellum (translation, 'little brain') can be subdivided into three anatomically separate regions. These can also be distinguished in terms of inputs and outputs: the medial regions modulate and 'smooth out' movements initiated elsewhere, whereas the lateral regions coordinate skilled movements enacted 'in time'. The cerebellum is involved in a wide range of motor skills including balance, posture, multi-limb movement and, of course, the acquisition and enacting of ballistic movements. It is important to realise that damage to the cerebellum does not eliminate movement per se: rather it seems that tasks that at one time were effortless become a struggle after cerebellar damage.

The basal ganglia

These are a group of subcortical structures that connect with each other and the cortex in a distributed control network.

Basal ganglia components

The main components include the caudate and putamen (referred to jointly as the striatum in some books), the globus pallidus, the subthalamic nucleus, and the substantia nigra (see Fig. 5.3). The main input to the basal ganglia is an excitatory one from the frontal lobes (especially the supplementary motor area, discussed later in this chapter). The caudate and putamen ordinarily inhibit the globus pallidus, whose principal output to the thalamus is also inhibitory. The final component in the loop is an excitatory one from the thalamus back to the

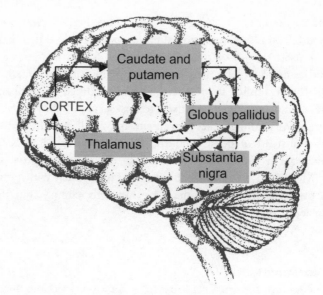

FIGURE 5.3 Components and connections of the basal ganglia

The figure shows the main components of the basal ganglia. The structures form a loop with the frontal cortex (particularly the supplementary motor area). A current idea is that plans and intentions for movement get channelled through the basal ganglia prior to being put into effect. The overall excitability of the basal ganglia can be influenced by release of dopamine from neurons originating in the substantia nigra (dotted line in figure). (Adapted from Wichmann & Delong, 1996.)

frontal lobes, and a smaller output direct to the spinal cord. The overall activity of the caudate/putamen is modulated (influenced) by inputs from the substantia nigra via the nigro–striatal pathway.

If this is not already sufficiently complicated, a further twist is that there are, in effect, parallel competing direct and indirect loops through the basal ganglia, which are shown in Fig. 5.4. The direct route is from the striatum to the internal region of the globus pallidus, then to the thalamus and back to the cortex. The indirect route takes a detour via the external portion of the globus pallidus and subthalamic nucleus (DeLong, 1993). Moreover, the release of a single neurotransmitter (dopamine) from the nigro–striatal pathway has opposite effects on the direct and indirect loops: it stimulates the direct loop by exciting **D1 dopamine receptors**, while inhibiting the indirect route by stimulating **D2 receptors**.

Basal ganglia functions

That the basal ganglia are important in movement seems self-evident when we consider the raft of movement-related disorders seen in people with damage to

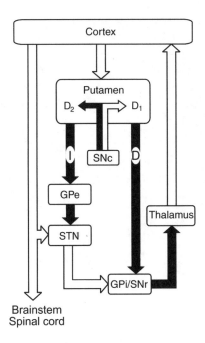

FIGURE 5.4 Direct and indirect basal ganglia pathways

Activation of the direct (D) pathway permits selection of the desired action, while stimulation of the indirect (I) pathway holds alternative possible actions in check. Although it appears that the two routes are in direct opposition to one another, the indirect route works more slowly. The consequence is that more excitation in the direct pathway is *followed* by less excitation in the indirect pathway. This mechanism explains the selective influence that the basal ganglia exert on the frontal cortex. (Key: GP = globus pallidus; STN = subthalamic nucleus; SN = substantia nigra.)

one or more components of them. However, at present there is still no firm agreement on exactly how the basal ganglia influence movement. At one time it was thought that they were concerned almost exclusively with slow medial postural adjustments because people with basal ganglia damage sometimes have 'writhing' like movements or other postural disturbances. Another idea was that they were important for initiating movements: damaged individuals certainly sometimes appear to struggle to start movements but are OK once they get going. However, a modern view of basal ganglia function, based on more extensive neurological investigation in human disease and experimental studies with animals, is that they operate rather like a 'gatekeeper' for action plans locked away in the motor and pre-motor regions of the frontal lobes (Bradshaw & Mattingley 1995). The upshot of the arrangements described above (and illustrated in Fig. 5.5) is that the direct loop effectively works as an 'enabling'

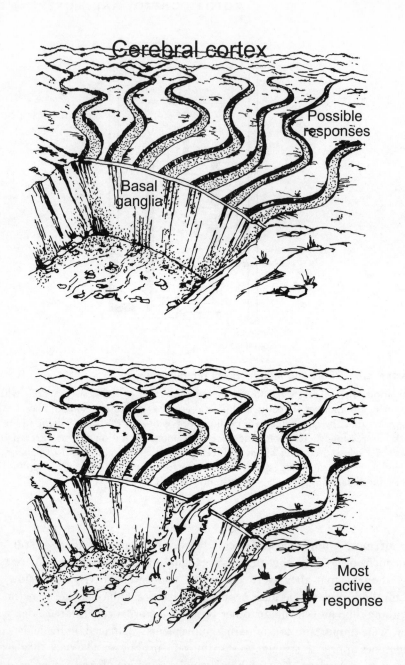

FIGURE 5.5 The basal ganglia as a facilitator/inhibitor of action plans

Conceptually, we might think of the basal ganglia as facilitating selection of the appropriate movement by holding in check all but the most desired response. Source: Figure 10.41 from Gazzaniga, M.S., Ivry, R.B., and Mangun, G.R. (1998). *Cognitive Neuroscience: The Biology of the Mind.* Copyright © 1998 by W.W. Norton & Company, Inc. Used by permission of W.W. Norton & Company, Inc.

mechanism, which, if active, facilitates ongoing or preferred activity. The indirect loop suppresses unwanted movements by preventing the plans for those actions (hatched in the frontal lobes) from being put into effect. This regulatory function is supported by the observation that electrical activity in the basal ganglia increases in anticipation of intended movements (Steg & Johnels, 1993).

The cortex

At one time, motor function (in the brain) was thought to involve all cortical tissue forward of the central sulcus – 'the motor unit' in Luria's terms (Luria, 1973). With more research, this view has required revision. First, it ignores the fact that the frontal lobes have various non-motor functions in addition to responsibilities for the control of movement (see Chapter 10). Secondly, it ignores the apparently critical role of regions of the parietal lobe, especially on the left side, in controlling movement in particular circumstances. Today, attention has turned to unraveling the relative responsibilities of different cortical regions in organising and controlling movement, and to trying to understand how these regions interact with each other and with the subcortical structures already mentioned. The model that is emerging is essentially hierarchical, with a particular focus on distinctions between internally generated movement and stimulus-driven or externally prompted movement.

The motor strip

As I mentioned earlier, the primary motor cortex or motor strip (Brodmann's area 4), like the somatosensory cortex, is highly topographically organised. All regions of the body are represented, and there is predominantly contralateral control; the right motor cortex coordinates muscles in the left side of the body, and vice versa. As with the somatosensory cortex, the relationship between cortical 'space' in the motor strip and body region is not proportionate: there is over-representation of regions capable of fine motor control, such as the hands and fingers, and the mouth area of the face, and under-representation of less 'movement-critical' regions such as the back and top of the head, the trunk and the upper limbs. The axons of pyramidal neurons, whose cell bodies are found here, make up much of the cortico–spinal and cortico–bulbar pathways I identified earlier. Remember, however, that output from this region can also influence activity in the indirect (extra-pyramidal) pathways via synaptic contacts in the brain stem. The region also has reciprocal connections with the basal ganglia.

With more precise instrumentation (basically amounting to finer electrodes), researchers have discovered that the primary motor strip comprises not one but several parallel bands of topographically mapped pyramidal neurons (as many as nine have been reported). Moreover, it appears that muscles actually require a pattern of activity in several adjacent cortical cells in order to bring about movement (Georgopoulos, Taira, & Lukashin, 1993). This explains why damage to one or a few pyramidal cells weakens, but rarely eliminates entirely, movement in the corresponding body region. It is also clear that more extensive damage to this region can bring about a widespread loss of muscle function and paralysis. In cases where accident or stroke has damaged the entire left or right primary motor cortex, the result is opposite side **hemiplegia**, which usually involves lasting impairments.

The supplementary motor area and pre-motor cortex

Having established the link between the primary motor cortex and muscles, we now need to consider how a person 'initiates' a movement. The answer to this question is only now emerging, and other brain regions in addition to the cortex are certainly involved. However, as I hinted earlier, within the cortex the control of movement is organised 'hierarchically' by different regions of the frontal lobes. The hierarchy works like this. As we have already seen, pyramidal cells in the primary motor cortex control muscle contractions via their connections with motor neurons in the spinal cord. But these pyramidal cells are, in turn, partly controlled by neurons in the region of frontal lobe just forward of the primary motor cortex. This area divides into two functionally distinct regions, both, occupying Brodmann's area 6; the more medial supplementary motor area or SMA (towards the top of the brain) and the more lateral pre-motor cortex or PMC (towards the sides). Cells in each region influence neurons in the motor strip when a particular movement is carried out. In other words, SMA and PMC neurons control hierarchically the activity of individual pyramidal cells (see Fig. 5.6). Individuals with damage to these regions retain fine motor control of fingers but are impaired on tasks that require the coordination of two hands (such as tying a knot).

The main outputs from the SMA are to the primary motor cortex bi-laterally. The main inputs are from the pre-frontal cortex and the basal ganglia. This arrangement places the SMA in a strategic position (in the hierarchy) to coordinate motor plans (that have been 'approved' by the basal ganglia for execution) via the pyramidal neurons of the primary motor strip. It provides a buffer store for such plans prior to their execution. Several important observations reinforce this view. First, it is possible to record a negative ERP (see Chapter 2) from the SMA that builds over a period of one or two seconds prior to intended movement. This is known as the *bereitshaftpotential,* and is observable even when movements are only imagined (Tyszka et al., 1994)! Secondly, stimulation of the SMA is reported to produce an urge to perform movements (Bradshaw &

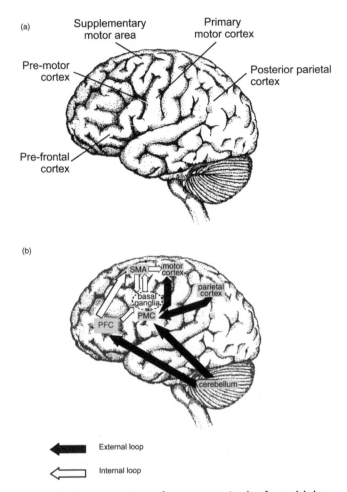

(a)

Supplementary
motor area

Primary
motor cortex

Pre-motor
cortex

Posterior parietal
cortex

Pre-frontal
cortex

(b)

SMA | motor cortex

basal ganglia

parietal cortex

PMC

PFC

cerebellum

External loop

Internal loop

FIGURE 5.6 Hierarchical organisation of movement in the frontal lobes

Fig. 5.6(a) identifies the four hierarchically organised areas of the frontal lobe (the pre-frontal cortex, the SMA, and PMC and the motor strip). In Fig. 5.6(b), 'motor' areas outside the frontal lobes are identified. In general terms, internal (self-generated) actions involve the pre-frontal cortex, SMA, and primary motor strip mediated by the subcortical basal ganglia (the internal loop). Actions prompted by external events engage the cerebellum and probably the parietal lobe, both of which send outputs to the PMC, which, in turn, outputs to the primary motor strip (the external loop).

Mattingley, 1995) and, thirdly, bi-lateral damage of the SMA can bring about complete loss of voluntary movement including speech (Freund, 1984).

In many respects, the PMC works in analogous fashion to the SMA, except that it is more concerned with coordinating motor plans related to externally cued events. Like the SMA, the main outputs from the PMC are to the primary motor strip. The main inputs are from the parietal lobe, the cerebellum and, to a lesser extent, the pre-frontal cortex. Activity is greater in the PMC in response to external cues (than internally generated plans). For example, Roland et al. (1980) showed that blood flow increased markedly in this region as the subject was required to keep a spring in a state of compression between fingers. This region, along with the pre-frontal cortex, also appears to be more active during the acquisition of skilled movements, whereas the SMA becomes more active when well-practised movements are required (Jenkins et al., 1994).

Other frontal regions involved in movement

As I mentioned earlier, both the SMA and, to a lesser extent, the PMC receive inputs from the area of frontal lobe *in front of them*. This area is known as the pre-frontal area, and it becomes active when an individual begins to plan a movement. Thus, there are three levels in the hierarchy; the intention or plan to act, the motor pattern and the movement of individual muscles. I illustrate this hierarchy in Box 5.1. Two other frontal regions also merit brief mention: as I describe in Chapter 9, the anterior cingulate is particularly activated when attentional effort needs to be directed towards novel stimuli that require effortful responses. An additional frontal lobe region, the frontal eye fields, is of critical importance in controlling **voluntary gaze**.

Box 5.1: Need a drink? The motor hierarchy for quenching your thirst:

- Dehydration leads to activation of 'osmoreceptors' in the anterior hypothalamus. This is translated into consciously feeling thirsty, leading to a motivational state represented in the pre-frontal areas as a *plan* or *intention* to drink.
- The act of raising a glass, tipping and swallowing (the appropriate *motor pattern*) is coordinated by the SMA and/or the pre-motor cortex. Remember that these areas control bi-laterally: after all, you could pick up the glass with either hand.
- The SMA and PMC control the pyramidal cells in the primary motor strip in the co-ordination of individual muscles as the glass is raised and the drink consumed.

Interim comment

Motor control is organised hierarchically. Plans or intentions to act are 'hatched' in the pre-frontal regions. Motor plans are coordinated in the SMA and PMC, and control of muscles is mediated by the primary motor strip. Although this organisational hierarchy has been speculated about for many years, the use of in-vivo imaging procedures such as SPECT and rCBF (see Chapter 2) has confirmed it. Roland (1993) reported that when an individual was asked to complete a simple repetitive movement such as wiggling a finger, only the contralateral primary motor cortex showed increased activity. However, if a more complex sequence such as touching the ends of each finger with the thumb was required, both the SMA and the pre-frontal cortex showed increased activity as well as the primary motor cortex. Even asking the subject to imagine the complex sequence caused increased activation in the SMA and pre-frontal regions.

The distinction between internally and externally cued movement also seems to be important. The basal ganglia interact with the SMA to enable (or inhibit) *internally* generated movement plans. The cerebellum interacts with the PMC to regulate actions related to *external* stimuli or events. Thus the novice tennis player will rely mainly on the second set of connections to return serve, hoping to make contact with the ball (the external stimulus) and hit it anywhere in their opponent's court. The experienced player, on the other hand, will use both systems: the cerebellar-cortical connections will control contact with the ball, and the basal ganglia-cortical connections will allow them (via internally generated intentions) to place their shot deliberately, to maximum advantage.

Parietal involvement in movement

The parietal lobes have long been regarded as having exclusively sensory functions, yet we now know that they make at least two independent contributions towards motor control (in addition to their primary role in somatosensation). Proprioceptive information from muscles and joints arrives in the primary somatosensory strip, relaying details about the position of body parts in relation to one another. This information is, in turn, fed to superior posterior parietal regions 5 and 7, which also receive 'feedback' from more anterior motor regions. This region is therefore in the position of being able to guide and correct movements, especially when actual movements do not correspond to those intended. A significant minority of pyramidal neurons' cell bodies originate in these parietal areas, and the region also has reciprocal links with motor regions in the frontal lobes.

More lateral regions of the left parietal lobe seem to have a different motor role, and damage to this area is associated with apraxia, the name for a collection of movement disorders in which the ability to perform certain movements on command is compromised. Although there is, as yet, no firm agreement either about the different types of apraxia or the brain regions that may be involved in the disorder, at least one form, sometimes referred to as ideational apraxia,

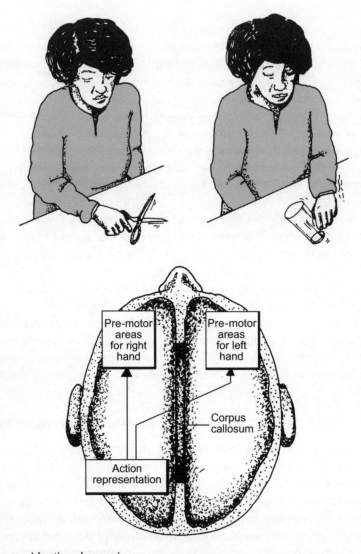

FIGURE 5.7 Ideational apraxia

Movement of the left and right hands is coordinated by the right and left motor cortex. Patients with motor apraxia may be unable to engage in purposeful movement with one (or both) hand(s), being clumsy or otherwise responding inappropriately. However, damage restricted to the left parietal lobe is sufficient to induce bi-lateral ideational apraxia. In this condition, the patient seems to have lost their internal representations for movements, so can neither recognise actions by others, nor implement movements on instruction. Source: Gazzaniga et al. (1998). *Cognitive Neuroscience: The Biology of the Mind*. Copyright © 1998 by W.W. Norton & Company, Inc. Reproduced by permission of W.W. Norton & Company, Inc.

is consistently associated with left parietal damage. In this form, the individual has difficulty following instructions to engage in complex action sequences, or even imitating them, although individual components may be executed on command or even spontaneously (Heilman & Rothi, 1993). According to these authors, representations of movement plans are stored in lateral regions of the left parietal lobe. People with damage to this area effectively lose their 'memory' for movement sequences, so can neither recognise a gesture made by others or implement a movement to order. At the beginning of the 20th century Liepmann distinguished ideational apraxia from a second less severe form that he called motor apraxia. In this disorder, gestures can usually be identified, but individual movements cannot be made on command. Motor apraxia is usually associated with left frontal rather than parietal damage (see Fig. 5.7).

Peripheral and spinal movement disorders

From our consideration of the neuroanatomy of movement, it should now be clear that movement disorders can result from damage or loss of function to many different regions of the nervous system. Literally dozens of movement disorders, often thankfully very rare, are described in the neurological literature, but for present purposes I will restrict my list to specific examples that either illustrate the importance of particular components of the motor system, or are of special interest to neuropsychologists. I begin the review in distal regions of the nervous system with a brief mention of some disorders related to peripheral or spinal cord abnormalities, before moving into the brain. Here, I will consider a small number of disorders related to cortical damage, but spend more time reviewing motor disorders associated with basal ganglia or other subcortical structures.

Myasthenia gravis

The main symptoms of myasthenia gravis (which are highly variable and range from mildly disabling to life threatening) are those of muscle weakness or fatigue, especially in the head–neck region. (A tell-tale early symptom is drooping eyelids.) The weakness results not from damage to, or loss of tissue from, the muscles themselves, but from impaired neuro-muscular synaptic transmission. In most cases, normal amounts of the neurotransmitter acetylcholine (ACH) are released from motor neurons but this fails to have the expected effect on the target muscles. In the 1970s it became apparent that myasthenic individuals have a reduced number of ACH receptors (Albuquerque et al., 1976), which is thought to occur as a result of an inappropriate immune response in which (for reasons that are not currently known) the body's immune system inadvertently attacks ACH receptors as if they were 'foreign'. Myasthenia gravis therefore joins a growing list of auto-immune diseases (Engel, 1984).

If the symptoms are mild, they can be treated quite effectively with drugs that have the effect of boosting activity in the synapses between motor neurons and muscles. At present it is not possible to promote the growth of new ACH receptors, but certain drugs can partially override the problem by ensuring that released neurotransmitter remains in the synapse for longer before it is inactivated. The drugs in question achieve this by inhibiting the enzyme that normally breaks down ACH soon after it is released. The enzyme is acetylcholine esterase (ACHE) and the drugs are therefore known as acetylcholine esterase inhibitors (ACHEIs). Examples include physostigmine and neostigmine. These medications are, however, far from ideal, because they influence all ACH synapses including many in the brain, where they may induce a raft of unwanted side effects including sleep disturbances, cognitive impairments and hallucinations.

Diseases associated with neuronal damage/loss

Multiple sclerosis (MS) is one of a group of demyelinating diseases, meaning that the principal pathological process involves the progressive loss of myelin. In MS, this can occur throughout the nervous system and affect all myelinated neurons. However, the progress of the disease is often slow, starting in the periphery and gradually working its way into more central locations including the spinal cord and (eventually) the brain. Early signs therefore include loss of (or disturbed) sensation in hands or lower limbs, and loss of, or impaired, muscle control. Blurred vision is also a common early feature. As the disease progresses, more widespread paralysis (and loss of sensation) will be seen, and there may be cognitive changes as well.

As the name implies, motor neuron disease (MND) is more restricted in terms of its targets, but also usually more aggressive, with death generally occurring within a few years of onset as the motor neurons that normally control respiration and swallowing become affected. MND actually comprises a group of related disorders with variable course. One of the most common forms, amyotrophic lateral sclerosis (ALS), is also known as Lou Gehrig's disease after the New York Yankees baseball player who developed this disorder. As motor neurons die, there is progressive and unremitting loss of muscle function, although intellectual abilities remain intact until later stages of the disease.

The causes of MS and MND remain a mystery, although a small proportion of MND cases are thought to be genetic. Other possible causal factors include auto-immune disease, as yet unknown viruses and possible exposure to toxins. It might be noted that poliomyelitis, an infectious disease caused by a virus and otherwise unrelated to MND, also targets motor neurons. Although rarely fatal, polio may leave lasting muscle wastage as a result of nerve damage and the resultant loss of innervation to the muscles.

Spinal damage

There are a number of rare diseases of the spinal cord but the most common damage to it results from accidental injury. Although the nerve tissue is normally well protected by the backbone which encases it, spinal injury often involves a displacement of vertebrae resulting in a 'shearing effect' in which axons are literally torn apart. Transection of the spinal cord brings about a permanent paraplegia (lower body paralysis) in which there is loss of sensation and motor control of the body regions below the point of damage. Ironically, spinal reflexes below that point may still be intact, and even more pronounced as a result of loss of inhibitory influence from the brain. Transection in the neck region resulting from injury (usually breaking of the neck) is likely to bring about quadriplegia; paralysis of all four limbs and trunk. The actor Christopher Reeve suffered such an injury in a riding accident. He is quadriplegic, unable even to breathe by himself.

Cortical movement disorders

Hemiplegia

This condition has already been described as a loss of contralateral voluntary control. This means that an affected individual is no longer able to intentionally move parts of their body on the side opposite to that of the brain damage. The most common cause of hemiplegia is interruption of blood supply via the mid-cerebral artery, due to **aneurysm, haemorrhage**, or **clot**. Other causes include accidental head injury, epilepsy and tumour. Hemiplegia can also occur after damage to subcortical structures, including the basal ganglia, which are also served by the mid-cerebral artery.

Usually with hemiplegia, there will be a discernible degree of recovery of function over time. This is because initial symptoms result not just from cell death due to loss of blood supply, but from temporary loss of function in adjacent neurons in which activity is affected by change in blood supply (and sometimes even by exposure to excess blood in the event of haemorrhage). Many of these neurons later appear to return to a normal or near normal level of functioning leading to (partial) behavioural recovery of function. Functional improvement may also occur as recovering patients develop entirely new ways of achieving movement, making use of quite different brain regions. A primary aim of physiotherapy is to promote recovery of function in this way, by teaching the use of alternative muscle systems to achieve the same goal.

Cerebral palsy

Cerebral palsy is not a unitary disorder, and may take a variety of forms encompassing many **signs** and **symptoms** depending on extent of damage. It usually results from trauma during foetal development or birth. Because of its heterogeneous nature, it is difficult to talk in general terms about the condition. However, a hallmark is motor disturbance, which may include poor muscle coordination, unwanted involuntary movements and excessively tensed muscles. These problems are probably also responsible for the speech difficulties that are often seen in cerebral palsy, although language difficulties may also be linked to more general intellectual impairment which is a frequent but by no means ubiquitous feature of the condition.

Subcortical movement disorders

Within a period of a few months in the early 1980s, a group of young patients came to the attention of a hospital in California. All presented with profound Parkinson's disease-like symptoms including marked and unremitting akinesia (immobility). Research indicated that each individual was a drug addict and had recently used synthetic heroin contaminated with a substance known as MPTP. This substance is converted in the brain to the closely related and highly toxic substance MPP, which has an affinity for cells that contain the pigment neuromelanin. The substantia nigra (as the name suggests) is rich in such cells, and these had been obliterated by the MPP. The individuals came to be known as 'the frozen addicts'. They had an unusually 'pure' and enduring drug-induced form of **Parkinsonism** (Martin & Hayden, 1987).

Most neurological disorders that affect the basal ganglia are less clear-cut than the self-inflicted damage seen in the frozen addicts: in these disorders, damage tends to be localised, and/or progress slowly. Because of this selectivity, there is rarely complete loss of function. Rather, we find a raft of intriguing disorders in which movement is compromised rather than abolished. Actions may still be possible but they now occur in unregulated or poorly coordinated ways.

Parkinson's disease (PD)

Of all the subcortical movement disorders, this is perhaps the best understood. It affects relatively few people under 50, but the incidence steadily increases to about 1% in 60 year olds and at least 2% in 85 year olds. It is a progressive and relentless disorder, although the symptoms may develop quite slowly. Indeed, although it is, in principle, a terminal illness, its progress is so slow that most people die of unrelated illnesses before PD has run its full course (thought to be about 15 years). The features of the disorder were recorded by the ancient Greeks, and the constellation of symptoms was known by is common name of 'shaking palsy' for many years before its full characterisation by the English physician, James Parkinson. Incidentally he did not name it after himself! This honour was suggested by the famous French neurologist Charcot.

Through careful observation of affected individuals, Parkinson realised that the disorder that came to bear his name comprised a cluster of movement-related symptoms. These need not all be present for the diagnosis to be appropriate, and the severity of symptoms will become more pronounced over time. The symptoms in question comprised resting tremor, rigidity, akinesia and postural disturbance. This list has now been expanded, and the full range of Parkinson's

---

Box 5.2: The positive and negative symptoms of PD

POSITIVE SYMPTOMS

- *Tremor at rest*: alternating movements that usually disappear during deliberate actions. The 'pill-rolling' action of fingers and thumb is common.
- *Muscular rigidity*: caused by antagonistic muscles being tensed at the same time. This is apparent when limbs are manipulated passively (by someone else). A resistance followed by loosening then further resistance is often found, giving rise to the term 'cog-wheel rigidity'.
- *Involuntary movements*: changes in posture, known as akathesia, may be almost continual, especially during inactivity. Involuntary turns to the side (of the head and eyes) are sometimes apparent.

NEGATIVE SYMPTOMS

- *Disordered posture*: for example, the inability to maintain a body part (such as the head) in the appropriate position, or failure to correct minor imbalances that may cause the patient to fall.
- *Loss of spontaneous movement*: akinesia is the inability to generate spontaneous intentional movement. A blank facial expression is another manifestation.
- *Slowness in movement*: bradykinesia is a marked slowing of repetitive movements such as tapping or clapping.
- *Disordered locomotion*: walking may be slow and poorly coordinated – more a shuffle than a stride.
- *Disturbed speech*: bradykinesia also affects the production of speech, which may slow markedly, sound atonal and be difficult to understand.

---

features are clustered into what are often referred to as positive and negative symptoms (see Box 5.2).

Resting tremor is so called because it disappears or at least becomes less marked when the person engages in some deliberate act. It can usually be seen in the hands or lower limbs. The rigidity (sometimes called cog-wheel rigidity because an external force can induce 'give' only for rigidity to reappear after a brief movement) is thought to be related to dysregulation of usually antagonistic actions of flexor and extensor muscles. Under normal circumstances, as one muscle is tensed, the opposite muscle passively extends. Rigidity occurs because both muscles are tensed at the same time.

Akinesia, and bradykinesia are two prominent negative symptoms that also merit close consideration. These terms describe absence or severe slowing of movement. They both become most apparent when the patient is required to act by his or her own volition. A classic illustration of akinesia depending on the failure of internally driven intentions is to ask a Parkinson's patient to throw a ball to you. Although they will certainly understand the instruction, they may find this (internally driven action) impossible. Toss the ball back to the patient and they might catch it without difficulty, which would, of course, be stimulus-driven movement. Bradykinesia might be observed by asking a PD patient to get out of their chair and walk across the room. Although, once again, the instruction will have been understood, they may find this simple task extremely effortful (even impossible). Curiously, a white line painted on the floor or some military marching music may do the trick. These, too, are external stimuli driving the action. The mask-like visage of the Parkinson patient is a further tell-tale sign of akinesia affecting facial expression.

That this set of diverse symptoms all depend (in some way) on dysfunction in the basal ganglia circuitry has been known for over 30 years. Indeed, post-mortem studies had shown clear evidence of loss of tissue in the caudate/ putamen region (particularly the putamen) even before this. The discovery by Hornykiewicz in 1966 that these changes may be secondary to loss of dopamine innervation from neurons originating in the substantia nigra (and making up the nigro–striatal pathway) led eventually to the development of drug treatments aimed at replacing missing dopamine or restoring the balance between dopamine and ACH in the striatum.

You might think that dopamine itself would be a suitable drug to treat PD. However, when taken orally most is broken down in the gut. But a related substance, L-Dopa, can be taken orally, does not get metabolised in the gut and is converted to dopamine by cells in the brain. This drug has therefore assumed a central role in the treatment of PD. It does not 'cure' the disease, but it does provide some symptomatic relief, although its effects lessen as the disease progresses.

A radically different treatment for PD involving the implantation of tissue from foetal brains has recently attracted interest. The idea (no matter how distasteful) is to implant cells that are dopaminergic (i.e. that manufacture and release dopamine). It is too early to judge the true effectiveness of this procedure: An initial review of more than 20 cases by Olanow, Kordower, and Freeman (1996) gave early cause for optimism, but a more recent study by Freed et al. (2001) suggests that the beneficial effects of grafts may be limited to young patients. More worryingly, Freed's research group found that about 15% of treated patients may develop side effects that are as debilitating as the disease itself.

Huntington's disease

This rare genetically determined disorder (which used to be known as Huntington's chorea) leads to death within about 12–15 years of onset of symptoms. The symptoms themselves take a particular course, although the exact transition point between 'choreic' and 'end-stage' is difficult to identify or predict. The 'choreic' stage of Huntington's is marked by the presence of unusual and intrusive movements (choreform movements). These may initially appear benign, taking the form of fidgeting or restlessness. But soon, involuntary movements are apparent in limbs, trunk, head and neck, to the extent that they interfere with 'normal' actions including walking, talking and even swallowing. Psychological and cognitive changes, which can sometimes lead to a misdiagnosis of mental illness, may also be apparent.

In the later stages of the disease, many of these involuntary movements disappear, but so too do voluntary movements. The upshot is that 'end-stage' Huntington's disease resembles, in certain respects, the negative symptoms of Parkinson's disease. The individual may be immobile, mute, bed-ridden, and even have difficulty breathing and swallowing. Memory and attentional impairments, **perseveration** and aphasia are also seen. Death is often due to **aspiration pneumonia**.

Although the disease remains rare, its **pathology** is now becoming somewhat better understood. In later stages, there are widespread changes involving loss of tissue to several regions of cortex. These probably account for the psychological and cognitive changes, which become progressively more prominent. However, these are thought to be secondary to more subtle and earlier changes to the striatum, or at least relatively independent of the main symptoms of movement disorder. Indeed, in early-stage Huntington's the only changes are found in the caudate where a progressive loss of so-called 'spiny' interneurons, initially in the medial region and later in more lateral regions, is observed. Because these neurons normally help to regulate the inhibitory output to the external part of the globus pallidus and substantia nigra, their demise brings about a dysregulation of the indirect (inhibitory) route through the basal ganglia, and the appearance of unwanted (disinhibited) involuntary movements (see Fig. 5.4). However, as the disease progresses to affect neurons throughout the striatum, the entire regulatory function of the basal ganglia is compromised including the 'enabling' facility of the direct route. Now, negative symptoms prevail as intentional actions (including basic vegetative processes such as breathing and swallowing) no longer gain the 'assent' of the basal ganglia.

As I mentioned earlier, the disease is entirely genetically determined, and depends on a single dominant gene on chromosome four. If one of your parents has Huntington's you have a 50% chance of developing it. You may therefore wonder why this disorder has persisted, as far as medical records tell us, for at least 300 years. The answer is that the symptoms do not appear until middle age (typically about 40) and most people have had children by that time. However, it is now possible to test for the presence of this gene (Gusella & MacDonald, 1994), and many people with a family history opt for it to help them decide in advance whether or not to start a family.

Tics, Tourette's syndrome and obsessive-compulsive disorder

Tics are brief, involuntary, unpredictable and purposeless repetitive gestures or movements that often seem to focus on the face and head. They may involve unusual facial grimacing, twitching or other stereotyped actions. Sometimes, vocal tics occur, wherein the individual makes clicks or grunts, or even barks. These are most common in children, and often disappear in adolescence. Evidence suggests that the appearance of tics is definitely associated with stress. If tics persist into adulthood the condition merges with Tourette's syndrome (TS).

TS is therefore a severe form of tic disorder. As well as the sort of tic already described, someone with Tourette's may display multiple involuntary mannerisms, echolalia (parrot-like mimicry) and, in the most severe cases, coprolalia (expletive use of foul language often of a sexual nature). Although this constellation of symptoms sounds completely bizarre, people with TS do not have a mental illness as such, and often have insight into their condition. Rather, they cannot 'control' action plans (including lewd thoughts) which therefore intrude on their other activities. Their manifestation is made worse by anxiety or stress, and ameliorated to some extent by relaxation and the use of dopamine blocking drugs.

Earlier I described the features of tics and TS as involuntary. Strictly speaking this is not the case. Most 'Touretters' can muster sufficient 'will-power' to inhibit a tic or mannerism for a short while, but the longer they hold off the worse the compulsion to engage in the action becomes. Although this seems a world away from 'normal experience', Bradshaw and Mattingley (1995) have likened this 'compulsion' to the infectious nature of yawning and the struggle to suppress it, with which all readers (by this stage of my book) will be familiar!

My inclusion of obsessive-compulsive disorder (OCD) alongside tics and TS may, on the face of it, seem a little fanciful. After all, OCD is a psychiatric disorder appearing in DSM4 (the current classification system) in the same section as other anxiety-related conditions, and the symptoms of OCD seem to support this. As the name suggests, people with this disorder display a range of symptoms including obsessive repetitive thoughts or feelings, and/or the compulsion to engage in ritualistic behaviour, such as repeatedly checking locks or handwashing. The obsessions or compulsions are so intense that they interfere with other more routine behaviours, so that day-to-day living becomes completely disrupted by them. If the individual is, for any reason, unable to engage in the behaviour, they are likely to experience spiralling levels of anxiety.

Yet there are, increasingly, serious doubts about the purely psychological origin of OCD. For one thing, psychological treatments tend to be relatively ineffective against it, whereas a new group of antidepressant drugs known as selective serotonin re-uptake inhibitors (SSRIs) can have dramatic effects in reducing or even eliminating the obsessional and compulsive behaviours (Kurlan et al., 1993). This has led to speculation that OCD may be related either to low levels of serotonin, or underactivity at serotonin synapses in the striatum. Serotonin is known to interact with dopamine in this region and is generally thought to have an inhibitory action. So an SSRI drug, which has the effect of boosting serotonin neurotransmission, will, in effect, replenish the inhibitory influence whose absence leads to obsessive and compulsive behaviours in the first place (Rapoport, 1990).

Secondly, there is considerable overlap between OCD, tics and TS. To start with, tics are, in effect, compulsive actions. Moreover, at least 25% of people with TS also meet the diagnostic criteria for OCD. Finally, if all other treatments for OCD fail, a surgical procedure known as the cingulotomy can effectively reduce symptoms in a proportion of those operated on (Martuza et al., 1990). The surgery involves severing (lesioning) the pathway that funnels cortical output from the cingulate gyrus and/or the orbito-frontal regions into the basal ganglia.

Interim comment

At the beginning of this section it was suggested that damage to the basal ganglia (or the neural networks or loops between the basal ganglia and the rest of the brain) would not bring about the abolition of movement, but rather its dysregulation. This, of course, is exactly what we see in both Parkinson's and Huntington's diseases. In the former, loss of dopamine input to the striatum from the substantia nigra leads to underactivity in the direct route and the negative symptoms of bradykinesia and akinesia. The positive symptoms are thought to be related to changes in output from the basal ganglia and thalamus to the spinal cord secondary to the functional changes in the striatum itself. In Huntington's disease there is intrinsic cell loss within the striatum, particularly in the caudate. Initially the indirect inhibitory pathway is affected, leading to the intrusion of unwanted (disinhibited) choreic movements. However, in the final stages of Huntington's the loss of cells in the striatum is so extensive that most output is compromised, and the symptoms now resemble the negative features of Parkinson's disease.

In the case of tics, TS and OCD, the basal ganglia and its inputs from the cortex are again central. There are relatively few functional imaging studies in tics and TS, but the available evidence points to underactivity in several frontal areas including the pre-frontal and the cingulate regions coupled with underactivity in the caudate (Moriarty et al., 1995). Three structural imaging studies have reported reduced size of the caudate and/or putamen (see Saxena et al. 1998 for a review). Despite this, dopamine blocking drugs acting in the striatum can modify TS symptoms (Wolf et al., 1996). In the case of OCD, there is compelling evidence of overactivity in the orbito-frontal and cingulate regions and the caudate, especially if the individual is challenged or provoked by the object/situation that induces their symptoms (Breiter et al., 1996). Symptomatic relief may be achieved by severing the pathway connecting these regions, or by SSRI drugs, which potentiate serotonergic inhibition in the striatum and/or the orbito-frontal lobes.

Summary

At the start of this chapter, I warned that the nervous system's control of movement is complex, yet we are probably all guilty of taking the skills that this control mechanism permits for granted. These skills are not solely the domain of Olympic gymnasts or concert pianists: with very little practice, we can all master skills quite beyond the scope of the most talented robots!

There are at least four major motor pathways carrying different types of motor information to various regions of the body. These in turn are innervated by different brain regions. At one time it was thought that there were two basic motor systems in the brain; the pyramidal and extra-pyramidal systems, controlling deliberate and automatic actions respectively. This distinction is not now thought especially helpful, because components of the two systems interact in the brain itself, and in the spinal cord and periphery.

In the brain, attention has focused on the various roles in movement of the cerebellum, the basal ganglia and the cortex. The cerebellum is important for posture, balance and skill acquisition, and it interacts with the spinal cord and the frontal lobes. The basal ganglia also interact with the frontal lobes with which they form a series of feedback loops. A current theory about basal ganglia function is that they play a vital role in the selection of appropriate actions and the inhibition of others. The actions in question are ones that are internally generated, rather than those that are driven by external stimuli.

Cortical control of movement is essentially hierarchical. The primary motor strip is innervated by the SMA and PMC. These regions are, in turn, influenced by the pre-frontal cortex. There is increasingly strong evidence that the parietal lobes also have at least two important roles in movement control. Areas 5 and 7 seem to be important in adapting movements in light of sensory feedback, and the more lateral regions, especially on the left, may be involved in the storage of representations of movement plans. Damage to this region leads to ideational apraxia, which is viewed as a problem of recognising or conceptualising movement plans in time/space.

In the frontal lobes, damage in the primary motor strip may cause weakness or loss of movement in very discrete contralateral muscles. Damage in the SMA and PMC disrupts internally or externally driven motor plans bi-laterally. Pre-frontal damage will be associated with absence of motor plans and other features of the dysexecutive syndrome (which I describe in Chapter 10).

Damage to components of the basal ganglia is usually associated with dysregulation of internally generated movements. Several well-characterised neurological diseases – including Parkinson's and Huntington's diseases, and probably Tics, Tourette's syndrome, and even OCD – are associated with damage, disease or disorder to components of the basal ganglia and/or its connections with the thalamus and cortex.

Chapter 6

Language and
the brain

■ Introduction   104

■ The classic neurological approach and
   aphasia   105
  Broca's aphasia   107
  Wernicke's aphasia   109

■ Connectionist models of language   109

■ The psycholinguistic approach   112

■ The modern era of language
   research   114
  The cognitive neuropsychology
    approach   114
  Neurophysiological approaches   118
  Neuroanatomical research   123

■ Language and laterality   125

■ Summary   127

Introduction

Think for a moment of the complex range of computational skills that are involved in understanding and generating language. Yet, by the age of four or five, most children can understand language (in their 'mother' tongue at least) spoken at a rate of several words per second. This stream of sounds is continuous – not conveniently broken up like words on a page – and the listener has to know the boundaries between words in order to make sense from them. By late adolescence most humans will have a working understanding of many thousands of words (up to 50,000 for English speakers). But humans start to produce language as soon as they begin to acquire their vocabulary. In fact, some psychologists argue that using language precedes knowledge of words, and they cite the verbal-babble interactions of mother and child as examples of pre-vocabulary 'speech'.

By about two to three years, children can effortlessly generate completely novel utterances according to implicit grammatical rules, and conduct meaningful conversations both with other children and with adults. Language development also seems to occur in the most adverse circumstances: consider, for example, the acquisition of complex language in deaf-mute children. Indeed, of all psychological attributes, language is surely the one that sets humans apart. Other animals may use gestures and sounds to communicate, but the sheer complexity and sophistication of human language suggests that extensive regions of the brain must be dedicated to dealing with it.

Scientific interest in language dates back to the earliest attempts by researchers to study the brain in a systematic way, with the work of Dax, Broca and Wernicke in the 19th century. Since then, interest in all aspects of language has intensified to the point where its psychological study (psycholinguistics) is now recognised as a discipline in its own right. The development of research tools such as the Wada test, and, more recently, structural and functional imaging procedures, has enabled researchers to examine language function in the brains of normal individuals (see Chapter 2). Perhaps predictably, this research has necessitated some revision of earlier ideas about how the brain deals with language: as usual, the more closely one looks, the more complicated things appear! However, despite the complexities, it is reassuring to note that research findings from several different perspectives are now producing converging results.

I start this Chapter with a review of the classic neurological studies of aphasia, a condition commonly seen following brain damage or disease (40%

of stroke victims develop some form of temporary or enduring language impairment). It is also seen in 'dementing' disorders such as Alzheimer's and Pick's diseases, and it can occur following head injury (for example, after a road traffic accident). More recently, there has been a move away from the strictly neurological approach that has focused on the organisation of the brain (for language). Instead, researchers have begun to examine the organisation of language (in the brain) and the specific language processes that may be lost after brain damage. I summarise the main areas of interest in psycholinguistics later in the chapter, and pick up this theme again when introducing the cognitive neuropsychological approach.

In-vivo imaging research into language is also reviewed. This work has tended to support the view that language is mediated by a series of interconnected cortical regions in the left hemisphere, much as the 19th century neurologists proposed. However, it has shown that many additional brain areas in the left hemisphere (and some in the right hemisphere) are also involved. The use of structural imaging techniques to study aphasia, as typified by the work of Dronkers and her colleagues, is also introduced. Like the functional imaging research it too has prompted revision and elaboration of earlier ideas about brain-language systems.

The classic neurological approach and aphasia

The phrenologist Franz Joseph Gall, working almost 200 years ago, noticed that some of his more articulate friends had protruding eyeballs! This, he reasoned, must be due to the brain behind the eyes having grown to accommodate a superior language faculty; and thus was born the idea that language 'resided' in the frontal lobes. Although interest in phrenology waxed and waned in the 19th century, Gall's ideas about localisation of language gained support when Broca was introduced to a patient with a serious leg infection, right **hemiparesis** and loss of speech. As I mentioned in Chapter 1, the patient was known as Tan because this was the only 'sound' he could utter. Broca realised that this patient could serve as a test of Gall's theory, and when he died, a rudimentary postmortem of Tan's brain revealed evidence of marked damage to the left posterior frontal gyrus (see Fig. 6.1). Actually, Broca noted that there was damage to other cortical regions too, but the brain was never dissected, so the true extent of Tan's lesion was not known.

In 1874 Karl Wernicke described two patients who had a quite different type of language disorder. Their speech was fluent but incomprehensible and they also had profound difficulties understanding spoken language. Wernicke later examined the brain of one of these patients and found damage in the posterior part of the superior temporal gyrus on the left (see Fig. 1.2 and Fig. 6.1). He argued that

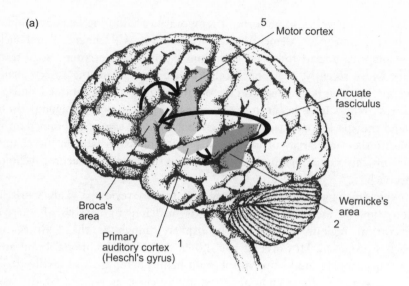

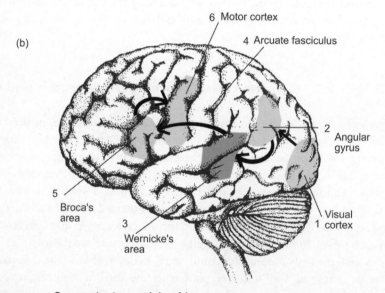

FIGURE 6.1 Connectionist models of language

Part (a) shows a connectionist model for speaking a heard word. Sounds are initially coded in the primary auditory cortex (1), then fed to Wernicke's area (2) to be linked to meanings. The arcuate fasciculus (3) conveys information about the heard word forward to Broca's area (4) to evoke programmes for articulation. Output from Broca's area is supplied to the primary motor strip to produce the necessary muscle movements in the mouth and throat. Part (b) shows a connectionist model for speaking a seen word. As above, except following initial processing in the visual cortex (1) input is then relayed to the angular gyrus (2) where the visual image of the word is associated with the corresponding auditory pattern in the adjacent Wernicke's area.

this patient's comprehension difficulties arose because the damaged region in question would ordinarily be involved in the auditory memory of words. His incomprehensible output was attributed to ineffective monitoring of self-generated speech.

At the same time as characterising this second form of language disorder, which we now call Wernicke's aphasia, Wernicke developed a theory of how the various brain regions with responsibility for receptive and expressive language function interact. His ideas were taken up and developed by Lichtheim and later, by Geschwind, and I return to consider their work after reviewing the clinical features of the two aphasic conditions I have already introduced. However, it is important to note that the following descriptions differ somewhat from those of the original authors, having broadened over the years to accommodate a wider band of aphasic features as more cases have come to light.

Broca's aphasia

In Broca's aphasia, as with most neurological conditions, impairment is a matter of degree, but the core feature is a marked difficulty in producing coherent speech (hence the alternative names of 'expressive' or 'non-fluent' aphasia). Although Tan's speech was limited to the one 'sound', most Broca's aphasics can speak a little, but they seem to have problems in finding the words they want to use, and prepositions, conjunctions and other relational words (words like 'in', 'and', 'but', 'about', 'above' and so on) are often omitted. As a result, speech is slow, effortful and deliberate, and may have only a very simple grammatical structure. The term **'telegraphic speech'** has often been used as a short-hand description for Broca's aphasia speech (' ... *in car* ... *off to the* ... *the match* ... *City play* ... *good watch* ... *like City* ...').

Despite these problems, some aspects of language function are well preserved. Broca's aphasics can use well-practised expressions without obvious difficulty (*'It never rains but it pours!'*), and they may also be able to sing a well-known song faultlessly. Reading aloud is usually unaffected. These abilities demonstrate that the problem is not related to 'the mechanics' of moving the muscles that are concerned with speech, and to underline this point, many Broca's aphasics have similar 'agrammatical' problems when trying to write. (See Box 6.1 for an illustration of some Broca's aphasia features.)

The alternative name of 'expressive' aphasia is a reminder that the most obvious features of this condition relate to difficulties in language production, especially of novel (as opposed to well-learned) utterances. However, some Broca's aphasics also have comprehension difficulties. For example, while the sentence '*the boy watched the girl talk with friends*' would probably not cause problems, a sentence such as: '*the girl, whom the boy was watching, was talking with friends*' might. (The test is to see if the respondent knows who was watching

Box 6.1: Broca's aphasia (adapted from Stirling, 1999)

Therapist: 'Tell me about your recent holiday.'

Patient: '. . . Well . . . Well now . . . (long pause). We . . . err . . . I . . . holiday . . . you know . . .'

Therapist: 'What happened?'

Patient: '. . . Oh, we . . . err . . . holiday . . . you know . . . seaside . . .'

Therapist: 'Tell me some more.'

Patient: 'Beautiful weather . . .' (shows off suntan on arm).

Therapist: 'Where did you get that?'

Patient: (bursts into song) 'Oh, I do like to be beside the seaside . . . Oh I do like to be beside the sea . . .' (broad grin)

Therapist: 'Did you go with your sister?'

Patient: 'Sister . . . yes . . . sister. To . . . On holi . . . holiday . . . In a cara . . . cara . . . cara- thingy . . . caravan! That's it! A cara . . . caravan.'

Therapist: 'Did you take her, or did she take you?'

Patient: 'Hey! You're . . . you're . . . trying to catch . . . catch me out . . .!' (grins broadly again).

Therapist: 'I just wondered who made the arrangements?'

Patient: 'We . . . we . . . you know, we go there . . . every . . . each . . . you know . . . year. Same place, same time, same girl.' (laughs at own joke).

Comment: This vignette includes instances of telegraphic and agrammatical speech, effortful word finding, faultless expression of familiar material and insight. Can you identify an example of each?

whom.) At present it is unclear whether this comprehension deficit is related to problems with grammatical processing of the more complex sentence, or to problems with working memory or even attention. However, it is generally accepted that comprehension problems in Broca's aphasia are both qualitatively and quantitatively distinct from those seen in Wernicke's aphasia (Dronkers, Redfern, & Knight, 2000). Finally, most Broca's patients are usually well aware of their own language difficulties and have 'insight' into their condition.

'Broca's area' is located in the left frontal lobe just forward from the primary motor cortex on the posterior surface of the third frontal gyrus, encompassing Brodmann's area 44 and part of area 6 (see Fig. 6.1a). It is roughly in front of, and slightly above, the left ear. However, recent research indicates that Broca's aphasia probably depends on more extensive damage than Broca originally thought. Adjacent cortical regions and/or areas of cortex normally hidden from view in the sulci (folds) under the surface have also been implicated. The insula is one candidate region, which I return to later. Incidentally, deaf people with brain damage in this region have trouble producing sign language!

Wernicke's aphasia

Wernicke's first patient had difficulty in understanding speech yet could speak fluently, although what he said usually did not make much sense. This form of aphasia clearly differed in several respects from that described by Broca. The problems for Wernicke's patient were related to comprehension and meaningful output rather than the agrammatical and telegraphic output seen in Broca's patients.

The fluent but nonsensical speech of someone with Wernicke's aphasia (as it became known) is all the harder to understand because of two further characteristic features. One is the patient's use of non-words or made-up words (known as 'neologisms'). A second is the use of 'paraphasias' – words that are semantically related to the desired word, but nevertheless inappropriate (binoculars instead of glasses for example). Most Wernicke's aphasics also have little or no 'insight' into their condition. They talk nonsense without realising it, being unaware that other people cannot understand them! (See Box 6.2.)

Wernicke thought that the underlying deficit in this condition was in linking sound images to stored representations (memories) of words. Although he only performed a post-mortem on one of his aphasic patients, damage was evident in the left posterior temporal region immediately behind Heschl's gyrus (the primary auditory cortex). Heschl's gyrus was known to receive massive inputs from the ears and is where speech sounds undergo initial analysis. Wernicke thought that the processed speech sounds would then be fed into the areas of cortex just behind Heschl's gyrus (the area we now call Wernicke's area) to be referenced to actual words (see Fig. 6.1a and b). More recent evidence suggests, once again, that this analysis may be somewhat simplistic, and that other areas of the cortex, in addition to Wernicke's area, may be important in understanding spoken language – a point that I return to later.

Connectionist models of language

Broca's and Wernicke's work generated considerable interest among fellow researchers. In 1885, Lichtheim proposed what has come to be known as the 'connectionist model of language' to explain the various forms of aphasia (seven in all) that had, by then, been characterised. Incidentally, the term 'connectionist' implies that different brain centres are interconnected, and that impaired language function may result either from damage to one of the centres or to the path-

---

Box 6.2: Wernicke's aphasia (adapted from Stirling, 1999)

Therapist: 'What's this for?' (shows patient a hammer)

Patient: 'Oh Boy! That's a ... that's a thingy for ... thing for ... for knocking things'

Therapist: 'Yes, but what is it?'

Patient: 'It? I dunno ... Umm ... It's a nisby thing though!' (chuckles to himself)

Therapist: 'How about this?' (shows patient a nail)

Patient: 'That? Well, see you have those all over the place ... In the doors, on the floors ... everywhere's got 'em ...'

Therapist: 'What is it?'

Patient: 'Mmm ... See, I don't really get there much see, so ... , you know, it's kind of hard for me to spray ...'

Therapist: (hands patient the nail) 'Do you recognise it now'?

Patient: 'Let's see now ... it's sort of sharp, and long ... could be a screw ...'

Therapist: 'Do you use this (points to the hammer again) with that?' (points to the nail)

Patient: 'Mmm. That's a good one! (laughs again) Let's see now, a screw and a nail eh? Maybe in a toolboss ... Yes! That's it; they all go in the toolboss in the back of the shed you see. In the garden ... the shed, in the toolboss.'

Comment: This vignette includes illustrations of paraphasia, neologisms, incoherent speech, and lack of insight. Can you identify one example of each?

---

ways between centres. It is thus similar to the idea of a 'distributed control network' which I introduced in Chapter 1.

In Lichtheim's model, Broca's and Wernicke's areas formed two points of a triangle. The third point represented a 'concept' centre (see below) where word meanings were stored and where auditory comprehension thus occurred. Each point was interconnected, so that damage, either to one of the centres (points), or to any of the pathways connecting them would induce some form of aphasia. Lichtheim's model explained many of the peculiarities of different forms of aphasia, and became, for a time, the dominant model of how the brain manages language comprehension and production (see Figs. 6.1 and Fig. 6.2). Although it fell out of favour in the early part of the 20th century, the model received renewed impetus in the 1960s following Geschwind's work (e.g. Geschwind, 1967).

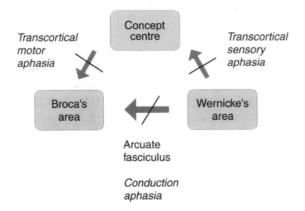

FIGURE 6.2 Lichtheim's model of connectivity serving language functions

In this model, Wernicke's area processed the sound image of words. This was fed forward via the arcuate fasciculus to Broca's area, which was responsible for the generation of speech output. Damage to this pathway led to conduction aphasia. A second route between Wernicke's and Broca's areas is via the concept centre, which Lichtheim envisaged as the part of the brain where meanings were stored. Damage to the pathway between Wernicke's area and the concept centre gave rise to transcortical sensory aphasia (marked by intact repetition but inability to understand auditory inputs). Damage to the pathway from the concept centre to Broca's area induced transcortical motor aphasia marked by loss of spontaneous speech.

Wernicke had actually been the first to suggest that the region of brain he had identified would be anatomically linked to Broca's area, and he reasoned that there could be a disconnection between the area for speech sounds (Wernicke's area), and the area for speech output (Broca's area), even if the two areas themselves were not damaged. The pathway in question is called the arcuate fasciculus, and Geschwind (1965) described a small number of aphasic individuals with apparent damage to it. Their disorder is known as conduction aphasia and, although comprehension and speech production may be substantially preserved, the ability to repeat words, especially if they are novel or unusual, is lost (see Fig. 6.1a and b and Fig. 6.2).

The exact location of the concept centre in Lichtheim's model was unclear, with Lichtheim himself arguing that concepts were actually distributed widely throughout the cortex. More recent interpretations (Geschwind, 1967) localised it to the left inferior parietal lobe encompassing the angular gyrus (see Fig. 6.1a) and the region just anterior to this known as the supramarginal gyrus. This area is connected to (but separate from) Wernicke's area, and patients with damage to this region certainly have 'receptive' language problems. However, this usually manifests as some form of 'alexia' (loss of reading ability). On the other hand, damage to area 37 (posterior medial temporal gyrus) in the left hemisphere *is* associated with lost access to semantic information about words that aphasics can nevertheless hear and repeat, making it a good candidate for the concept centre (Damasio & Damasio, 1989). (See Figs. 6.1a and b and Fig. 2.1.)

Geschwind (1972) proposed that damage to the concept centre, or the connections between it and the other centres, readily explained the features of two further rare aphasic conditions; motor and sensory transcortical aphasia. The motor form is similar to Broca's aphasia, but, in addition, spontaneous speech is absent. Another feature is a marked tendency (which sometimes appears almost compulsive) to repeat things aloud. This is called 'echolalia'. Damage to the pathway between the supplementary motor area (SMA) and Broca's area can bring about this disorder (Bradshaw & Mattingley, 1995). In the sensory form, difficulty with comprehension resembles that seen in Wernicke's aphasia but repetition is intact. Indeed, as with the motor form, echolalia may even be prominent. The loss of connections between Wernicke's area and area 37 (which I mentioned earlier) may be responsible for transcortical sensory aphasia. To complete the picture, extensive damage to multiple parts of Lichtheim's system could account for global aphasia; a profound aphasic disorder affecting both comprehension and production of language.

Interim comment

The study of language impairment in people with brain damage has provided a wealth of information about the role(s) of left-sided cortical regions in language. The types of aphasia identified over 100 years ago are still seen today, although careful case study has revealed additional forms of language disorder that may be related to lesions/damage to other components of the brain's language system. As we shall see, recent research has led neuropsychologists to conclude that the forms of aphasia identified by Broca and Wernicke probably depend on more extensive damage to either frontal or posterior regions than was initially thought. It also seems that other 'centres' (and interconnecting pathways) in addition to Broca's and Wernicke's areas and the arcuate fasciculus contribute to a distributed control network responsible for the full range of language skills, which is considerably more complex than the triangular connectionist model of Lichtheim. Finally, it is worth mentioning again that there is potential danger in relying on the study of damaged brains to form an understanding of normal brain function.

The psycholinguistic approach

Psycholinguistics is, primarily, the study of the structure of language in normal individuals rather than the study of language dysfunction in neurological patients.

(We could describe it as a 'top-down' approach, whereas the neurological approach is 'bottom-up'.) As the discipline grew, psycholinguists developed theories about the form and structure of language that were relatively independent of the neurological work described in the previous section: in fact, the two approaches initially represented quite distinct levels of inquiry into the study of language. Although it is beyond the scope of this book to provide a detailed account of contemporary psycholinguistic thinking, an understanding of some psycholinguistic concepts and terminology is important, and will inform our discussion of the neuropsychology of language.

Psycholinguists generally divide language into four major domains:

1. *Phonology* is the investigation of basic speech sounds (*ba*, *pa*, and *ta*, are all phonemes).
2. The study of meaning in language is known as *semantics*.
3. Words are strung together to form sentences according to particular implicit rules of grammar, known as *syntax* (*syntactic* is the adjective).
4. The study of using language in a natural social setting is known as *pragmatics*.

Phonemes are combined to form words, and our word store, which includes information about pronunciation, meaning and relations with other words is known as our lexicon. The structure of our mental lexicon has been a major research topic in psycholinguistics and evidence suggests that it is partly organised in terms of meaning.

From this summary you can see that psycholinguistics has a distinct approach and different level of inquiry. However, it is still of interest to ask whether there is any common ground between it and the classic neurological approach. Earlier, for example, we noted how Wernicke's and other 'posterior' aphasias involve speech, which, despite being correctly structured, is difficult to understand. There is also poor comprehension. A psycholinguistic interpretation would be that these aphasias are related to deficits in *semantic* processing rather than to problems with the brain's *syntactic* mechanisms. This may, in turn, imply that semantic processing was a function of these posterior regions.

Similarly, I earlier described individuals with damage to frontal regions (including Broca's area) as having non-fluent agrammatical aphasia. In psycholinguistic terms, this type of aphasia could be attributed to impaired *syntactic* processing. We know that some non-fluent aphasics have difficulties in understanding language, which would imply a problem with semantics too: however, these problems become apparent when understanding depends on precise grammatical analysis in the absence of other semantic clues. Broca's aphasics would, for example, probably be able to distinguish between the meaningful sentence '*the boy ate the cake*' and the meaningless sentence '*the cake ate the boy*'.

Actually, Linebarger, Schwarz, and Saffran (1983) have shown that Broca's aphasics can also distinguish accurately between grammatical and agrammatical sentences. So, it seems that the problem for individuals with this form of aphasia is not that grammatical processing mechanisms have been lost, but rather that they cannot be easily accessed, or alternatively cannot be accessed quickly enough.

Interim comment

Psycholinguistics is a complex and somewhat isolated discipline. Progress has certainly been made in identifying the structure and form of language(s), its universal features, its acquisition and so on, but, until recently, this work has tended to ignore pathologies of language. More recently, as we have just seen, neuropsychologists have begun to draw parallels between aphasic disorders and disruption to specific linguistic processes. This data provides evidence of a double dissociation between semantic and syntactic processes, and illustrates clearly that no single brain 'language centre' exists. This approach has been the springboard for cognitive neuropsychologists to study individual cases of language disorder in detail, and, in the process, further unravel or tease apart specific components of the language system that may be selectively impaired.

The modern era of language research

The cognitive neuropsychological approach mentioned earlier is a relatively recent development (dating back no more than 20 to 30 years) and is considered in the following section. However, this is just one of three important contemporary lines of investigation that we need to review. In addition, we must consider recent explorations of language functions in the brain using neurophysiological and imaging techniques, and revisit some more carefully conducted neuroanatomical research.

The cognitive neuropsychology approach

In this approach, which is exemplified in the work of Caplan (1992) and Ellis and Young (1996), researchers try to understand the true nature of language disturbances in relation to underlying cognitive dysfunctions. Although this approach has evolved from the psycholinguistic approach reviewed earlier, it differs in two important respects. First, it tries to relate language and cognitive processes, and, secondly, it focuses on pathologies of language rather than normal language.

Because cognitive neuropsychologists focus on specific language impairments, **syndromal** (multi-faceted) conditions like Broca's and Wernicke's aphasia are of little direct interest. Indeed, as I mentioned in Chapter 1, although researchers are divided on the matter, some, at least, argue that studying groups of people with Broca's or Wernicke's aphasia is pointless because the conditions are both broad and poorly defined. Ellis and Young (1996) argue that as brain damage is inherently variable, potentially informative individual differences are lost in 'group' based research (see also Caramazza, 1984), so it makes more sense to conduct detailed case study investigations on individuals with very specific language impairments.

Although cognitive neuropsychologists have made progress in understanding many aspects of language impairment, I will illustrate their approach with reference to just one condition – **anomia** – which is defined as a problem in naming objects. If you followed the descriptions of the classic aphasias that I gave earlier, you will be aware that some form of anomia is common to both Wernicke's and Broca's aphasias, which, on the face of it, is not a promising start. Yet detailed case study reveals several subtly different forms of anomia, and thorough neuropsychological testing indicates that they may have quite distinct origins in terms of cognitive dysfunction.

Consider, first, patient JBR, reported by Warrington and Shallice (1984). He had developed widespread temporal lobe damage following **herpes simplex infection.** He was impaired at naming living things (such as a daffodil or lion) but not inanimate objects (like torch or umbrella). His problem was not, however, limited to naming because he also struggled to understand the spoken names of items that he himself couldn't name.

Compare JBR with Hart et al.'s patient MD, who also had a deficit in naming animate objects, yet could sort pictures of animate and inanimate items well, and could also discriminate heard and read words from each category (Hart, Berndt, & Caramazza, 1985). This subtle distinction suggests that whereas JBR might have incurred loss (or degradation) of semantic knowledge of specific categories, MD had retained the semantic representations but his access to it from pictures or actual objects was impaired.

A third anomic patient, JCU, reported by Howard and Orchard-Lisle (1984), seemed at first glance to have a widespread generalised anomia for objects from various categories, yet could often be prompted to name items correctly if given the initial phoneme (sound) of the word. However, he was also prone to naming semantically related items if given the wrong phoneme! For example when asked to name a tiger, and given the phoneme 'l' he incorrectly said lion.

In contrast, patient EST, studied by Kay and Ellis (1987), had pronounced anomia with no apparent damage to semantic representations, similar to what we might see in Broca's aphasia. Although he clearly struggled to name objects from many categories, he nevertheless retained semantic information about items,

TABLE 6.1 The underlying difficulties of five anomic patients

Patient	Can understand speech?	Can generate speech?	Can name living things?	Can name inanimate things?	Has semantic knowledge about things?	Likely underlying problem
JBR	Yes	Yes	Only poorly	Yes	Not about living things	Loss of semantic knowledge for specific categories
MD	Yes	Yes	Not fruit or vegetables	Yes	Yes	Loss of access (via pictures or objects) to preserved semantic knowledge
JCU	Yes	Yes	No (unless prompted with auditory cues)	No (unless prompted with auditory cues)	Partial at best	Object recognition and comprehension relatively intact but a general non-specific impairment to semantic representations
EST	Yes	Yes (only high frequency words)	No	No	Yes	Loss of access to speech output lexicon for low-frequency words
RD	No	No (produces neologisms)	No	No	Yes	Failure to understand speech or monitor own speech

voluntarily providing associated semantic information about an object even if the name eluded him. This suggests that EST's anomia was related to a problem in generating the actual words (perhaps through inaccessibility to his speech output lexicon) rather than any loss of semantic representation. To reinforce this view, patients like EST know when they have generated an approximation to the required word rather than the correct word itself, and will comment to this effect, saying *'that's not quite it ... it's like that but I forget what it actually is'*.

Yet another word production disturbance, often encountered in Wernicke's aphasia, is known as 'neologistic jargonaphasia'. Patient RD, studied by Ellis, Miller, and Sin (1983) was anomic, especially for rare or unusual items, yet evidence from other tests indicated that he retained semantic knowledge of the un-namable items. He could name items he had used before or was very familiar with, but for other items he generated phonological approximations – neologisms that sounded similar to the target word ('peharst' for 'perhaps' for example). The major difference between EST and RD is that the former could understand speech well, but RD could not: in fact, his comprehension had to be assessed using written words. His neologisms are likely to be the result of a failure to properly monitor his own speech, which explains his lack of awareness of his own errors.

These types of observation have enabled researchers to develop detailed models of the cognitive processing stages involved (in this instance) in object naming. We can see, for example, that JBR's anomia appeared to be related to a problem with specific components (categories?) of his semantic system. Other operations were intact. EST, on the other hand, had problems accessing his speech output lexicon, especially for rare words, while the lexicon itself and his semantic system were probably intact. These examples also show us that, with appropriate testing, subtle differences can be identified in the form of anomia that a patient presents with. I have summarised the cases described above in Table 6.1.

Interim comment

Earlier I said that the cognitive neuropsychological approach focused on language dysfunction in brain-damaged individuals. However, Ellis and Young (1996) have pointed out that the anomic disturbances seen in brain-damaged individuals are, in certain respects, simply more pronounced forms of disturbance that we all experience from time to time. Slips of the tongue, malapropisms, spoonerisms, and the 'tip of the tongue' phenomenon are all features of 'normal' language usage, and may be related to brief disruptions of the same processes (or components) that are more severely affected in cases of clinical anomia. At present, the cognitive neuropsychological approach continues to lean more towards psychology than neurophysiology. Its interest is in cognitive models and hypothetical processes rather than anatomical locations and neural pathways. However, this is quite likely to change as researchers become more aware of the potential advantages of the in-vivo imaging techniques for exploring brain-language relations, discussed in the following section.

Neurophysiological approaches

Structural and functional in-vivo imaging techniques, such as CT, MRI and PET (see Chapter 2), allow researchers to observe the living brain. These approaches are gradually leading to important discoveries about many aspects of brain function, and language is no exception.

CT and MRI scan data tend to reinforce the classic post-mortem findings of extensive damage and loss of tissue to frontal areas in people with Broca's aphasia and posterior damage in individuals with Wernicke's aphasia (Damasio & Damasio, 1989; Naeser & Hayward, 1978). When PET is used to examine 'resting' brain function, patients with non-fluent (Broca's type) aphasia show underactivation in left frontal regions, while patients with fluent aphasia show underactivation in more posterior regions. However, when anatomical and activation data are compared in the same individuals, underactivity is sometimes observed in areas that are not damaged. Moreover, the functional measures correlate more closely with language disturbance than do the anatomical measures. This is a reminder that visible anatomical lesions may only reveal part of the story.

PET has also been used to examine functional activity in normal individuals while they undertake different types of linguistic task. Petersen and Fiez (1993) asked subjects to perform one of two tasks: in the first, they had to decide whether (or not) pairs of nonsense syllables ended in the same consonant (which effectively made the subjects say the words to themselves); in the second, subjects had to interpret syntactically complex sentences. The researchers found that both tasks led to increased activity in and around Broca's area, showing the importance of this cortical region in speech production and grammatical processes. However, other researchers, including Mazoyer et al. (1993) and Bavelier et al. (1997), have questioned the importance of Broca's area for syntactic processing, and, on the basis of their imaging studies, have suggested that a region of the anterior superior temporal lobe (on the left) may be the key area for grammar (see Fig. 6.3).

Petersen et al. (1988) reported what has come to be acknowledged as a classic PET study of language and it is worth spending a little time considering

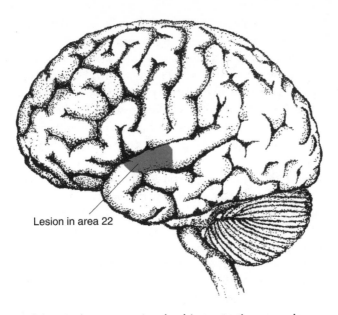

Lesion in area 22

FIGURE 6.3 Left hemisphere areas involved in syntactic processing

PET and lesion studies by Mazoyer et al. (1993) and Dronkers et al. (2000) respectively identify Brodmann's area 22 on the left side as a candidate region involved in grammatical processing.

their method more closely. Subjects were normal volunteers with no known language impairments. There were four conditions, each undertaken while the subject lay in the scanner. In condition one, subjects passively viewed a fixation point on a screen. In condition two, subjects listened passively to a series of nouns, or observed a similar series of nouns displayed on a TV monitor. In condition three, subjects had to repeat aloud the words they heard or saw. Finally, in condition four, subjects had to generate (and speak aloud) a 'related' verb for every noun they heard/saw. The researchers used 'subtraction logic' to generate PET images. In simple terms this means that activity recorded during the control condition is (literally) subtracted by a computer from the activity recorded during the task so that any remaining activity can be attributed specifically to the task. Thus, for example, the PET activity produced when subjects repeated words was subtracted from the activity when subjects generated verbs. In this way the researchers could be confident that the remaining activity was linked to the process of generation rather than simply repetition/verbalisation.

As we might expect, the two passive conditions of seeing and hearing words activated quite distinct cortical regions. Viewing words led to greatest activation bi-laterally in the primary and secondary visual areas and the angular gyrus. Hearing words led to bi-lateral activation in the primary and secondary auditory areas in the temporal lobes, and uni-laterally in left temporo parietal regions.

The areas in question encompassed the angular and supramarginal gyri in addition to Wernicke's area. The hearing condition then served as control for the word repetition condition. Now, there was bi-lateral activation in the motor cortex and supplementary motor area (SMA) controlling face and mouth, and some other regions more usually related to attention than language. In condition four (for which condition three served as control), there was activation of Broca's area, and two additional regions that had not hitherto been identified as important language centres – the anterior cingulate gyrus and the cerebellum (see Box 6.3).

The results of this study offer some support to the classic connectionist view of interconnected language centres with specific and distinct responsibilities, although the apparent failure to activate Wernicke's area unless words were presented auditorally was both puzzling and counter-intuitive. In another sense, the study also illustrates the weakness of a strict localisationist theory of brain-language function: despite the apparently straightforward nature of the tasks, each appeared to induce activity in many cortical areas. The established regions were activated, but so too were other regions such as the cingulate, which is more normally associated with attention, and the cerebellum, which is usually associated with motor learning (see Box 6.3).

The relative inactivity in Wernicke's area reported by Petersen's group has been hotly debated, with commentators suggesting either that the use of subtraction logic itself was responsible (Wise et al., 1991), or that the control conditions were inappropriate. In fact, several subsequent PET and fMRI studies have reported activity in Wernicke's area during tasks of speech perception (e.g. Bavelier et al., 1997; Mazoyer et al., 1993). In any case, the anatomical location of Wernicke's area is somewhat vague, with many neuroanatomists accepting that it includes the supramarginal gyrus (Brodmann's area 40), and arguably even area 37 (posterior medial temporal gyrus) (Chertkow & Murtha, 1997). Nevertheless, collectively, such studies show that several areas in the left hemisphere that have not previously been identified as 'language areas' become active during tasks that involve aspects of comprehension. Imaging studies are ongoing to establish their precise roles.

Petersen's group deliberately chose word generation because they thought it was a 'simple' task to examine with PET. However, psycholinguists such as Levelt (1989) have long argued that word generation is, in fact, a task of considerable complexity involving multi-tiered processing components. Although the precise details of Levelt's theory need not concern us (but see Levelt, Roeloffs, & Meyer, 1999 for further information), a version of his model of word generation does merit consideration and is summarised in Box 6.4.

This summary should leave us in no doubt that the task of selecting a single word (in response to a picture, word or other stimulus) does indeed involve multiple processing stages, and is an enormously complex undertaking. Does this

Box 6.3: Flow diagram of Petersen et al.'s PET study and findings

Level 1: Passive viewing of a visual fixation spot
(Level 1 served as subtraction control for level 2)

Level 2: Passive presentation of words (visually or aurally)
(Level 2 served as subtraction control for level 3)

Level 3: Repetition of presented words
(Level 3 served as subtraction control for level 4)

Level 4: Generation of appropriate verbs to presented nouns

Following subtraction:

- Passive viewing/listening to words activated visual occipital regions and the supramarginal and angular gyri respectively. Listening activated Wernicke's area.
- Repeating words led to bi-lateral activation of motor and sensory face areas and the cerebellum.
- Generating verbs activated Broca's area (and surrounding frontal regions on the left side), regions of posterior temporal cortex around but not specifically including Wernicke's area, and the cerebellum and anterior cingulate.

mean that the functional imaging studies of word generation need to be completely rethought? According to Indefrey and Levelt (2000), it is still possible to make sense of this data by taking advantage of the fact that most of the studies have used slightly different experimental procedures. For example, some, like Petersen et al.'s, have used verb/word generation. Others have employed word repetition, or picture naming. Sometimes, word generation has been overt, while in other studies silent, or delayed. The different procedures involve different core processing stages; so, for example, word repetition does not make demands on conceptual preparation. Similarly, the first core process implicated in reading pseudo-words (non-words that sound like words) is phonological encoding, and so on. Thus, it is possible to tease apart the individual components involved in different word generation studies, and Indefrey and Levelt (2000) have presented such a provisional meta-analysis.

In their model, the conceptual processing stage involves occipital, ventro-temporal and anterior frontal regions, which become active within 250 msec of stimulus presentation. The middle region of the left temporal gyrus seems to be involved in the lexical selection process. Activation then spreads to Wernicke's area and area 37, which the authors argue are the location for storage of phonological codes of words and meanings respectively. This information is then fed

---

Box 6.4: A summary of Levelt's model of word generation

- First, the speaker needs to be aware of the social context in which word generation is occurring, to remember the rules of the experimental task, and to know what is expected of him/her.

- Next, there must be some conceptual preparation, which may depend on semantic processing of the stimulus material that is to be responded to: e.g. *'generate a verb which relates to the following noun'*.

- Since there may be many alternatives (i.e. lots of potential verbs), the mental lexicon must be accessed, and some form of selection undertaken.

- Once selected, the mental representation of the word must be articulated. But word articulation is itself a compound task, involving the sequential processing of phonemes.

- These in turn permit the generation of syllables. (Although most spoken English is based on reassembling no more than 500 syllables, the language itself contains about 50,000 words.)

- Quite how these are translated into sounds is not known, but it is clear that the actual articulation process is flexible – people can make themselves understood with their mouth full, or when smoking a cigarette for example!

- Humans can produce about 12 speech sounds per second, and this involves the precise coordinated control of at least 100 different muscles.

- Generated speech is also monitored by the speaker, and, if necessary, corrected for errors, sometimes before the errors are even articulated.

- Speech is also effortlessly adjusted for volume and speed of delivery to suit the particular environment.

---

forward to Broca's area and the mid-superior temporal gyrus for phonetic encoding. The SMA, cerebellum and primary sensory motor areas will also be recruited at this stage to produce articulated output.

Interim comment

Indefrey and Levelt's model is tentative and will, no doubt, be subject to amendment in the light of future research findings. Its great strength is its recognition of the true complexity of apparently simple linguistic tasks. The emerging picture of the still predominantly left-sided cerebral network underlying word generation updates and dramatically elaborates Lichtheim's connectionist model that served as the template for brain-language research for much of the last century.

Neuroanatomical research

The 'neurological/neuroanatomical' approach was an obvious choice for the early researchers who relied on case studies of individuals with brain damage. Cases of Broca's and Wernicke's aphasia have been reported and described for over 100 years and are relatively commonplace today. Each is widely accepted as a legitimate clinical entity. But the real question is not how many cases of these syndromes conform to the description and anatomical model of Lichtheim, but how many do not.

This matter has been carefully explored by Dronkers and her colleagues at the University of California (Dronkers, Redfern, & Ludy, 1995; Dronkers, Redfern, & Knight, 2000). Her starting point was the realisation that certain problems with the connectionist model have been routinely 'forgotten' in the quest to find supportive evidence for it. For example, the grammar-based comprehension difficulty of many Broca's cases does not fit well with the idea of this aphasia as a disturbance of expressive language function. Moreover, the connectionist model has somewhat conveniently ignored the fact that many Wernicke's aphasics make significant recoveries, ending up with few lasting comprehension problems despite obvious posterior damage. The true neuroanatomical locations of Broca's and Wernicke's areas have even been questioned.

By 1992, Dronkers' group had detailed evidence on 12 right-handed Broca's aphasics, two of which had lesions that completely spared Broca's area. Ten more cases were identified in which damage to Broca's area was apparent, but who had no true Broca's aphasic features! In a similar vein, Dronkers et al. (1995) reported seven cases of Wernicke's aphasia of which two had no damage to Wernicke's area at all, and seven additional cases with damage to Wernicke's area but without the persistent features of Wernicke's aphasia.

Dronkers' patient pool comprises over 100 very clearly defined and extensively imaged aphasics, and it has been possible to look for anatomical commonalities within aphasic groups. For example, every subject who met the diagnostic criteria for Broca's aphasia had damage to a specific part of a deep cortical region in the left frontal lobe known as the insula (the superior tip, see Fig. 6.4). The immediate conclusion from this observation might be that this is the true location of Broca's area, but this would be incorrect because the research group also had a small number of patients with damage to this part of the insula who did not have Broca's aphasia! However, they all had a language abnormality known as **speech apraxia** (an articulatory speech programming disorder in which the individual generates neologisms – i.e. approximations to the correct word, rather than the word itself). This is, of course, a common though not defining feature of Broca's aphasia. The most parsimonious explanation for this finding is that if, as is often the case, frontal damage includes this region of the insula, the individual is likely to experience speech apraxia as one of the features of their aphasia.

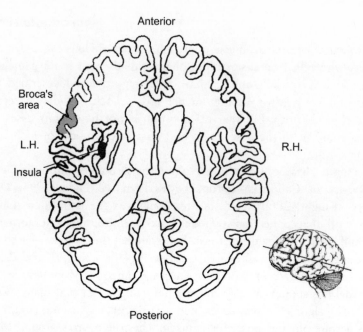

Anterior

Broca's
area

L.H.

R.H.

Insula

Posterior

FIGURE 6.4 The location of the superior tip of the insula (on the left)

This region, identified by Dronkers et al., is consistently damaged in aphasics with speech apraxia. Broca's area is indicated for reference.

Dronkers' group has also explored the anatomical basis of the comprehension difficulties often reported in Broca's aphasia. Almost all such cases have damage to anterior regions of the superior temporal gyrus (on the left). This area is frequently damaged in Broca's aphasia, but is in the temporal rather than frontal lobe. At present it is difficult to ascertain whether this region is truly a grammar 'node' in the language network, or part of a working memory network that is needed to process longer sentences. However, functional imaging studies by Mazoyer et al. (1993) and Bavelier et al. (1997) have also confirmed the importance of this region in sentence comprehension in normal individuals. As for Broca's area itself, the most likely explanation for the function of this region is that it is involved in the motor control of speech musculature, which, ironically, is the function that Broca originally ascribed to it!

In the case of Wernicke's aphasia, enduring symptoms are only found in individuals with extensive damage to the posterior regions of the mid-temporal gyrus and underlying white matter. Smaller lesions, either in Wernicke's area itself or to other posterior temporal sites, usually produce only transient aphasic features that resolve in a matter of months. According to Dronkers et al. (1998), damage to Wernicke's area alone is more likely to be associated with repetition deficits than comprehension problems. The authors have suggested that this deficit could primarily be an auditory short-term memory problem in which the individual cannot hold on to the **echoic trace** of an item long enough to repeat it.

Dronkers' approach has shown that it is possible to draw conclusions about brain-language relations if one has access to aphasic individuals with carefully characterised symptoms/features and anatomically accurate information about brain lesions. The work of her group indicates that in addition to Broca's and Wernicke's areas and the arcuate fasciculus, many other regions, mainly on the left in the temporal lobe, contribute to both receptive and expressive language functions. Like Levelt, Dronkers et al. (2000) acknowledge that the neuropsychology of language has, for too long, been guided by an oversimplified model of how the brain deals with language. The emerging model must integrate the new language areas with the traditional ones, but also factor in attentional, executive and working memory processes in order to provide a more realistic framework of brain-language networks.

Interim comment

Three recent lines of research have taken our understanding of the neuropsychology of language well beyond the revised connectionist model of the early 1970s. The cognitive neuropsychology approach has shown how, by careful observation and neuropsychological testing, it is possible (and informative) to distinguish between subtly different forms of language dysfunction. The neuro-imaging approach has not only tended to reinforce, but also to extend, classic models of how the brain processes language. In particular, this approach has led to the identification of brain regions not previously thought to be involved in language. The neuroanatomical approach of Dronkers has shown how it is possible to relate loss of function to cortical damage, provided that subjects are thoroughly tested and the damage is precisely mapped. A picture emerging from all three approaches is that language itself is far more complicated than the early researchers thought. Thus, the neural networks serving language comprise many more discrete regions, albeit mainly on the left side, than earlier models suggested.

Language and laterality

From my review of brain-language research, it would be reasonable to conclude that language is mediated by a series of interconnected regions in the left hemisphere. This pattern of 'distributed control' is found in almost all right-handers, and the majority of left-handers (Rasmussen & Milner, 1977). Over 100 years ago Broca declared '*nous parlons avec l'hemisphere gauche*', and both the functional and structural imaging findings bear this out, but so too does much of the research on language function in the split-brain syndrome and data derived from the Wada test (see Chapters 2 and 3).

So is the left hemisphere *the* language hemisphere? Not exclusively, for there is evidence to show that certain *emotional* aspects of language are managed, perhaps predominantly, by the right hemisphere. For example, individuals with right hemisphere damage, and with otherwise intact language skills, may speak in a monotone, despite *understanding* the emotional connotations of what they are saying (Behrens, 1988). The region of right cortex in question is in the equivalent location to Broca's on the left. In other words, damage to Broca's area impairs fluent speech. Damage to the equivalent area on the right impairs emotionally intoned (**prosodic**) **speech,** which instead is said to be 'aprosodic'. More posterior right-sided damage (in regions roughly equivalent to Wernicke's area on the left side) can lead to difficulties in the interpretation of emotional tone. Regional blood flow studies with normal individuals have also highlighted this double dissociation: speech production requiring emotional tone activates frontal regions on the right (Wallesch et al., 1985), whereas comprehension of emotionally intoned speech activates posterior regions on the right (Lechevalier et al., 1989).

Obviously, the actual message may convey enough meaning to be understood without having to decode the emotional tone too, but sometimes appreciation of tone is critical in understanding the true message. 'Thanks very much!' can mean 'thank you' or 'thanks for nothing' depending on the speaker's tone of voice. The right hemisphere's interpretation of 'prosodic cues' appears to be closely related to more fundamental skills in detecting tonal differences, or changes to pitch, which are also mediated primarily by the right hemisphere. Recently, our research group (Stirling, Cavill, & Wilkinson, 2000) reported a left ear (right hemisphere) advantage in normal individuals for the detection of emotional tone in a dichotic listening task (this sort of experiment is described in Chapter 9 and illustrated in Fig. 9.1): a finding that reinforces the view that the processing of emotional voice cues may be preferentially a right hemisphere task.

There is growing evidence linking inferential skills (filling in the blanks, or 'putting two and two together') and even 'sense of humour' to the right hemisphere too. Individuals with right hemisphere damage are less adept at following the thread of a story (Kaplan et al., 1990) or understanding the non-literal aspects of language, such as metaphors (Brownell, 1988). They also struggle to rearrange sentences into coherent paragraphs (Schneiderman, Murasugi, & Saddy, 1992). The idea that the right hemisphere may be critically involved in more abstract aspects of language is one that is gaining ground, and is, in certain respects, reminiscent of the idea (discussed in Chapter 3) that the two hemispheres have different processing styles.

Summary

The classic neurological approach to understanding the role of the brain in language relied on case studies of people with localised damage, usually to the left hemisphere. Broca and Wernicke described differing forms of aphasia, the prominent features of the former being non-fluent agrammatical speech, and those of the latter being fluent but usually unintelligible speech. Their work led to the development of Lichtheim's 'connectionist' model of language, which emphasised both localisation of function and the connections between functional areas. Connectionist models gained renewed impetus with the work of Geschwind in the 1960s.

Three new lines of inquiry – the cognitive neuropsychology approach, the functional neuro-imaging research of Petersen, Raichle and colleagues, and the neuroanatomical work of Dronkers and colleagues – have prompted new ideas about the networks of brain regions that mediate language. The cognitive neuropsychological approach has underlined the subtle differences in cognitive processes that may give rise to specific language disorders. The functional imaging research has identified a wider set of left brain (and some right brain) regions that are clearly active as subjects undertake language tasks. The newer structural imaging work has also prompted this conclusion, as well as necessitating a re-evaluation of the functional roles of Broca's and Wernicke's areas.

The emerging view from these diverse research approaches is that language is a far more complex and sophisticated skill than was once thought. Many left-sided cortical regions collaborate in a truly distributed network to facilitate receptive and expressive language functions. Their work is supplemented by right hemisphere regions with particular responsibilities for emotional and inferential aspects of language processing.

Chapter 7

Memory and amnesia

■ Introduction   130

■ Psychological investigations of
    memory   131
  Working memory approaches   132

■ Long-term memory   134

■ Neuropsychological approaches   136
  The case of HM   137
  The case of RB   138
  The case of CW   138

■ Diencephalic amnesia   139
  The case of NA   140
  Korsakoff's syndrome   140
  STM and amnesia   142

■ Imaging studies   142
  Imaging and LTM   143
  Imaging and implicit memory   144
  Imaging studies of working memory   144

■ Some other forms of amnesia   147
  Concussion amnesia   147

ECT-induced amnesia	148
The explicit-declarative implicit-procedural debate revisited	148
■ Summary	150

Introduction

WITHOUT MEMORY WE WOULD be unable to acquire skills, learn languages or remember faces. It is hard to imagine how the processes of thinking and perception could happen at all without at least some reference to prior experience or events. Planning future events or actions would be pointless because unless you acted immediately, you would have forgotten your intentions by the time you wanted to put them into effect! In short, life would be spent perpetually in the 'here and now'.

It is quite difficult to make a clear distinction between psychological and neuropsychological approaches to memory. On the one hand, many psychological concepts about memory have drawn on anecdotal observations of memory impairment in brain-damaged individuals, while, on the other, neuropsychologists have adopted many of the ideas about the structure and processes of memory from psychological investigations. If there is a difference in emphasis, it is that psychological research into memory function has tended to focus more on the structure and integrity of memory in 'normal' individuals, whereas the neuropsychological approach has concentrated primarily on the effects of brain damage or injury on memory function.

In this Chapter I concentrate on the neuropsychological approach, but I start with a brief summary of some of the ideas and theories emerging from investigations into the psychology of memory. (Readers wanting to know more about the psychological approach should refer to a specialised textbook such as Baddeley's *Human Memory: Theory and Practice* [1997] or Groeger's *Memory and Remembering: Everyday Memory in Context* [1997].) I then focus on case studies of amnesia, and later consider the extent to which data from in-vivo imaging research is beginning to shed fresh light on the brain substrates of human memory. My coverage is intentionally selective, and some interesting areas of memory research have been omitted. For example, the extensive literature on animal memory has not been included. Similarly, in the human domain, I have not dwelt on lifetime changes in memory function or on how memory may be affected by degenerative disorders such as Alzheimer's disease or by cumulative brain damage as observed in boxers who develop **dementia pugilistica**. Finally, I have decided not to include material relating to **psychogenic amnesia**.

Psychological investigations of memory

Whatever the exact model of memory adopted, there is broad agreement that at least three processes must be involved:

- the act of committing something to memory involves 'encoding' (input);
- holding the material in memory requires 'storage'; and
- remembering (recalling) that material involves 'retrieval' (output) (see Fig. 7.1a).

Memory can thus be defined as the process of storing and retaining information for possible recall/use at some later date, and its fundamental importance for psychological functioning was recognised more than a century ago by William James (1890). He proposed that human memory comprised two distinct stores, which he called primary and secondary memory. The former was his term for the transient immediate 'stream of consciousness' retention that some modern-day psychologists call short-term memory (STM), and the latter corresponded to retention of information over a longer and possibly indefinite period of time, beyond conscious awareness. Today, we might think of James' secondary memory as equating to long-term memory (LTM).

Although not all psychologists would agree about the exact structure of memory, most accept that it does make sense to distinguish between short-term/working memory (STM/WM) and LTM. Evidence also indicates that LTM should be further divided into different sub-types, of which the most important distinction is between declarative and non-declarative (procedural) memory. These terms loosely equate to memory for explicit factual knowledge, such as the capital of Australia, and memory for implicit procedural skills, such as the ability to ride a bicycle.

Psychological research into memory really took off after World War II, and this era was marked by the reporting of literally hundreds of experiments in which the parameters of different memory systems were examined. Because many of these studies are described in standard introductory texts, they will not be revisited here. However, the impact of this work on the new discipline of cognitive psychology was considerable, leading to the generation of various multi-store models of memory, all of which (to a greater or lesser extent) conceptualised the route to long-term storage as requiring the passage of 'information' through a series of earlier linear short-term stores. Atkinson and Shiffrin's (1968) 'multi-store' model (see Fig. 7.1b) is one of the most widely cited examples.

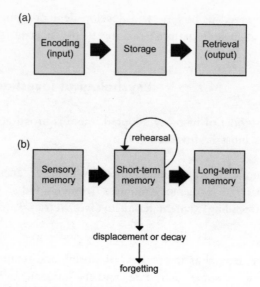

FIGURE 7.1 Psychological models of memory

(a) A generic model of the key processes in memory systems.

(b) A schematic diagram of Atkinson and Shiffrin's modal (multi-store) model of human memory in which sensory input was conceptualised as passing from a sensory register into short-term storage. If the material was rehearsed it would be consolidated in long-term memory. Otherwise, it would be quickly forgotten.

Working memory approaches

Although multi-store models could account effectively for many of the experimental findings reported by researchers such as Brown (1958), Petersen and Petersen (1959) and Glanzer and Cunitz (1966), other features of these models seemed, on closer inspection, counter-intuitive. For example, the uni-directional flow of information through the various 'boxes' in Atkinson and Shiffrin's model implied that items could be registered in LTM only after rehearsal in STM. Yet personal experience suggests that we are able to remember certain things indefinitely without any rehearsal. Moreover, multi-store models also said relatively little about how material, once lodged in LTM, could be accessed. The concept of working memory, developed by Baddeley and colleagues (Baddeley & Hitch, 1974), provided an alternative framework which, the authors suggested, overcame many of the shortcomings of the earlier multi-store models.

Proponents of the working memory approach argued that both short-term storage of new information and 'on-line' access to previously stored information depended on the operation of a common system comprising at least three separate components: a central executive, and two 'slave' systems; a phonological loop; and a visuo-spatial scratch pad. The central executive is a command and control centre that oversees the activities of the two subordinate loops and also permits interaction with LTM. It is able to allocate resources to working memory tasks, and can also update what is 'in' working memory. Another way of thinking about the central executive is as a 'director' of conscious attention, and it is of interest to note that a similar mechanism (called the supervisory attention system) has been proposed in the information-processing model of Norman and Shallice (1980) outlined in Chapter 10. The central executive is also inevitably involved in many 'higher order' mental processes such as planning and coordinating actions, and other aspects of executive function (such as directing attention) not traditionally considered in the of STM research.

The phonological loop was proposed to explain the observation that if subjects are asked to recall visually presented letters, errors in recall neverthe-less tend to be acoustic (based on the letters' sound rather than on their physical appearance). Moreover, immediate recall of similar sounding words is worse than that of distinct sounding words. Taken together, these observations suggest that this component of memory is based neither on physical appearance nor meaning of the material, but on sounds. It is the component of short-term memory that we bring into play when trying to remember a telephone number long enough to dial it, and it relies on silent articulation (rehearsal) to keep the material in mind. The capacity of the phonological loop is limited (perhaps to the amount of information that can be rehearsed in two seconds [Baddeley, Thomson, & Buchanan, 1975]) so contents will be displaced as new material is attended to.

Parallel evidence has been offered in support of a visual-based memory (the visuo-spatial scratch pad). We can, for example, view objects or simple draw-ings, hold the image in mind after they are removed from sight and then draw them 'from memory' without difficulty. Although once again, by attending to new objects (or even objects recalled from LTM) the current contents of the scratch pad will quickly be displaced. Several researchers have suggested that at least two forms (or components) of visuo-spatial scratch pad may exist; one for pattern-based images, and a second for spatial locations, although research on this is still at an early stage (see Farah, 1988 and Goldman-Rakic, 1992).

Whatever the exact structure of working memory eventually agreed upon, there is good evidence for the relative independence of the two principal 'slave' components from dual-task experiments in which (within certain limits) the requirement to engage in an additional visual task while currently maintaining material in the articulatory loop does not cause interference. A schematic diagram of the main components of working memory is shown in Fig. 7.2.

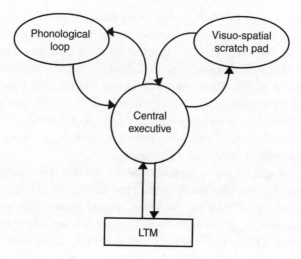

FIGURE 7.2 The key components in Baddeley's model of working memory

The central executive coordinates activity in two slave systems to keep 'in mind' visual or auditory material. This operates either for newly presented material or for existing material already in LTM that requires conscious attention.

Interim comment

As we will see later in this chapter, the use of functional imaging procedures has led to recent debate about the components of working memory: are there separate visual-object and spatial loops for example? Can verbal and spatial working memory functions be attributed to different cortical regions in the left and right cortex as Goldman-Rakic et al. (1993) and Jonides et al. (1993) have suggested? Whatever structural network finally emerges, it is interesting to note that most cognitive psychologists favour working memory over earlier models of STM as a means of conceptualising the ability to hold 'in mind' and manipulate or rehearse information that is either newly presented or drawn out of LTM.

Long-term memory

Whatever the mechanisms of short-term storage, most psychologists agree that information retained for a significant period of time resides in a separate long-term store or stores. The main questions in this area are thus concerned less with capacity or duration than with how material in LTM is organised, and whether it is appropriate to subdivide LTM into distinct components or systems.

There is broad agreement that LTM can be divided along the lines of 'explicit-declarative' (*what*) and 'implicit-procedural-non declarative' (*how to*) memory. The explicit-implicit taxonomy is originally attributed to Tulving, Schacter, and Stark (1982) and Graf, Squire, and Mandler (1984), and the declarative-procedural distinction was coined by Cohen and Squire (1980). The impetus for this was, as we shall see, the observation that many brain-damaged individuals suffer impairments to explicit memory while implicit memory is spared. (The reverse pattern is rarely observed, but see the case of MS reported by Gabrieli et al. 1995.) Explicit and declarative are terms referring to personal recollections of events, facts, categories and so on. Implicit and procedural fall under the general heading of non-declarative memory. Although different, they both refer to knowledge that we have no true conscious access to – an acquired skill such as swimming or riding a bike, learned behaviours such as habits, and so on. I revisit the declarative-procedural distinction later in this chapter.

Tulving (1972) proposed a further distinction within LTM between episodic and semantic memory. In his view, episodic memory referred to 'one-off' events in our personal history, such as going to the theatre or a train journey; a conscious awareness of prior episodes of one's life. Semantic memory, on the other hand, referred to acquired world knowledge, such as the rules of chess, the name of your team's goalkeeper, or tools associated with woodwork. Initially, there was considerable interest in the semantic-episodic distinction, bolstered by Tulving's suggestion that some **amnesics** showed impaired episodic memory yet retained an intact semantic memory (Tulving, 1989). However, his measures of semantic memory relied heavily on vocabulary, which, of course, is acquired early in life. Gabrieli, Cohen, and Corkin (1988) have shown that many amnesics do have difficulty assimilating new words (i.e. words, like 'internet' or 'laptop', that have entered the vocabulary after the date of the trauma leading to amnesia). Moreover, semantic and episodic memory are both usually impaired in amnesics lending weight to the argument that both should be considered as elements of explicit/declarative memory.

Implicit-procedural memory refers to stored knowledge that does not require intentional conscious recollection. Skill acquisition is one example. A second is seen in research into '**priming**'. In a typical study, subjects are shown a list of words and later complete a recognition test in which they have to identify previously presented words from new non-target words. Depending on list length, participants will typically recognise some but not all of the words from the original list. However, if, later still, the same participants are given a list comprising fragmented or partial versions of words from the original list (e.g. c_pb_a_d: for *cupboard*), and simply asked to write down any words that come to mind, more words from the original list are produced. This shows that there must have been implicit memory for these additional words despite a failure to retrieve them during the recognition test.

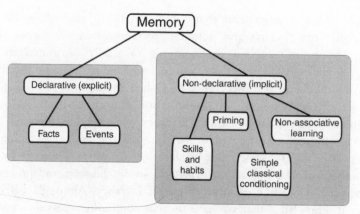

FIGURE 7.3 The subdivisions of long-term memory

This general model distinguishes between the main domains of long-term memory, combining the ideas of Tulving (1985) and Cohen and Squire (1980). (Adapted from Gazzaniga et al., 1998.)

Interim comment

Further evidence in support of an explicit-declarative implicit-procedural distinction has been provided by Tulving (1972) who showed that although recognition was generally better than fragment completion in the short term (same day), the reverse was true if testing occurred seven days after presentation. This suggests that information may be retained in long-term storage at an unconscious level for varying periods, although our ability to access it probably declines with time. Fig. 7.3 provides a generalised diagram of the major subdivisions of LTM based on psychological research. Later in the chapter we will revisit this diagram, adding information about possible underlying brain systems that are involved in the various components of the model.

Neuropsychological approaches

Memory deficit, whatever the cause, is referred to as **amnesia**, and it can result from brain damage, disease or injury. There may be a selective or generalised loss of memory, which can be temporary or permanent, and the deficit may affect short-term storage, long-term storage or both. Obviously, amnesia is not something that can be experimentally manipulated in humans so we must rely on acquiring information from particular individuals who, for whatever reason, are amnesic. Although amnesia is quite rare, sufficient numbers of amnesic cases have now been studied (often in considerable detail and for many years) for neuropsychologists to contribute significantly to the debate about the nature of human memory. In the following section I describe three cases whose amnesic disorders have helped to delineate the relationships between amnesia and brain structure.

The case of HM

In 1953, at the age of 27, HM underwent a 'last-ditch' operation for the relief of intractable drug-resistant epilepsy that he had suffered from since childhood. His surgeon decided to remove the tissue that was responsible for precipitating the seizures; in his case, the medial temporal lobes on both sides. The bi-lateral temporal lobectomy not only removed a significant amount of cortical tissue, but also both amygdalae, and several centimetres from the front (anterior) region of HM's hippocampus, again on both sides. After a period of recovery, it was clear that the surgery had been quite effective in relation to HM's seizure activity, the intensity of which was much reduced, permitting a reduction in his anti-convulsant medication. His IQ score rose and certain reasoning and perceptual skills normalised. Unfortunately, the surgery had also brought about a profound and permanent amnesic condition. HM could no longer form long-term declar-ative memories.

The extent of HM's amnesia was apparent to anyone with whom he came into contact. On returning to the hospital two years after his surgery, he reported the date to be March 1953 (a month before his operation) and his age to be 27 (he was now 29). If a person he met left the room for a few minutes and then returned, HM failed to recognise him. He would read the same magazine article over and over again without realising that he had read it before, and without being able to remember anything of the story if quizzed later. When his parents, with whom he lived, moved house, HM was never able to learn the new address and frequently got lost or arrived expectantly at his old house.

The psychological investigations of HM, reported by Milner and others (see Milner, 1965) revealed the true nature of his memory deficit. He had a profound anterograde amnesia meaning that he could not form memories for explicit-declarative material from the date of his surgery (see Fig. 7.4). He also had retrograde amnesia, meaning that he could not remember things that happened in the period leading up to his operation. This was more or less 'total' for about 2 years pre-surgery, and was 'partial' back to about 10 years pre-surgery. On the other hand, his short-term retention, as measured by digit span for example, was normal, and so was his remote long-term memory for events up to his mid-teens. Of particular interest in the light of the earlier discussion about the distinction between implicit and explicit memory, HM could learn and retain new skills although he had no recollection of prior experience with the test materials. For example, Milner reported that HM's improvement over a period of several days at 'mirror drawing' (where a person must trace round

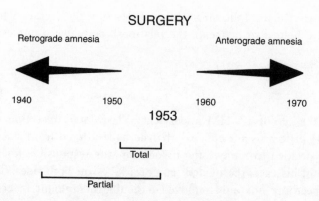

FIGURE 7.4 HM's retrograde and anterograde amnesia

HM underwent surgery in 1953. He developed a marked anterograde amnesia for learning new material thereafter. He also showed an almost total retrograde amnesia for events one to two years prior to surgery, and a partial amnesia for several years before that. (Adapted from Groome, 1999.)

a shape such as a star that they can only see in a mirror) was within normal range, yet at the end of the training he could not remember ever having seen the mirror drawing equipment on earlier occasions. This is a very good illustration that HM's amnesia did not generalise to affect his implicit-procedural LTM.

The case of RB

HM's surgery was extensive, and he had suffered from epilepsy for many years, so one could not attribute his amnesia with certainty to any particular area of removed tissue. However, his is not (by any means) the only documented case of medial temporal lobe damage. Consider RB (Zola-Morgan et al., 1986). The blood supply to RB's brain was temporarily interrupted while he underwent heart by-pass surgery. This episode induced localised but permanent damage restricted to a region of his hippocampus (bi-laterally) where a particular type of neuron (the CA1 type) is found. He died shortly after his operation but not before his amnesia had been investigated by psychologists. His memory dysfunction closely resembled that of HM, especially in his inability to form new memories. He also had a retrograde amnesia, although this was not as extensive as HM's, going back only one to two years.

The case of CW

Occasionally, amnesia can result from complications associated with herpes simplex infection, giving rise to a condition known as HSE (encephalitis) when the virus attacks the brain. HSE causes widespread bi-lateral damage to the temporal lobes (within which the amygdala and hippocampus reside). The well-documented case of CW graphically illustrates the devastating effects of this disease. CW was a respected musician at the time he developed HSE. Brain scans indicated that the infection had completely 'wiped out' his left temporal lobe, had caused some damage to his right temporal lobe and had also damaged his frontal lobes. Like HM, CW developed profound anterograde amnesia, being unable to learn any new material. Unlike HM, he also had an extensive retrograde amnesia, and his knowledge of events and people, even from his childhood, was poor. Intriguingly, CW retained particular musical skills including playing the piano, and sight-reading, despite having little or no recollection of his earlier career as a musician. (See Wilson and Wearing [1995] for a full account of this case.)

Interim comment

Taken together, these three cases offer key insights into the likely role(s) of the medial temporal lobes in memory. First, this region seems not to be involved in STM. Secondly, the hippocampus (rather than other medial temporal structures such as the amygdala) seems to be important in the formation of new explicit-declarative long-term memories. This process is sometimes referred to as 'consolidation', and has been likened to a cementing or strengthening of information into LTM. One hypothesis is that consolidation leads to stronger associations between new stimulus inputs and activations of previously stored material. Whatever its exact nature, the duration of anterograde amnesia experienced by HM and RB suggests that consolidation may take several months or even years to be completed. Thirdly, long-term memories are not stored in the hippocampus, although the temporal lobes that surround them may provide storage space.

Diencephalic amnesia

The medial temporal lobes are not the only brain regions associated with amnesia. Damage to so-called diencephalic structures – notably the thalamus and the mamillary bodies – can also lead to memory impairments. The damage may result from disease such as stroke or tumour, but the best-documented case is that of patient NA, who suffered very localised damage following a fencing accident. We also need to consider the large numbers of cases of individuals who develop Korsakoff's syndrome as a result of chronic alcohol consumption.

The case of NA

NA developed amnesia following a freak accident in which a fencing foil entered his brain (via his nostril) damaging his left dorsal thalamus, his mamillary bodies (bi-laterally), and his mamillo–thalamic tract, which connects the mamillary bodies to the thalamus. Like HM, NA showed normal STM, but had a profound impairment in declarative LTM. He became markedly amnesic particularly for verbal material. In fact, in many ways his amnesia closely resembled that of HM, with a pronounced anterograde amnesia. However, his retrograde amnesia was less severe and his recollection for events prior to his accident (in 1960) was good.

Korsakoff's syndrome

Long-term alcohol abuse, especially in combination with poor diet, can lead to an amnesic syndrome first characterised by Korsakoff in the late 1890s. This disorder can take a variety of forms, but encompasses three core features:

- There is marked anterograde amnesia. This may be quite sudden in onset despite a long history of alcohol abuse, or there may be an insidious onset.
- There is a significant retrograde amnesia that may go back many years, or even extend to most of the person's life. Korsakoff's cases do very poorly on a test of remote memory known as the 'famous faces' test, which requires recognition of photographs of famous film stars, politicians and other notable individuals. HM did quite well on this test.
- Confabulation is common. Korsakoff's patients tend unwittingly to fill in gaps in their memory with plausible but untrue stories as a result of confusion between semantic knowledge and their own episodic memory. Problems with source memory also make confabulation more likely.

In addition, Korsakoff's patients tend to be apathetic and (unlike HM) lack insight. However, in other respects their IQ is preserved, their reasoning ability seems unimpaired, and they are usually well-motivated and cooperative. Some of these features, including the apathy and confabulation, are probably related to the extensive damage to frontal areas, which is apparent in about three-quarters of Korsakoff's cases (Moscovitch, 1989). However, the amnesic features appear to be related to damage to the medial thalamus, and possibly the mamillary bodies as well.

Interim comment

Clearly there are similarities (as well as some differences) in the amnesic disorders related to medial temporal and diencephalic damage. Why should damage to two distinct brain regions lead to similar types of amnesia? At present, the answer is that we do not really know, although it is unlikely that both regions do the same job. A more probable explanation is that they serve different functions within the explicit-declarative LTM system. One suggestion, based on the known connections between the hippocampus, the diencephalic structures and the cortex, is that while the hippocampus is important in the formation and storage of new long-term memories, the diencephalic structures are more important in processing and retrieving memories from storage. However, the honest answer is that 'the jury is still out'. The question of the relative contributions of medial temporal and diencephalic structures to the encoding and retrieval of long-term memory remains unresolved.

In similar vein, it remains a matter of debate as to what actually is impaired in such cases of retrograde amnesia. Some researchers have argued that a disruption to the consolidation process explains both anterograde and retrograde effects, and therefore that amnesia is, fundamentally, an encoding deficit (e.g. Milner, 1966). The main problem with this viewpoint is that retrograde amnesia sometimes appears to stretch over many years, and this would imply that consolidation also happens over a similar period of time; something which many researchers think unlikely.

An alternative explanation of amnesia is that it results from a failure in retrieval (Warrington & Weiskrantz, 1970). This has particular appeal because we know that amnesics' memories can be improved with the use of prompts or cues. Unfortunately, this observation in itself does not 'prove' the retrieval-deficit hypothesis of amnesia: it could be that memories that were not encoded properly, or were stored in fragmentary fashion, can nevertheless be retrieved with the help of sufficiently strong cues. Moreover, a retrieval deficit model would predict equally strong retrograde and anterograde effects, which is certainly not supported by the literature. At present, we simply do not know whether the problem is one of encoding or retrieval. Explanations based on encoding failure struggle to account for phenomena like cued (or spontaneous) retrieval, while adherents of the retrieval failure explanation may be mistaken in assuming that the memory process was entirely normal up to the moment of retrieval. Incidentally, this argument also applies to forgetting in normal individuals too.

STM and amnesia

So far, most of the examples of amnesia that I have reviewed have related to LTM difficulties. Very occasionally, selective STM impairments are also found. One of the first examples was reported by Shallice and Warrington (1969). Their patient had damage to the left hemisphere in the vicinity of the Sylvian fissure, and had a markedly reduced **digit span** of about two items. Verbal list recall was also impaired. Interestingly, this patient retained the ability to form long-term memories. Today, we would interpret this as evidence of damage to the phonological loop component of the working memory system, and since Shallice and Warrington's report, other cases have come to light suggesting that this stems from damage in and around Brodmann's area 40 (the supra-marginal gyrus) especially on the left side (see also Chapter 6). Conversely, individuals with damage restricted to the right parietal-occipital boundaries have difficulties with visuo-spatial working memory tasks. As we shall see shortly, imaging research has also identified locations in the dorso-lateral pre-frontal regions that probably represent the anatomical substrate of the central executive.

Interim comment

There are two key points that emerge from research into STM amnesia. First, there is accumulating evidence linking discrete damage in different cortical regions to the different components of working memory. Damage to one component need not impair functions that depend on the other components of the system. Secondly, STM impairments can co-occur with normal LTM, which suggests that the systems operate in a parallel processing manner rather than serially as suggested in Atkinson and Shiffrin's model.

Imaging studies

On the face of it, one might think that in-vivo imaging would finally provide the technological solution to Lashley's infamous quest for the engram (see Chapter 1); the location of memory traces in the brain. After a lifelong search involving hundreds of experiments, Lashley himself concluded, somewhat unsatisfactorily, that it was not possible to localise particular memory traces at all, and that they must be distributed throughout the cortex. By using procedures such as PET and fMRI, researchers should be able to establish which brain regions are most (and least) active during different types of memory test. However, before reviewing recent work using in-vivo imaging, it is wise to recall the practical and method-ological limitations of these procedures that I described in Chapter 2.

Imaging and LTM

Several research groups have adopted PET (and more recently fMRI) in an effort to pinpoint the anatomical substrates of memory. Squire et al. (1992) investigated the role of the hippocampus in retrieval. Participants first studied a list of words. Some then took part in a procedure (known as stem-completion) in which they were shown a list comprising the first few letters (word stems) of some of the words they had just seen mixed up with word stems for new words, and asked to complete the stems with the 'first word that came to mind' (an implicit measure). Others completed a routine recall in which stems were available as explicit memory aids. Activation was greater in the right hippocampus during explicit recall, although it was still apparent during the implicit test. In a second experiment in which the task was made more fundamentally 'verbal' by repeating the presentation of word lists several times (Squire, 1992), retrieval was associated with activation in the left hippocampus, as well as both the left and right frontal lobes. Taken together, these results have been interpreted as showing that both left and right hippocampi are active during retrieval although there may be some laterality effect with verbal material making a preferential demand on the left hippocampus. If you are wondering why the hippocampus is active at all during retrieval, the answer is that the memorised material was 'recent', and most researchers acknowledge that retrieving recently acquired information still depends on hippocampal activation.

In-vivo procedures have also illustrated the role of the hippocampus in the process of encoding. Haxby et al. (1996) presented participants with pictures of faces or nonsense images (juggled up faces) to be memorised. The left hippocampus and the left pre-frontal cortex were most active during the encoding (learning) phase. The right pre-frontal cortex but not the hippocampus was active during the recognition test.

I mentioned previously that Squire et al. (1992) found some activation of the hippocampus during both implicit and explicit memory retrieval, whereas we might have predicted that activation would only be seen in explicit procedures. To revisit this issue with a different (and arguably better) implicit procedure, Schacter et al. (1996) presented participants with a list of words that they had to analyse for only physical features (the number of T-junctions in the letters). A stem completion test then followed during which subjects were scanned. Although implicit learning had obviously taken place (because of the number of correct stem completions) there was no significant hippocampal activation on either side. In a separate study in which explicit memory was tested by requiring participants to engage in detailed semantic analysis of the to-be-remembered material, bi-lateral hippocampal activation was apparent. Schacter et al. argued that their findings reinforced the view that hippocampal activation only occurs in explicit retrieval. Perhaps the participants in Squire et al.'s study intermittently engaged in explicit memory of target items which 'contaminated' their results.

Can in-vivo imaging be used to study cortical activation in memory tasks? Nyberg et al. (1996) required participants to engage in either superficial or semantic coding of words. The superficial coding required participants to say if the word contained a particular letter, and the semantic coding required a judgement as to whether the word was an animate or inanimate object. Words were presented one at a time, and results indicated markedly greater PET activation for the deeper level of processing. The activation was most marked in the inferior pre-frontal cortex on the left side. There was no increase in right pre-frontal regions. In a further study of episodic memory (for sentences), the recognition phase, which occurred 24 hours after the learning stage, was associated with more activation in the right dorsolateral pre-frontal cortex than the left.

Imaging and implicit memory

Far less time and effort has gone into exploring the anatomical correlates of implicit memory. We have already seen that priming failed to activate the hippocampus in Schacter et al.'s (1996) study. Converging evidence suggests that implicit skill acquisition, such as mirror drawing or learning to follow a moving illuminated target with a light-sensitive pen (the pursuit rotor test), activates brain regions including the motor cortex (Grafton et al., 1992), the basal ganglia (striatum) (Doyon et al., 1997) and the cerebellum (Flament et al., 1996). Eye blink conditioning studies have generated more equivocal findings, but the strongest evidence implicates the cerebellum (particularly the vermis) and basal ganglia (Logan & Grafton, 1995).

Imaging studies of working memory

Baddeley's model of working memory was proposed to account for our ability to hold, manage and manipulate either new or old information from different modalities for short periods of time. Working memory allows us to keep information 'on-line', in mind or in conscious awareness for seconds. Initial investigations into the physiological basis of working memory were conducted on primates by researchers such as Goldman-Rakic (1992). One of her experiments is illustrated in Fig. 7.5. Monkeys were shown the location of some food (in one of two food wells outside the cage). The food wells were then covered and the cage window closed. After various (short) delays, the window was reopened and the monkey could choose the food well containing the food. Animals with lesions in Brodmann area 46 (lateral pre-frontal cortex) did particularly poorly at this working memory test, but not at other tests that assessed associative long-term recognition memory. This test is essentially one of object

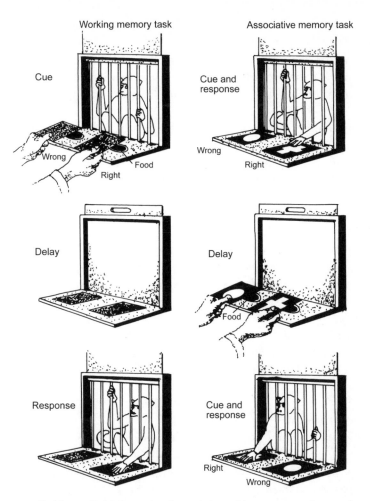

FIGURE 7.5 Goldman-Rakic's study of spatial working memory in monkeys

Monkeys with pre-frontal lesions show a selective impairment on a working memory task (left-hand figures) but not on an associative memory task (right-hand figures). In the working memory task, the monkey must remember the position of the 'baited' food well during a delay period when a screen hiding the food wells descends. In the associative task, the monkey must learn to associate a particular symbol with the 'baited' well even if the physical position of the well is changed. (Adapted from Goldman-Rakic, 1992.)

permanence: the animal has to keep in mind the location of the reward when it is out of sight for a short while.

Goldman-Rakic's paradigm is too simple to use with humans, but McCarthy et al. (1994) reported an equivalent neuro-imaging study in which participants viewed a series of abstract coloured shapes on a computer screen, one at a time every 1.5 seconds. The shapes could appear in one of twenty positions, and the task was to indicate whenever a stimulus occupied a position that a previous stimulus had appeared in. (A control condition required participants to respond whenever a particular coloured shape was presented.) The researchers used fMRI to show that the memory task induced greater activation in area 46 bi-laterally, although activation for this spatial working memory task was greatest on the right side.

A study similar to that of McCarthy et al.'s was reported by Smith, Jonides, and Koeppe (1996), although this group employed PET to compare spatial and verbal working memory. In the spatial condition, subjects saw a brief array of three dots on the screen. After a three second delay, a single circle appeared on the screen, and participants had to decide whether its location would have encompassed any of the dots. In the verbal condition, four letters were shown briefly, followed by a similar delay. Participants were then shown a single letter and they had to say whether or not it had appeared initially. PET activation was more marked at several locations on the right side for the spatial task, and more marked on the left side for the verbal working memory task. However, in both conditions, area 46 was activated.

Braver et al. (1997) used fMRI in a verbal working memory test in which subjects had to 'keep in mind' the order and identity of sequences of letters. As the burden on working memory increased, so too did activity levels in several left brain areas including area 46.

Interim comment

Researchers have made good progress by employing functional imaging in studies of explicit and implicit memory, and also in relation to working memory. The studies of explicit memory indicate that the hippocampus is involved both in the encoding of new information, and in the retrieval of recently stored information where explicit recollection is required. According to a recent review by Lepage, Habib, and Tulving (1998) hippocampal activation during encoding is most marked in rostral (front) regions, whereas activation during explicit retrieval is greater in caudal (rear) areas. Lepage's meta-analysis also identified a laterality effect for encoding in which explicitly verbal material activated only the left hippocampus, whereas non-verbal material preferentially (though not exclusively) activated the right hippocampus. This laterality effect was not evident during retrieval. Cortical regions are also clearly involved in both encoding and retrieval, and there is evidence of an asymmetry that has given rise to the acronym HERA (hemispheric encoding retrieval asymmetry). It represents the idea that the left dorso-lateral pre-frontal cortex is more active during encoding, and the right more active during retrieval.

Imaging of different types of implicit memory process has implicated a quite distinct set of brain regions including the motor cortex, components of the basal ganglia and the cerebellum. Consistent evidence of hippocampal and dorso-lateral frontal activation in implicit-procedural memory is not yet forthcoming, suggesting that the distinction between explicit and implicit memory derived from psychological research extends to non-overlapping anatomical substrates.

Arguably, most progress from the application of imaging procedures has come from research into working memory. PET and fMRI investigations repeatedly implicate area 46 as the likely location of the 'central executive'. These same studies also indicate that parietal, temporal and even occipital regions (mainly on the right side in tests of spatial working memory, and the left side for verbal working memory) are activated. A picture is emerging in which pre-frontal areas can serve as a temporary repository for 'reactivated' representations drawn from remote cortical regions on both sides of the brain. This scheme fits in well with the observation that there are complex reciprocal connections between area 46 and the association areas of both temporal and parietal lobes. However, researchers have yet to resolve the matter as to whether there is one single 'central executive' as Petrides (1996) has argued, or whether this is fractionated (subdivided) on a modality specific basis, as Goldman-Rakic (1996) has concluded.

Some other forms of amnesia

Concussion amnesia

A bang on the head is actually one of the most common causes of amnesia, although memory impairment is almost always temporary, unless, of course, the accident has caused organic damage to the brain. In a typical case (such as a cyclist who collides with a tree and loses consciousness for a few minutes) there may be both anterograde and retrograde amnesia. The anterograde amnesia will extend beyond the point of recovering consciousness. It may include being unable to remember the ambulance journey, or being checked over at the hospital. In addition to the traumatic event itself, the retrograde amnesia may encompass a period of a few minutes leading up to the accident. A curious feature of concussion amnesia is that it usually shrinks with time, although there is nearly always some permanent loss of memory for the period just before the event.

Concussion amnesia is, in many respects, akin to a temporary form of organic amnesia. Indeed, during the anterograde amnesia phase, STM seems to be preserved (Regard & Landis, 1984). The limited nature of retrograde amnesia suggests that the main effect of the concussion is to impair the consolidation of new information from STM to LTM, although the shrinkage of it over time is suggestive of a retrieval failure. Perhaps the non-specific nature of concussion amnesia can effect both consolidation and retrieval.

ECT-induced amnesia

ECT is an effective treatment for individuals with a particular form of depression. Nevertheless, the process is somewhat drastic, involving the induction of an epileptic seizure by passing an electrical current through frontal and temporal cortical regions, so its use is mainly restricted to individuals who fail to respond to other forms of treatment. An oft reported side effect of ECT is memory impairment. In most cases, this resembles the amnesic pattern seen in cases of concussion amnesia. There is loss of memory for events following the administration of ECT (anterograde amnesia), and sometimes some retrograde amnesia too, so that the person may not recall the events leading up to the treatment. As with concussion amnesia, there is invariably shrinkage over time, and usually, a brief retrograde amnesia (of a day or two) is all that remains (Squire, Slater, & Miller, 1981). Ironically, and despite occasional subjective impressions to the contrary, there is accumulating evidence that memory actually improves following ECT (Warren & Groome, 1984). However, it is very difficult to say whether the improvement is a direct consequence of ECT or linked to the general improvement in psychological functioning as the depression dissipates.

The explicit-declarative implicit-procedural debate revisited

Evidence from investigations of people with organic amnesias tends to show that certain skill-based learning may be preserved while factual/knowledge-based material is lost, and the imaging research suggests that different circuitry may be involved in these two types of memory. Earlier in this chapter I commented on the ways researchers had proposed LTM may be subdivided, and suggested that there was considerable overlap between the explicit-implicit distinction and the declarative-procedural distinction. Now that we have reviewed more material, can we be any more precise about the best way to distinguish what is lost from what is retained in amnesia?

The explicit-implicit distinction certainly has a basic intuitive appeal. HM *explicitly* failed to learn his new address, yet *implicitly* acquired procedural skills such as learning to mirror-draw, while denying all knowledge of the equipment! For some psychologists the distinction between conscious and unconscious processing (in explicit and implicit memory respectively) is pivotal. Mandler (1989), for example, has distinguished between controlled (explicit/conscious) and automatic (implicit/unconscious) processes, arguing that organic amnesia is, in effect, a manifestation of impaired consciousness: the amnesic has lost the ability to engage in conscious control of material in memory, while unconscious automatic processing is unimpaired

For others, such as Cohen (1997), the issue of consciousness muddies the waters. For example, the hippocampal system is not, so far as we can tell, directly related to consciousness at all: people with massive hippocampal damage still experience consciousness. A second concern relates to amnesia in animals, who show just as marked a dissociation between so-called explicit memory tasks (such as spatial memory), and implicit memory tasks (such as conditioning or skill learning). While the question of animal consciousness goes well beyond the remit of this book, most animal behaviourists would be surprised if animal consciousness turns out to be identical to human consciousness. Thus, the parallel memory disturbances jibe poorly with the argument that explicit memory is different from implicit memory simply because it relies on conscious processes.

A third problem is that the so-called implicit memory skills of amnesics can, in fact, be shown to be defective under certain test conditions. In a study by Whitlow, Althoff, and Cohen (1995) normal control and amnesic participants viewed a series of scenes twice. Then, a week later, they were shown another set of scenes, half of which were identical to the first set. The remainder were identical except that certain vital elements had been rearranged. Although most subjects now failed to distinguish between original scenes and those that had been rearranged, an analysis of the eye movements of the control subjects still suggested they were concentrating on areas of the scene where an object or person had appeared in the original! This is evidence of implicit memory. The amnesics on the other hand failed to direct their eye movements to the critical regions of the amended scenes, suggesting impaired implicit memory.

According to Cohen and colleagues (see Cohen, 1997), amnesics struggle with certain memory tasks not necessarily because of impaired consciousness, but because the tasks in question are fundamentally 'relational' in nature. Declarative memory (Cohen prefers the declarative-procedural distinction for the reasons given above) is relational in the sense that tasks not only require associations to be formed between objects in a scene or words in a list, but also between the new material and existing memories. Indeed, related declarative memories can be activated by any number of new stimuli or old memories, regardless of the current context, and the neural structure that facilitates this process is the hippocampus. This structure receives converging input from vast areas of sensory, motor and association cortex. Its role is 'metaphorically' to bind these converging inputs together, to facilitate remembering of links or relationships between potentially disparate objects, stimuli or events – i.e. to create a web, or perhaps more accurately, a network of related memories. Procedural memory on the other hand is neither associative or relational. On the contrary, it is inflexible and tied only to the processing operations that were invoked on earlier trials.

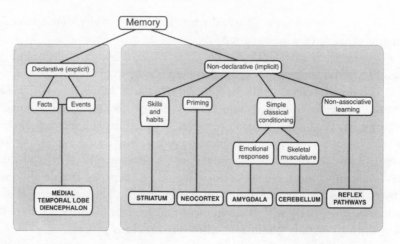

FIGURE 7.6 Subdivisions of long-term memory indicating possible anatomical substrates of different components. (Adapted from Gazzaniga et al., 1998.)

Most of the research I have reviewed in this chapter fits well with the declarative-procedural distinction when it is reinterpreted in terms of relational and non-relational processes. Animal work on the role of the hippocampus in spatial memory can also be readily understood in these terms because researchers have shown that hippocampal neurons become 'tuned' not to individual elements in the environment but to the relative spatial locations of multiple elements (see O'Keefe & Speakman, 1987). Although the forming of relationships may involve conscious processes – as for example in the use of **mnemonics** to aid memory – it need not necessarily do so. Contextual cues may aid recall even if the respondent cannot say why! The putative anatomical substrates of these different components of memory are illustrated in Fig. 7.6.

Summary

Our consideration of memory and amnesia has taken us from the formative experimental work of cognitive psychologists via the classic case studies of amnesia and brain damage to in-vivo imaging of memory functions in the brain. The psychological approach led to the development of models of memory in which the distinct capacities and duration of short and long-term storage were emphasised. The development of an alternative 'working memory' system to account for both short-term processing of new material and on-line processing of previously learned material was also considered. Psychologists have also developed theories to account for the organisation of LTM. Here, the emphasis has been on the distinction between declarative (explicit) and procedural (implicit) LTM.

Case studies of organic amnesia vividly illustrate the selective loss of function that can result from damage to temporal and/or diencephalic regions. The specificity of lesion suffered by RB pinpoints the key role of the hippocampus (especially CA1 neurons) in the process of consolidating material into LTM. Other cases provide less anatomically precise but nevertheless compelling evidence of the effects of brain damage on both retrograde and anterograde amnesia.

The in-vivo studies have, for procedural reasons, tended to focus on working memory and LTM. Both animal and human investigations of working memory have identified regions in the pre-frontal cortex (especially area 46) as a likely location for the central executive component of working memory, although this region is probably involved in other non-memory functions as well. The role of the hippocampus both in the consolidation of new material and the retrieval of previously presented material has also been confirmed by PET and fMRI studies. The weight of evidence supports the view that hippocampal activation is not involved in implicit (procedural) memory processes.

The chapter concluded with brief consideration of Cohen's ideas about the role of the hippocampus in consolidation (and retrieval), and the distinction between declarative and procedural memory. According to this hypothesis, the key function of the hippocampus is to bind together links between stimuli (and between new stimuli and established memories) to create a network of related memories. This happens when new material has to be memorised, but continues for a considerable period after initial memorisation as LTM consolidates. Procedural memory differs fundamentally from declarative memory because it is non-relational.

Visual object recognition and spatial processing

■ Introduction   154

■ The 'what' and 'where' streams and
    visual perception   155

■ The ventral stream and object
    recognition   158
   Classic descriptions of visual agnosia   159
   Recent concerns about visual agnosia   162
   Modern ideas about visual agnosia   164
   Recognition of faces and prosopagnosia   166
   Co-occurrence of different forms of agnosia   169
   Prosopagnosia and the brain   170
   Capgras syndrome   172

■ Evaluation of the ventral stream and
    the agnosias   173

■ Spatial functions and the 'where' stream   173
   Basic spatial processes   174
   Constructional skills   175
   Route-finding   177
   Spatial memory   178
   The left hemisphere and spatial processing   178

■ Summary   180

chapter 8

Introduction

THE PRIMACY OF THE VISUAL system in humans is reinforced by the observation that up to half of the cerebral cortex is directly or indirectly involved in visual processing. It is important at the outset to distinguish between the sensory mechanisms of vision and the perceptual processes that permit recognition of the visual input. Visual sensation is about input 'getting registered' in the brain. Perception is concerned with the interpretation of the input (Mesulam, 1998). To understand the former we would need to know about the structure of the eye, and the route that visual input takes from the retina to the occipital cortex. To understand the latter (or perhaps begin to understand, since so much more is yet to be learned), we will consider some research findings from case studies of people who have lost certain perceptual functions, usually after damage or disease to key cortical regions.

Although the distinction between 'sensation' and 'perception' sounds clear-cut, it is, to some extent, artificial, because a good deal of 'processing' of visual input takes place almost as soon as light enters the eye. In the retina, a network of cells interacts to provide the brain with evidence of contrast, colour and boundaries (edges). Retinal output, in the form of millions of nerve impulses, travels via the optic nerve and tract to the lateral geniculate nuclei (one on each side) of the thalamus. Here, information from the two eyes begins to coalesce, with input from the central fovic retinal regions being separated from peripheral retinal regions. Most lateral geniculate output is relayed on to the primary visual cortex where two vast 'sheets' of cells (in the left and right occipital lobes) map out the entire visual field (see Fig. 3.3). Cells in this region are arranged in columns and respond preferentially, and in some cases exclusively to particular types of visual input, such as the orientation of lines, whether the input conveys information about colour, or contrast, and so on. Thanks in no small part to the pioneering work of Hubel and Weisel in the 1960s and 1970s, the route from eye to brain is reasonably well understood, although I do not intend to provide detailed coverage of it in this chapter. Readers wishing to learn more should refer to one of the many excellent reviews of this research area, such as Chapter 4 of Gazzaniga et al. (1998).

Neuropsychologists tend to be more interested in the processes after sensory registration that lead to perception. In order to begin to understand these stages of processing, we need to look beyond V1 and V2 of the occipital lobe to other cortical regions that are implicated in the interpretation of visual sensation. There are separate cortical regions to deal with colour and movement, and additional regions to coordinate reading, object recognition and probably facial recognition too. In fact, visual areas seem to be scattered throughout the occipital, parietal and even temporal lobes.

There is substantial evidence that these areas divide (to some extent) into two separate processing streams, commonly referred to as the 'what' and 'where' streams (Ungerleider & Mishkin, 1982). Later in the chapter I introduce some brain disorders that seem to be anatomically and functionally linked to one or other stream. These are of interest in their own right, but they also provide clues about the sort of visual perceptual processing that must occur in 'intact' brains. However, I start with a brief review of Ungerleider and Mishkin's model of parallel, but functionally distinct, visual processing streams.

The 'what' and 'where' streams and visual perception

In the mammalian brain, there is extensive output from the occipital lobes to other cortical regions that is carried primarily by two major fibre bundles. The inferior route follows a ventral course (round the side and particularly underneath) into the temporal lobes, whereas the superior route takes a dorsal course (over the top) into the posterior regions of the parietal lobes. In 1982, Ungerleider and Mishkin suggested that these anatomically distinct routes could also be distinguished in terms of the types of 'processing' they mediated. On the basis of data gleaned largely from lesion studies and electrical recording in monkeys, they proposed that the ventral stream is specialised for object recognition and perception, whereas the dorsal stream is specialised for spatial perception – i.e. for determining the locations of objects and their positions relative to one another

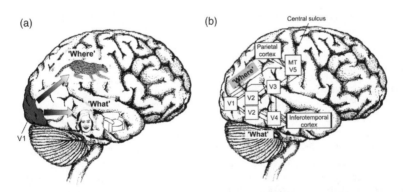

FIGURE 8.1 The 'what' and 'where' streams of visual perception

(a) Ungerleider and Mishkin's 'what' and 'where' streams, and (b) a slightly more detailed flow diagram of some of the cortical regions implicated in these two processing streams.

and to the viewer. The two streams operate in parallel to allow us to address the fundamental questions of 'what' we are looking at, and 'where' it is located in our field of vision (see Fig. 8.1).

Pohl's (1973) discrimination learning study is typical of the research from which Ungerleider and Mishkin developed their model. It had two conditions: in the landmark task, monkeys learned to associate the presence of food in one of two food wells with a landmark such as a cone, which was always positioned near the baited well. After a period of learning the rule was reversed so that food now only appeared in the well furthest away from the cone. In the object discrimination condition, there were two landmarks such as a cone and a cube. In the training phase, food was only hidden in the food well near to one particular landmark, then when this had been learned, the relationship between cue

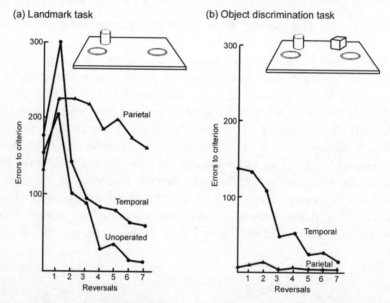

FIGURE 8.2 Pohl's double-dissociation study of landmark and object discrimination in macaques

In the landmark experiment, monkeys learned to associate the presence of food in a well identified by a particular marker (in this case a cylinder). Once learned, the rule was reversed so that now the food was in the well furthest away from the marker. Although control animals and those with temporal lesions quickly learned the reversal, animals with bi-lateral parietal lobe lesions failed to improve. In the object discrimination experiment, monkeys learned to associate the presence of food with one of two markers (say, the cube). Once learned, the rule was reversed, and food was now associated with the other object (the cylinder). Monkeys with parietal lesions were untroubled by this reversal, whereas those with bi-lateral temporal lobe lesions took several trials to learn the new association. The former experiment relies on processing in the 'where' stream, the latter on processing in the 'what' stream. (Adapted from Pohl, 1973.)

and food was reversed. Pohl found evidence of a double dissociation: performance on the 'spatial' landmark task was disrupted by parietal but not temporal lesions, whereas performance in the object discrimination was impaired by temporal but not parietal lesions (see Fig. 8.2).

Although Ungerleider and Mishkin's model was initially well received, it has undergone both anatomical and conceptual revision as more has been learned about cortical regions involved in visual perception. Anatomically, it is certain that more cortical modules (i.e. functionally and anatomically distinct localised cortical regions, of which more than 30 have now been identified) are involved in the two streams than was initially thought. Moreover, modules within the two streams appear to interact with one another (i.e. send and receive projections) rather more extensively than Ungerleider and Mishkin anticipated. Finally, there is growing evidence that a third pathway, projecting into the superior temporal sulcus area (STS) is involved. The role of this stream is unclear, but the neurons in the STS that it projects to are **poly-sensory**, meaning that they respond to inputs from multiple sensory channels. It is therefore likely that this route is important in the integration of perceptual information about stimuli arising from different sensory inputs, such as appearance and touch (Boussaoud, Ungerleider, & Desimone, 1990).

Conceptually, the main challenge to the model has concerned the nature of information processing in the dorsal stream. In the early version, Ungerleider and Mishkin proposed that this stream was concerned with identifying the location of objects in space. But according to Goodale and Milner (1992) this may be to underestimate the true importance of this pathway. They have argued that the dorsal stream's true purpose is to guide the on-line control of action. In other words, while knowing about the location of objects is an important component, some neurons in this pathway become particularly active only when a visual stimulus prompts a motor response, such as reaching for an object. This observation has prompted some researchers to suggest that this route should be referred to as the 'how' stream. It is of interest to note that a major projection from the parietal lobe is to frontal areas, which, as we have seen, are critical in planning purposeful movements.

Interim comment

At present, Ungerleider and Mishkin's model is accepted as offering a heuristic framework for understanding the lines of demarcation between object recognition and spatial processing. However, many neuropsychologists anticipate further revisions to the model as more is learned about the nuances of visual perception. We return to consider spatial processing in the dorsal stream later in this chapter. For the time being, we need to consider some of the characteristics of the ventral stream, and the effects that damage to different components of it can have on object recognition.

The ventral stream and object recognition

It is worth pausing to consider briefly the computational processes that must be involved in object recognition. For example, 3D objects in our field of vision are projected on to our retina(s), which only work in 2D. So the brain must 'reconstruct' a third dimension from the retinal projections in order for us to see in 3D. Secondly, objects must (within limits) be recognised as such irrespective of where their image falls on the retina, their distance from the viewer and their orientation. For example, a tree is still usually *perceived* as a tree whether it is at the end of your garden, on the other side of a field or on the horizon. Thirdly, you must also be able to recognise objects when they are moving in different directions. A horse moving across your line of vision projects a quite different image to one galloping directly towards you, yet you are able to recognise that each image is of the same object (a horse!). Finally, your brain must be able to link the percept (of the horse for example) with stored representations of horses in order for you to make the semantic leap towards recognition of the object as a horse.

The ventral stream runs bilaterally from area V1 of the occipital lobes via areas V2 and V4 into the inferior regions of the temporal lobes (see Fig. 8.1). If we examine the response characteristics of neurons in this stream, three clear trends emerge. The first is that neurons in posterior regions (at the beginning of the stream) fire in response to relatively simple stimulus characteristics such as width, shading and texture, whereas neurons later on in the stream only respond to much more complex visual stimuli. Remarkable as it may seem, cells towards the front parts of the temporal lobe (the anterior and polar regions as they are known) only respond to very specific shapes of stimuli such as a hand, or even particular faces (Gross, Rocha-Miranda, & Bender, 1972).

A second feature is that the further forward one looks along this stream, the less important is the physical position of the object in the visual field. We could describe cells in these forward regions as having large **receptive fields**, and in the case of some anterior temporal neurons, almost the entire retina appears to be covered. So, no matter where the object falls on the retina, cortical cells will respond to (i.e. be excited by) the object (assuming they are tuned to it in the first place). Even earlier on in the stream, V4 cells seem to be tuned to particular colours irrespective of stimulus orientation, location or movement, and they have receptive fields estimated to be between 16 and 36 times larger than those of neurons in the primary visual cortex (Desimone & Gross, 1979).

A final point, which I hinted at earlier, is that cells in this stream make considerable use of colour. This attribute is tremendously important for object recognition, not least because it often allows us to distinguish **figure** from **ground,** providing additional clues about the edges (and thus the shape) of objects (Zeki, 1980).

Classic descriptions of visual agnosia

In order to understand better the sort of processing that occurs in this stream, it is helpful to consider some classic neurological disorders that appear to stem from dysfunction or damage to it. In the 1890s, on the basis of a small number of detailed case studies, Lissauer described two forms of object recognition failure which he called apperceptive and associative agnosia. Some 100 years on, we think that the two disorders are linked to damage at different stages in the ventral stream, and reflect different types of perceptual disturbance. Although there is a growing awareness that Lissauer's binary classification of agnosias oversimplifies the true diversity of these conditions, the distinction at least provides a starting point for our consideration of visual agnosia and I will retain it for the moment.

Apperceptive agnosia

When shown a photograph of a cup, someone with this type of agnosia will probably be able to describe some of the physical features of it such as its size, the presence of a handle, the colour of designs with which it is decorated and so on. However, they will be unable to identify the object. Obviously, the degree of impairment depends on the extent of damage, but in the worst cases, when damage to occipital and surrounding posterior regions (especially in the right hemisphere) is widespread, apperceptive agnosics cannot even copy simple shapes, match them, or discriminate between them. A case in point is Mr S (studied by Benson & Greenberg, 1969) who had become agnosic following accidental carbon monoxide poisoning. Although he clearly had some rudimentary impression of form – describing a safety-pin as 'silver and shiny like a watch or nail clippers' – he could not recognise objects, letters, numbers or faces. He could, however, recognise objects from touch. Moreover, there was no evident deficit in his speech, memory or comprehension.

People with apperceptive agnosia are described as being unable to put individual parts of a visual stimulus together to form what psychologists call a 'percept'. The problem is regarded as 'perceptual' rather than 'sensory' because apperceptive agnosics can describe individual elements of an object. They can distinguish light and dark, and can detect the presence/absence of simple visual stimuli. What they seem unable to do is 'bind' together individual components of a visual stimulus into a meaningful perceptual whole.

Associative agnosia

Individuals with this form of agnosia can copy objects relatively well, and detect similar items from a visual display. In some cases, they may even be able to sort items into groupings (animals, items of cutlery, tools, etc.). The problem in associative agnosia is an inability to identify (and name) the object in question. Consider the following situation: a patient is shown an assortment of cutlery. He picks up a fork, and, when asked, draws a recognisable sketch of it. This shows that perception of the item is relatively complete, and therefore that the individual does not have apperceptive agnosia. He may, if asked, be able to find another similar item from the cutlery drawer. However, he would still be unable to identify the item as a fork! Moreover, if later asked to draw the object from memory, he may be unable to do so, although if actually asked to draw a fork, he probably could. Even at this point, he may not realise that the object he was holding and the drawing he has just made were of the same item! This problem is not necessarily related to general deficits in semantic memory because subjects can sometimes describe in great detail functional (or other semantic) information about objects from memory. One associative agnosic (MS) who was unable to draw an anchor from memory, was nevertheless able to define the item as a 'a brake for ships' (Ratcliff & Newcombe, 1982).

On the other hand, some associative agnosics certainly do have problems with their semantic memory. Patient AB (studied by Warrington, 1975) could match objects and distinguish shapes, and he could also match different views of faces reasonably well. He was, though, unable to name any of a series of 12 common objects shown to him. Evidence of AB's semantic memory impairment stems from the observation that although he could determine whether photographs depicted animals or objects, he was unable to name or distinguish between different types of animal whether presented visually or aurally.

An insight into the cognitive deficit found in associative agnosia is provided by the work of Warrington and her colleagues. In one study by Warrington and Taylor (1978), agnosics had to match objects according to function. They were shown a picture of a particular object, such as a rolled-up umbrella, and two other objects (an open umbrella and a walking stick) from which to choose a match. The correct functional match would be the open umbrella, but people with associative agnosia usually chose the walking stick (which looked more similar). This suggests that the core problem in associative agnosia is one of linking percepts to meaning. Object recognition is certainly more complete than for someone with apperceptive agnosia. However, the remaining problem is one of forming links between the 'percept' and stored semantic information about such items.

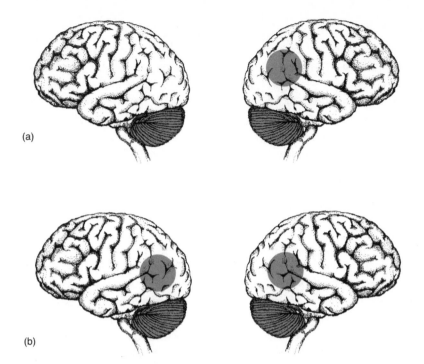

FIGURE 8.3 Cortical regions typically damaged in apperceptive and associative agnosia (Adapted from Kolb & Whishaw, 1996.)

(a) Uni-lateral damage in posterior regions of the right hemisphere is more likely to be associated with apperceptive agnosia than equivalent damage on the left (although damage is often bi-lateral).

(b) In associative agnosia, damage can be to either hemisphere, although the location is typically more ventral than that seen in apperceptive agnosia (in the vicinity of the occipital-temporal boundaries).

Interim comment

Both apperceptive and associative agnosics struggle to recognise objects, and are thus unable to relate visually presented items to stored knowledge about those items. In practice, a key distinction between the two forms has been whether or not individuals could copy drawings. Associative agnosics could, but apperceptive agnosics could not. Lissauer's distinction between the two forms of agnosia can be related to our model of processing in the ventral stream. Apperceptive agnosia occurs because of damage at an early stage in the ventral processing stream, and although many people with this form of agnosia have bi-lateral damage, cases of people with uni-lateral damage suggest that it is the right hemisphere that is most critical. People with this form of agnosia have only the most rudimentary visual perceptual functions, and damage to the occipital lobes and adjacent cortical regions is often apparent. Associative agnosia is related to a somewhat later stage in perceptual processing in the ventral stream. The percept is relatively complete, but a problem is apparent in the linking of the percept with stored information of objects. This may be related to damage to semantic systems in the left hemisphere or to damage to the pathways connecting the occipito-temporal border regions of the right and left hemispheres (see Fig. 8.3).

Recent concerns about visual agnosia

An unresolved problem concerning the classification of visual agnosia is related to the inherently imprecise nature of brain damage. Recall that in Lissauer's original characterisations both apperceptive and associative agnosia were considered to be 'post-sensory' disorders. Yet the reality is that many visual agnosics have sensory impairments such as colour blindness or small blind spots (scotomas) in addition to their perceptual problems. This is particularly so in apperceptive agnosia, which is frequently associated with accidental carbon monoxide poisoning (see the case of Mr S discussed earlier). The poisoning also leads to widely spread but minor lesions (sometimes called salt and pepper lesions) in posterior regions that are linked to sensory impairments such as those mentioned above. Clearly, it is important to ensure that the apparently perceptual deficits seen in agnosia are not, after all, caused by more fundamental sensory impairments as some writers have suggested (e.g. Bay, 1953).

Perhaps the main problem with Lissauer's classification of visual agnosia is that it is too simple, and therefore fails to distinguish satisfactorily between subtly different forms. Consider first apperceptive agnosia: although the classic description emphasises the failure to bind together individual elements into a perceptual whole, cases have more recently come to light where correct perception of the whole appears to depend on the orientation of the objects, the shading or shadowing that is apparent or even the extent to which images are degraded. Some agnosics may, for example, be able to identify an object when viewed in a normal (standard) orientation, yet be unable to identify the same object if it is shown end-on, upside-down, or in some other unusual orientation. Patient JL, studied by Humphreys and Riddoch (1984), struggled to match normal views of objects with foreshortened views (end-on) (see Fig. 8.4a). Moreover, when shown items from the Gollin picture test, which comprises intact and partially degraded line drawings of familiar objects, some agnosics can identify the intact drawings but not the degraded ones (Warrington & Taylor, 1973, and see Fig. 8.4b).

Associative agnosia also seems too simple a concept to account for the subtle differences in deficit that are seen in this condition. As we have seen,

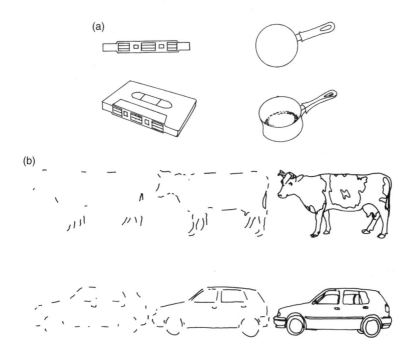

FIGURE 8.4 Unusual views of objects, and items from the Gollin test (Adapted from Gollin, 1960.)

(a)   All people find it easier to recognise objects when viewed from a 'normal' angle than an 'unusual' angle. However, some agnosics cannot recognise objects at all when shown the 'unusual' view.

(b)   The Gollin figures also present particular difficulties for some agnosics, although recognition for the complete figures may be unaffected.

Patient AB studied by Warrington (1975) could draw and match objects, and was good at recognising unusual views of objects. He was, however, profoundly impaired at object or picture naming, and he was also almost equally poor at describing functions of objects when given their names aurally. HJA, studied by Humphreys and Riddoch (1984), could, on the other hand, define a carrot when asked to do so verbally, yet fail to identify a picture of one, guessing that it was a sort of brush! Moreover, he could often name objects by touch (when blind-folded) that he could not identify visually. These two examples illustrate that similar perceptual frailties may, on closer observation, take subtly different forms, and be related to different cognitive processing impairments. AB's problems involved semantic memory deficits, whereas HJA had an intact memory but seemed unable to access it from visually presented material.

A third problem is related to the question of how complete the percept actually is for individuals who would otherwise receive a diagnosis of associa-tive agnosia. Recall that the acid test of this form has, historically, been whether or not the person can copy whole drawings. HJA, mentioned earlier, was able to produce an accurate copy of an etching of London, but the process took six hours and he completed the exercise is a laborious, slavish, line-by-line manner, which seemed to be independent of any 'knowledge' of the actual form of objects in the sketch. Humphreys and Riddoch acknowledged that HJA was an unusual case. They argued that he had a particular problem in the integration of overall form with local detail, and other test findings showed that HJA was often 'thrown' by the presence of detail in drawings or pictures that he was trying to copy or recognise: for example, he found silhouettes easier to recognise than line drawings. Of course, it is likely that normal individuals make extensive use of their semantic memory (which HJA could not do) when copying a drawing. This may make the copy less accurate, but a lot faster. The point is that, which ever way we look at it, HJA does not fit conveniently into either of Lissauer's agnosic types.

Modern ideas about visual agnosia

Most researchers now acknowledge that Lissauer's classification is in need of revision and/or expansion. Farah (1990) has, for example, proposed that visual object agnosia needs to be considered in relation to deficits in both word and face recognition. Warrington has emphasised the importance of perceptual categorisation as a stage in object recognition that may be impaired in apperceptive agnosics (Warrington & Taylor, 1978). Humphreys and Riddoch (1987) have argued that there are at least five sub-types of agnosia, and Ellis and Young (1996) also found it necessary to disaggregate Lissauer's two forms into several sub-types.

Ellis and Young's ideas merit special attention. Their cognitive neuropsychological model of object recognition is an attempt to integrate much of the case study reports (from their own patients, and those of Warrington, Humphreys and others) with an influential theory of visual perception proposed by Marr (1982). Although the details of his model need not concern us, it comprises three sequential stages. The first is the generation of a unified 'primal sketch' from the two 2D retinal images. It includes information about boundaries, contours and brightness fluctuations, but not overall form. The second stage involves the generation of what Marr called a 2.5D image. This is viewer-centred (from the viewer's perspective), and contains information about form and contour, but not object constancy or perceptual classification. The final stage is the 3D representation. This is a true object (rather than viewer) centred mental representation. It is independent of the viewer's position, and specifies the real 3D shape of an object from any view, enabling true object recognition.

Ellis and Young's model of object recognition is shown in Fig. 8.5. It takes Marr's three stages as axiomatic, but adds in a key additional element that permits identification. 'Object recognition units' are stored mental representa-

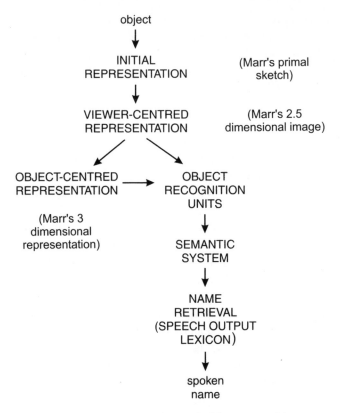

FIGURE 8.5 Ellis and Young's model of visual object recognition

tions of objects, and we may have only one for any given object. For example, you will probably have an object recognition unit for 'bicycle'. When either the 2.5D or 3D representation of a bicycle (that you form when you see a bike) corresponds to your stored object recognition unit for it, access to your semantic store (for information about bicycles) is achieved. In the Ellis and Young model, naming the object relies on an additional lexical component separate from the semantic system. This is necessary to accommodate some 'anomic' individuals who clearly have semantic knowledge of objects but still cannot name them when they see them (a condition called optical aphasia).

The point of this lengthy diversion is that Marr's model (plus Ellis and Young's modifications) serves as a useful template for understanding the various forms of agnosia that have now been described in the literature, and, *inter alia*, provides a heuristic model for visual object recognition in the intact brain. For example, Lissauer's apperceptive agnosia can be related to a failure early in the stream involving an inability to form either a primal sketch or a 2.5D viewer-centred image (e.g. Mr S). An inability to recognise degraded objects or unusual views of objects with preserved ability to recognise form may be related to a failure in forming a 3D object-centred image (e.g. JL). Associative agnosia may occur either because of problems in accessing semantic memory despite the formation of an intact object-centred image (e.g. HJA), or because of impairments to semantic memory itself (e.g. AB).

Interim comment

Ellis and Young have offered a dynamic multi-stage scheme of visual object recognition that accounts for many of the apparent contradictions or inexactitudes of earlier models. However, the authors acknowledge that much more research is required to resolve remaining uncertainties about agnosic disorders, and, in the process, about normal object recognition. Two examples bear mention. The first relates to the formation of a true object-centred image. Recall that the copying style of agnosics like HJA, though accurate, was painstaking and laborious. Humphreys and Riddoch have taken this as an indication that HJA did not, in fact, have normal form recognition, because of his problems in integrating fine detail into the global form. This in turn implies that normal object recognition involves both the encoding of a global form, and the integration of fine detail into that form. Humphreys and Riddoch coined the term 'integrative agnosia' to describe HJA's deficit and suggested that such a 'processing' failure was, in fact, a hallmark of many agnosic patients.

The second outstanding issue concerns the nature of semantic memory (or access) impairments that contribute to agnosia, because, astonishing though it may seem, there is evidence to suggest that such impairments may, in some cases, be category specific. We have already seen that AB's agnosia was linked to deficits in his semantic memory and his inability to make intra-class distinctions. However, a handful of cases have come to light suggesting that category specific semantic impairments may also occur in agnosia. Warrington and McCarthy (1994) have described a small number of agnosic patients, some of whom have a naming deficit for living things, and others who have a deficit for inanimate objects (see also Table 6.1). It remains to be seen whether this is evidence of a genuine double dissociation (and hence of the existence of category specific agnosia) or an artefact linked to the inherently greater similarity of animals than objects.

Recognition of faces and prosopagnosia

The ability to recognise faces is a skill that has long intrigued psychologists, partly because humans seem to be so good at it. Consider the following lines of evidence. First, humans have a phenomenal memory for faces. Most readers will be aware of that moment of recognition when spotting the face of someone not encountered for many years. Secondly, research indicates that humans can memorise face information very quickly and with very little effort. People tested on Warrington's facial memory test, in which they look briefly at 50 anonymous black and white photographs of people, can correctly recognise most (or even all) of them in a later test. Thirdly, although the distinctions between faces are subtle (all humans have two eyes, a nose and a mouth), humans are able to scan large numbers of photographs very quickly to find the one famous face in the crowd. This last observation is a reminder that the key to effective face processing is 'individuation'; that is, being able to distinguish between the subtle variations in form, size shape, and alignment of the components of a human face.

A small number of people suffer from a form of agnosia that involves the inability to perceive faces. In prosopagnosia (as it is known) the degree of impairment is, as with object recognition, variable. In some cases, people may be unable to match pairs of faces, or say whether two photographs are of the same individual. In other cases, recognition of particular individuals such as film stars or members of the person's own family may be affected. In the most extreme and perplexing form of the disorder, the person may even lose the ability to recognise themselves from photographs or in the mirror. Prosopagnosia is a rare condition, so the diverse forms of it have yet to be delineated to the satisfaction of all neuropsychologists. However, enough is known to indicate that at least two broad forms exist. In the former, the basic perception of faces is impaired. In the latter, face perception seems relatively intact but individuals still cannot recognise (or in other ways semantically process) faces (see Box 8.1).

Consider the following cases. Soldier S was studied by Bodamer (1947). Despite making an otherwise reasonable recovery following head injury, he was unable to recognise once-familiar faces. He could differentiate between faces and other objects, although he was prone to errors in recognising animals from photographs of their head, once misidentifying a dog as an unusually hairy person! When it came to humans, he complained that all faces looked very much alike, describing them as routinely flat white ovals with dark eyes. He was unable to interpret facial expressions although he could see the movements (of the face) that led to changed expressions. He was unable to recognise his own face in a mirror.

Now consider Mr W, who was studied by Bruyer et al. (1983). He developed prosopagnosia in middle-age following a period of illness. He retained the ability to copy line drawings of faces, and he could match photographs of faces taken from different perspectives. He could also select faces correctly given a verbal description, and his performance on this task deteriorated (as it would for normal subjects) if the faces were partly obscured. His particular problem only became apparent when he was asked to identify faces either of famous

Box 8.1: A case study of prosopagnosia (adapted from Stirling, 1999)

Therapist: (Shows patient a picture of a cow and horse) 'Which is the horse?'

Patient: 'That's easy . . . the one on the right without horns.'

Therapist: (shows photograph of Elvis Presley) 'Do you know who this is?'

Patient: 'Is it a famous person?'

Therapist: 'Yes.'

Patient: 'Is it the Pope?'

Therapist: 'No, this person is no longer alive . . . Describe the face to me.'

Patient: 'Well, he's tall, and has got black hair swept back with lots of grease . . .'

Therapist: 'Does he have a moustache?'

Patient: 'No, but he has long sideburns . . . and a guitar.'

Therapist: 'It's Elvis Presley!' (Patient nods, but doesn't appear to connect the face to the name.)

Therapist: 'Now, who's this?' (Shows photograph of patient's wife.)

Patient: 'I dunno . . . some woman . . . about my age with grey hair and nice eyes . . .'

Therapist: 'It's your wife.' (Patient once again seems unable to connect the picture to the identification.)

Therapist: 'O.K. Who's this?' (Shows photograph of patient.)

Patient: 'No idea . . .'

Therapist: 'Describe him . . .'

Patient: 'Well, he looks quite old, and has lost a lot of hair. He looks like he needs a holiday, with those bags under his eyes . . . A good long rest . . .'

Therapist: 'It's you!'

Patient: 'No . . . you are kidding me! It's a very poor photograph. I don't look a bit like that!'

people or people he knew personally. For example, he identified only one of ten photographs of famous people. He also failed to recognise any familiar acquaintances from video vignettes, although he could recognise them from their names or even from hearing their voices. This showed that Mr W had 'semantic knowledge' of these acquaintances, so his prosopagnosia was not simply an amnesic condition. Ellis and Young (1996) suggested that his problem was one of accessing memories about the person (including his/her name) from the image of the face. A fault in the operation of 'facial recognition units' (the facial equivalent to object recognition units in their model of object recognition) would account for Mr W's prosopagnosia.

The varying deficits of Soldier S and Mr W clearly illustrate the existence of (at least two) different forms of prosopagnosia. Soldier S's problems are, in certain respects, analogous to the object recognition deficits seen in apperceptive agnosia. Mr W's prosopagnosia, on the other hand, parallels the object recognition deficit of associative agnosia.

Co-occurrence of different forms of agnosia

Many people with prosopagnosia also show other abnormalities of object recognition, and when these conditions coincide the prosopagnosia is, typically, more severe. This has led to the suggestion that prosopagnosia is just a particular type of object recognition failure involving a breakdown of within-category recognition. However, the test of this hypothesis is not the number of individuals who show both forms of agnosia, but whether individuals can be found with one but not the other form. In fact, several individuals have now been studied in which there is evidence of a double dissociation between object recognition and facial recognition, which suggests that facial recognition is a separate skill that need not overlap with object recognition. One such case was reported by Assal, Favre, and Anders (1984). Their patient MX developed a marked agnosia for livestock (he was a farmer), places and faces. Within six months his prosopagnosia had disappeared although he remained agnosic for animals. Prosopagnosic patient WJ (McNeil & Warrington, 1993) showed almost the exact opposite pattern of deficit. His performance on a version of the **famous faces recognition test** was at chance level, although his ability to recognise objects such as cars, breeds of dog or flowers was normal. After developing the disorder, he acquired a flock of 36 sheep which could be identified by number. On a series of recognition tests WJ clearly retained his knowledge of individual sheep despite his profound prosopagnosia for human faces!

Farah (1990) has conducted a meta-analysis of the coincidence of object agnosia, prosopagnosia and **acquired alexia** (inability to recognise written words after brain injury/damage) by reviewing every published study detailing cases of any of these disorders between 1966 and 1989. As I hinted earlier, the purpose of her research was to test her hypothesis that alexia and prosopagnosia could be linked to fundamentally different deficits in analytical and holistic processing respectively, whereas object agnosia could result from deficits in either system. One prediction from this intriguing hypothesis is that object agnosia should not occur independent of either alexia or prosopagnosia (one or other must be present). The results of her analysis are shown in Table 8.1. Clearly, many people have deficits in all three areas. Numerous instances of alexia alone and prosopagnosia alone were also identified. But the most interesting findings were that only a single case of object agnosia alone could be identified, and there was one possible case of alexia and prosopagnosia without object agnosia. Since

TABLE 8.1 The results of Farah's meta-analysis of the co-occurrence of prosopagnosia, visual agnosia and alexia

Deficits in	Number of patients
Face, object and word recognition	21
Faces and objects	14
Words and objects	15
Faces and words	1?
Faces only	Many
Objects only	1?

publication of this research a small number of additional 'exceptions' have been reported casting doubt on Farah's hypothesis. Nevertheless, the co-occurrence (and mutual exclusivity) of different forms of agnosia merits further investigation.

Prosopagnosia and the brain

The evidence reviewed thus far indicates that although prosopagnosia often coincides with other agnosic disorders, it can occur independently. This raises the question as to whether (or not) specialised processing regions in the ventral stream (or elsewhere) exist to deal with faces. The question can be addressed by examining brain activation in individuals during tasks that involve object and face processing. In a PET study by Sergent, Ohta, and MacDonald (1992), the researchers found several regions in both hemispheres that became active when subjects completed tests of face and object recognition. However, when subjects had to group photographs of people by sex, only the ventral occipital/temporal regions of the right hemisphere were activated. And when specific faces had to be identified, temporal regions further forward in the right hemisphere (only) were activated. This ties in with the finding that cells in anterior ventral regions of the temporal lobe in the right hemisphere seem to be especially sensitive to person-related items including faces. (Sergent et al.'s (1992) data are summarised in Fig. 8.6.) However, the results of a study by Baylis, Rolls, and Leonard (1985) using single cell recording techniques with macaque monkeys suggest that this is probably a preferential rather than exclusive response pattern. This group found that most of the cells of interest (in the superior temporal sulcus) responded to multiple inputs, although some showed a distinct preference for faces (of other macaques).

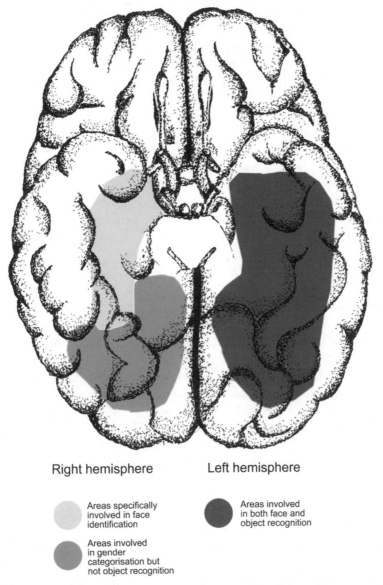

Right hemisphere   Left hemisphere

○ Areas specifically involved in face identification

○ Areas involved in both face and object recognition

○ Areas involved in gender categorisation but not object recognition

FIGURE 8.6 A view of ventral regions involved in object and face recognition

Several areas of ventral cortex are involved in the processing of objects and faces. In the left hemisphere, the areas (indicated) are involved apparently non-specifically in both object and face recognition. In the right hemisphere ventral temporal regions (also indicated) seem to have a specific responsibility for face recognition (Sergent, Ohta, & MacDonald, 1992).

If we consider the question of location of brain damage and prosopag-nosia, the following picture emerges: many cases have bi-lateral damage, and this is predominantly to occipital or temporal lobes. Of those prosopagnosics with uni-lateral lesions, the vast majority have right hemisphere damage, again mainly to ventral occipital and/or temporal regions (DeRenzi et al., 1994). In fact Farah (1990) could find only 4 cases (6% of her sample) of prosopagnosia following uni-lateral left-sided damage. Overall, this is quite strong evidence of a specialised role for the right hemisphere in face recognition. This view is further supported by data from a small number of imaging case studies of prosopag-nosia reported by Sergent and Signoret (1992). For two prosopagnosics with problems similar to Soldier S (see above) but no object agnosia, damage was localised to occipital and medial temporal regions of the right hemisphere. For two additional prosopagnosics with intact face perception but impaired access to memory (like Mr W) damage was found in more anterior regions of the right temporal lobe.

Interim comment

In summary, the available evidence suggests that face recognition is more than just a sophisticated form of object recognition. Prosopagnosia also seems to be linked to damage to brain regions that may be specialised to deal pref-erentially with faces. These areas include ventral regions of the occipital and temporal lobes on the right side. One interpretation of this data is that poste-rior regions (early in the ventral stream) deal with the integrative process of putting together the face from its component parts, whereas areas further forward, but still on the right side, are concerned with identification, and linking this with other semantic and biographic information about the person.

Capgras syndrome

We cannot leave the issue of face recognition without a brief mention of Capgras syndrome. The hallmark sign of this rare and curious disorder is the delusional belief that a close acquaintance or relative has been replaced by an impostor pretending to be that person. Because it is an occasional feature of psychiatric conditions such as schizophrenia, it has tended to be categorised as a mental rather than neurological disorder. However, Capgras syndrome is occasionally seen both in epilepsy and following brain damage, suggesting an organic origin. Ramachandran (1998) has proposed that Capgras syndrome might occur if normal face processing can no longer activate brain regions that deal with emotion, perhaps because of a disconnection between right anterior temporal regions and the right amygdala (which is a processing centre for emotional input).

If a familiar face no longer 'evokes' the appropriate emotional response the individual may rationalise this by concluding that the person in question must be an impostor! Although more research is needed to evaluate this hypothesis properly, early results suggest that such a disconnection may indeed contribute to Capgras features.

Evaluation of the ventral stream and the agnosias

I have described the ventral 'what' stream as a processing pathway along which visual information must be channelled in order for object recognition to occur. It includes a large area of the ventral regions of cortex on both sides of the brain. In general terms it seems that regions further away from the primary visual cortex deal with progressively more subtle aspects of object recognition. It clearly involves multiple stages, as exemplified by Ellis and Young's model, and specialised faculties seem to be built into the stream at different points. Some forms of object agnosia such as Lissauer's apperceptive type result from problems that occur relatively 'early on' in perceptual processing. The individual struggles to put together the 'whole' (the percept) from its component parts. Other forms of object agnosia probably result from damage further along in the processing stream because the percept seems reasonably well formed. Now, the problem is one of linking the percept to meaning. Although some researchers have argued that face recognition is just a particular form of object recognition, most regard the various forms of prosopagnosia as disorders to specialised faculties (for face recognition) within the ventral stream. Converging evidence identifies ventral regions in the right temporal lobe that are involved in this aspect of perception. Whether cells in these regions respond exclusively to faces or just preferentially to them remains a moot point, although evidence from single cell studies with primates favours the latter suggestion (Baylis et al., 1985).

Spatial functions and the 'where' stream

Earlier in this chapter, I reviewed some of the evidence that led to Ungerleider and Mishkin's proposal of separate 'what' and 'where' visual processing streams. The agnosic conditions described so far illustrate the effects of disturbances to functioning at different stages of the 'what' (perhaps it should be what and who) stream, but we now need to consider the other stream which is concerned with a range of spatial functions.

The 'where' stream takes a more 'northerly' route from the occipital cortex into the parietal lobe (see Fig. 8.1). Output travels via V2 and V3 into area V5 (also known as the mid-temporal sulcus or MT). From there, it is channelled into various modular regions within the posterior parietal cortex. In V5, for example, we find cells that are exquisitely sensitive to stimuli moving in a particular direction irrespective of their exact location in the visual field. Cells in a parietal region known as V7 have even more extensive receptive fields and are selectively responsive to objects moving in particular directions at particular speeds. Other cells in the inferior parietal region are responsive to a combination of input signalling spatial location of objects in the viewer's field of vision and the position of the viewer's own head and eyes. This is important because it allows the viewer to reference object location in space regardless of head or eye position or orientation; so, for example, you do not 'see' the world as tilted when you bend your head to the left or right (Motter & Mountcastle, 1981).

The right hemisphere is often referred to as the spatial hemisphere although the left hemisphere also engages in spatial processing. The available evidence leads to the intriguing possibility that the left and right hemispheres may actually have complementary responsibilities when it comes to dealing with spatial information, and we revisit the question of 'laterality' effects in spatial processing towards the end of the chapter. First, however, we need to consider briefly some basic spatial processes related to perception. Then we review some of the more integrative skills that nevertheless make substantial demands on spatial processing, such as constructional skills and negotiating routes. Finally, we consider briefly the general role of the left and right hemispheres in spatial memory.

Basic spatial processes

Localising points in space

Individuals with damage to superior regions of parietal cortex have difficulty reaching towards a visual stimulus. Left-sided damage affects ability to reach towards the right side, and vice versa. If we remove the movement component, and simply measure perception of left or right-side space (i.e. detection of stimuli in the left or right visual fields), we find that uni-lateral damage to the right parietal regions is most likely to adversely effect this ability.

Depth perception

Local depth perception, meaning the ability to detect depth of close objects because of the different images falling on each eye (binocular disparity) can be disrupted by both right and left hemisphere lesions (Danta, Hilton, & O'Boyle, 1978). Global depth perception, which refers to detection of depth (as in a landscape) where binocular disparity for individual items is not helpful, appears to be disrupted by right hemisphere damage (Benton & Hecaen, 1970).

Line orientation and geometric relations

The ability to judge angles or orientations of lines is affected following right (but not left) parietal damage (Benton, Hannay, & Varney, 1975). Similarly, the ability to remember novel complex shapes of geometric patterns (especially those that cannot be named) is also affected after right parietal damage.

Motion

It is very rare for humans to lose their ability to detect motion yet retain other perceptual abilities. In the handful of well-documented cases, there is usually damage to both left and right parietal lobes. Patient MP, reported by Zihl, Von Cramon, and Mai (1983) had extensive damage that included areas of the mid-temporal gyrus and adjacent regions of the parietal lobes on both sides. She described her motion blindness as like seeing movements as a series of jerky still photographs (similar to what we might see in strobe lighting conditions). Interestingly, other spatial skills such as localisation of objects in space were relatively spared, which supports the idea of distinct movement processing modules in each hemisphere.

Rotation

PET imaging research, both with normal subjects engaged in tasks that involve mental rotation and analysis of the performance of brain-damaged subjects on similar tasks, once again points to the involvement of the right parietal lobe. In a classic study by Deutsch et al. (1988) participants had to decide which hand a 'cartoon man' was holding a ball in. The cartoon was shown in various orientations, and in front and rear view. Patients with right hemisphere lesions made more errors and had slower reaction times on this task.

Constructional skills

The skills involved in completing constructional tasks are more complex than those needed to undertake the spatial-perceptual tests mentioned above. They involve spatial perception, but in addition require the production or generation of some tangible output. There are several standard neuropsychological assessments of these skills and evidence suggests that right parietal damage is most likely to impair performance on them. However, some caution is required in interpreting test results because, in moving away from the purely perceptual, we introduce other psychological factors. The following two tests certainly involve hand–eye coordination and attention, and arguably even memory (which depend on other cortical functions), in addition to spatial skills.

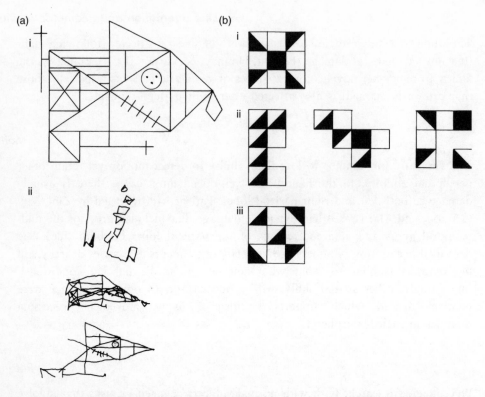

FIGURE 8.7 Rey-Osterreith figure and WAIS blocks test, and patients' attempts to complete these tests

(a)   This apparently simple copying task is quite beyond some patients with right temporal-parietal damage.

(b)   In the WAIS block design test, respondents must 'construct' the nine square pattern using individual blocks. Patients with right hemisphere damage are prone to errors in which they ignore the overall form of the pattern (ii). Left-hemisphere patients may get the overall form correct but get the detail wrong (iii).

The Rey-Osterreith complex figure is a detailed line drawing that looks a little like the Union Jack flag, with other elements such as extra triangles and lines attached (see Fig. 8.7a) The subject simply has to copy the figure. Normal individuals often complete this task almost faultlessly within a few minutes. However, it presents major difficulties for some patients with damage in the right temporo-parietal region (Benton, 1967). Damage here also adversely affects individuals on the block design test (a test taken from the WAIS) in which subjects have to copy a simple pattern by assembling coloured blocks (see Fig. 8.7b). Right hemisphere patients sometimes even fail to appreciate that the configuration of the nine blocks must be 3×3. Left hemisphere damage can also affect block design performance but in this case the basic configuration is usually correct; and it is more likely that individual blocks will be incorrectly oriented.

Route-finding

Researchers have developed a number of tests to assess route-finding. They range from simple **finger mazes** (where a blindfolded subject has to learn a route by trial and error, usually by guiding his finger through a small maze) to following directions using standardised maps. As with the construction tests mentioned earlier, we must, in interpreting results, be aware that the different tasks assess other skills in addition to basic spatial ones. Moreover, depending on the particular task, it may be possible to use non-spatial strategies as well as, or even instead of, spatial ones, which further complicates interpretation. An additional complication is that some people struggle with certain types of route-finding tasks and not with others. This has necessitated a distinction between those measures that 'tap' perception of spatial relationships in extra-personal space (like finger mazes) and measures that require respondents to guide themselves in three dimensional space.

Performance on variants of the finger maze is compromised following damage to the right parietal lobe (Milner, 1962), but, in addition, where there is a significant memory demand (a complex maze for example) performance can be affected by damage to right temporal or frontal areas. A variant of the finger maze is where the subject has to find their way through a proper maze. In Semmes et al.'s (1955) maze test, nine dots are placed on the floor of a large room and participants are given a plan of the route (via the dots) to follow. For reference, one wall of the room is designated 'north' and the person is not allowed to rotate the map as they follow the route. Typically, right parietal damage affects performance on this test (Semmes et al., 1963), although Ratcliff and Newcombe (1973) only found marked impairments in individuals with bilateral damage. A possible explanation for this apparent contradiction is that in this type of task respondents can adopt different strategies. A 'spatial' strategy is one way, but a verbal strategy (*turn right ... go straight on ... turn right again ...*) can also be employed.

In Money's (1976) standardised road map test, participants are given a fictitious map that shows a route marked on it. At every junction they must 'say' which direction (left, right, straight on) to go in. This test requires planning and memory as well as spatial skill, and performance is affected by damage to the frontal areas of the right hemisphere in addition to the more posterior parietal regions. Finally, there is even some evidence that basic geographic knowledge about entire countries can be adversely affected following right-sided damage.

> **Interim comment**
>
> Taken together, these observations illustrate the range of spatial perceptual abilities that humans possess, and which we tend to take for granted until a problem arises. Spatial perception depends on the ability to form an internal representation of the outside world, and sometimes to locate oneself in it. The formation of that internal representation, and the ability to manipulate it or 'mentally' move around it depends on effective processing in the 'where' stream.

Spatial memory

Spatial memory span can be assessed using Corsi's block-tapping test, which I introduced in Chapter 2. The wooden blocks are conveniently numbered on the tester's side, but the side facing the subject is blank. The experimenter taps a sequence of blocks, which the respondent must immediately duplicate. The experimenter increases the length of the sequence (in the classic manner) in order to establish spatial memory span. DeRenzi and Nichelli (1975) have found that patients with posterior damage on either side have a reduced span.

Tests that assess spatial working memory appear to 'tap' right hemisphere function, and usually present particular difficulties for respondents with right frontal damage. Recall from the previous chapter a study by Smith, Jonides, and Koeppe (1996) in which normal participants were shown a brief array of dots (for 200 msec) then 3 seconds later a circle appeared on the screen. Respondents had to decide whether (or not) the circle would have surrounded one of the dots. PET activation during this test (when compared with a non-working memory condition) was most marked in the right frontal lobe. When we move beyond short-term retention, we find evidence of marked impairment in people with more posterior right hemisphere damage. For example, if recall on the Corsi tapping test is delayed by as little as 16 seconds, patients with right temporal and parietal hemisphere damage show the largest deficits.

The left hemisphere and spatial processing

An insight into the operation of the left hemisphere in spatial tasks can be gleaned from observing the compensatory procedures adopted by individuals who have incurred right-sided damage. A classic case study of one such individual was reported by Clarke et al. (1993). Despite an extensive right-sided lesion resulting from a brain tumour the Swiss woman in question hoped to become an architect, and the researchers were able to observe her as she tried to overcome (or circumvent) her spatial deficits by making greater use of left-sided functions. When copying arrays like the Rey-Osterreith figure, she used a piece-meal strategy (akin to HJA's copying strategy described earlier). As a result, although basic elements of the figure were included, fine detail was often misplaced or omitted. She also used a feature-by-feature (as opposed to holistic) strategy in trying to recognise a series of Swiss towns from photographs. This worked well if a town had a distinctive or unique feature, but broke down when she tried to identify towns with similar but spatially distinct features. Related to these problems, her geographic knowledge and route-finding skills were also impaired, and in order to get around she developed a verbal point-by-point (landmarks) strategy.

Interim comment

The weight of evidence considered in the previous sections underlines the importance of right hemisphere structures in processing all kinds of spatial information. However, we also saw that once we moved away from purely perceptual types of task it became possible to solve or complete tasks using various strategies – essentially spatial, verbal, or perhaps a combination of both. Studies such as that reported by Clarke et al. remind us that both hemispheres can participate in spatial processing. Spatial skills are not the exclusive preserve of the right hemisphere. We might describe the processing responsibilities of the left and right hemispheres as verbal and spatial respectively, but this confuses the issue in view of the fact that we have been talking about how each hemisphere contributes to dealing with spatial tasks. We might, alternatively, invoke the idea of processing styles (see Chapter 3), by comparing the holistic approach of the right hemisphere with the analytical style of the left. Once again, this does not entirely work because some of the spatial skills that are affected by right hemisphere damage (such as spatial location) make no particular demands on holistic skills. Kosslyn (1987) has suggested a cerebral division of labour such that the right hemisphere is specialised for dealing with 'coordinate' spatial relations whereas the left is specialised for 'categorical' spatial relations. By 'coordinate' he means the relative distance of objects whereas his use of the term 'categorical' refers to the relative positions of objects (in front, behind, above, below and so on). Unfortunately, another way of distinguishing between 'coordinate' and 'categorical' is to say that the former does not readily lend itself to verbal description whereas the latter does – which brings us back to the spatial-verbal distinction we initially dismissed!

Summary

Visual perception of objects depends on activity in two parallel but separate processing streams. The 'what' stream deals with object recognition and links with stored memories of related objects. The 'where' stream deals with various aspects of spatial processing, both of perceived objects, and of the individual in space. This distinction is apparent if you consider the situation of reaching to select a particular object from a group of items: the 'where' stream guides your hand to the object, and the 'what' stream allows you to select the correct object. The visual agnosias appear to result from disturbances to different stages of processing in the 'what' stream. Lissauer's original distinction between apperceptive and associative agnosia is now considered an oversimplification of the true diversity of (object) agnosic conditions. Ellis and Young's model of object recognition is better able to explain many of these subtly distinct conditions.

Prosopagnosia often co-occurs with object agnosia but the weight of available evidence suggests that it is a distinct condition that is linked anatomically to ventral regions in the right hemisphere. In fact, many neuropsychologists think that it actually comprises at least two disorders: one related to a failure to construct the facial image from its component parts, and a second concerned with an inability to relate facial images with semantic information about the person in question. Capgras syndrome may arise due to a 'disconnection' between the face processing areas of the cortex and the emotional processing areas; notably the amygdala.

Spatial processing is sub-served by a dorsal stream that terminates in the parietal lobes. Damage to this stream affects the perception of objects in space, detection of motion and mental rotation. This stream interacts with other cortical regions to mediate spatial constructional skills, route-finding and spatial memory. Although available evidence tends to emphasise the importance of the right hemisphere for spatial processing, the left hemisphere can make important contributions to the overall processing effort through the employment of complementary processing styles.

Chapter 9

Attention

■ Introduction   182

■ Types of attention   182

■ Issues in psychological investigations
   of attention   183
  Early or late selective attention?   183
  Space or object-based selection?   187
  Attention as a resource   188

■ Attention and the brain   189
  Event-related potentials (ERPs) and
   attention   189
  Brain structures and attention   192
  Neuropsychological models of attention   195

■ Neurological attentional disorders   197
  Hemineglect   197
  Balint's syndrome   199

■ Towards an integrated model of
  attention   202

■ Summary   204

Introduction

COMMON SENSE TELLS US THAT we cannot pay attention to every item of sensory information that impinges on our sense organs. In order to deal with incoming information, we must be choosy, attending to some things at the expense of others. Attention refers to selecting, focusing and homing-in on certain inputs, and filtering out or inhibiting others, and an apt metaphor for this process is the 'attentional spotlight'. However, it is complicated by at least two additional considerations. First, we can also attend to internally generated ideas, thoughts or plans – indeed, it could be argued that consciousness itself is closely related to self-attending. Secondly, our own experience tells us that no matter how hard we may try to focus our attention on one 'thing', we can be easily distracted by an unexpected but salient event or stimulus occurring elsewhere. In other words, attention can be directed by both deliberate and accidental processes.

Despite our intuitive sense of what attention involves, neither psychologists nor neuropsychologists have yet developed a unified theory of it. Psychologists have worked on the development of theories about how different aspects of attention may work, and neuropsychologists have focused on trying to understand about the brain regions that may be involved. Neurology has provided additional data about neurological disorders in which attentional mechanisms seem to be damaged or impaired, and each of these areas is considered later in this chapter. However, I start on a point of consensus: there seems to be broad agreement that the general domain of attention needs to be subdivided into at least three more specific areas – selective attention, vigilance and arousal (LaBerge, 1990).

Types of attention

Selective attention

This refers to the phenomenon alluded to at the start of the introduction. Our sensory apparatus is constantly bombarded with input, yet we more or less automatically seem able to invoke a process that allows us to focus on one channel of input at the expense of others. As you read this page, I hope you are attending sufficiently carefully not to be distracted by the noises coming from outside, the smells wafting up from the kitchen, or the dull pain from that tooth that might need filling – not, at least, until I point them out to you! As we will see, psychologists have used experiments in selective attention and the related field of visual search to learn more about the way attentional processes operate.

Vigilance

This refers to our ability to sustain attention over time. Every time you go to a lecture your vigilance is put to the test as you try to stay 'on track' with the lecturer right to the end of the class. Obviously, this is different from selective attention; it requires more conscious effort for one thing, but it is clearly an aspect of attention, and variability in vigilance skill is certainly related to neurological disease and possibly psychiatric disorder too.

Arousal and alertness

These are terms that have usually been linked to physiological states that may vary in relation to attention. Consider your own circadian pattern of alertness for example. Every 24 hours you experience 6–8 hours of sleep during which time you are relatively unresponsive to external stimuli, although a clap of thunder or a loud firework may nevertheless disturb you. During your waking hours, you are certainly more alert at some times than others. Research has shown that alertness generally improves through the day, reaching a peak in early evening, and then diminishing towards bedtime.

Sudden unexpected events can interfere with your level of alertness when you are awake, just as they can when you are asleep. Researchers refer to the response that ensues as 'orienting', and as we shall see, the evoking of an **orienting response** has been used as a research paradigm by psychologists trying to understand this aspect of attention.

Issues in psychological investigations of attention

Early or late selective attention?

Most people will be aware of the effort required to converse with someone in a noisy and crowded room (sometimes referred to as 'the cocktail party phenomenon'), and of suddenly becoming aware of a salient word or term used by another speaker on the far side of a room (Cherry, 1953; Moray, 1959). This apparently innocent phenomenon shows that 'unattended' material can, under certain circumstances, attract our attention. In the 1950s, the pre-eminent model of attention held that 'attended' material is selected at a very early stage of information processing (Broadbent, 1958), but the cocktail party phenom-enon confounds this 'early selection' model because the so-called unattended input must have undergone a certain amount of processing in order to cause a shift of our attention. If it had been subject to early selection, we might simply not have 'heard' it.

An effective way of investigating selective attention experimentally is to use the dichotic listening paradigm. In a typical variant of this procedure a partici-pant may be presented with two simultaneous streams of verbal input (one to each ear), but be required to attend to only one stream (sometimes called 'a channel'). By later testing the participant on what they heard, or by requiring them to 'shadow' one channel (i.e. repeat aloud the 'attended' channel) the exper-imenter can assess the extent to which information in the unattended channel 'gets through'. Not surprisingly, there is nearly always much better recall from the attended than the unattended channel, but in situations where the unattended channel material is 'salient' or semantically related to the material in the attended channel, it is often recalled, and sometimes described (erroneously) as having been presented in the attended channel. This shows that the unattended channel may undergo quite extensive processing because the material is presented too quickly for the result to be explained simply on the basis of divided attention (see Fig. 9.1).

Most cognitive psychologists now accept that although the evidence from dichotic listening experiments clearly supports some sort of selecting or filtering

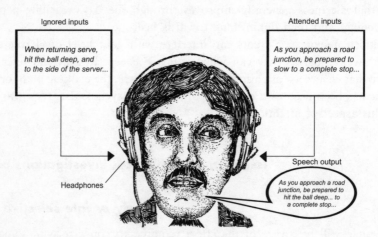

FIGURE 9.1 A typical dichotic listening experiment

In this 'shadowing' study, the respondent hears two verbal messages simultaneously, and he must repeat aloud only one of the 'channels'. Respondents usually notice little or nothing about the unattended input, but occasionally salient or personally significant material is recognised and sometimes even intrudes into the speech output! (Adapted from Gazzaniga et al., 1998.)

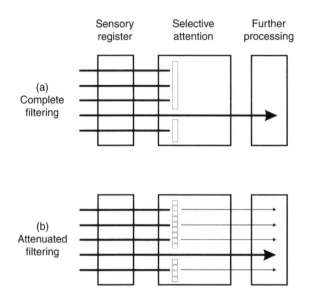

FIGURE 9.2 Two filtering models of attention

(a)   Following sensory registration, only one 'channel' of input is selected for further processing. This is akin to Broadbent's model of early selective attention.

(b)   One channel is selected for 'priority' processing. However, the other channels of input are not filtered out; rather they are attenuated. This is similar to Treisman's attenuation model of selective attention.

of attended over unattended material (because relatively little of the unattended message is recalled) it does not fit well with a strict 'early selection' model of attention like Broadbent's. An alternative model was proposed by Treisman (1964) who argued that although a particular channel might be selected early on in the processing stream, the unattended channel, rather than being shut down, was 'attenuated', meaning it received less attentional effort than the attended channel. Thus, salient, or personally relevant material in this channel would not necessarily be lost and may undergo semantic processing, at which point a shift in attention to the unattended channel may occur. Treisman's model has received widespread support, even from Broadbent (1970), and is the dominant theory for selective attention in the auditory modality. Fig. 9.2 illustrates the differences between the various models of selective attention.

In studies of visual attention, the evidence also suggests that selection may occur relatively early in the processing stream, especially when attention is directed towards stimulus location. The logic of visual search studies is that the more 'distractor' items present in a visual field, the longer it should take to identify the particular target. Consider, for example, a study by Treisman and Gelade (1980). Participants viewed a series of visual arrays comprising red Os and green

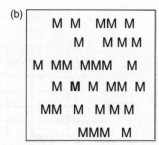

FIGURE 9.3 The type of array used in visual search studies

(a) The 'odd one out' target is a conjunctive one combining attributes of other targets. Visual search proceeds in a place-by-place manner until the target (**B**) is found.

(b) The target letter (**M**) almost jumps out of this array. Little conscious effort is required to locate it, giving rise to the expression 'pre-attentive' to characterise the processing requirements of the task.

Xs, and they had to identify the presence (or absence) of a red X. For such 'conjunctive targets' (targets combining stimulus attributes shared by non-targets), the time taken to identify presence/absence is proportionate to the number of non-targets shown, because attention must be directed around the array item-by-item until the target is found. This shows that attention to a spatial location precedes identification, supporting the idea of early selection of location. A conjunctive search array similar to Triesman and Gelade's is shown in Fig. 9.3a.

There is, however, an exception to this finding that occurs when the target is distinguishable on the basis of one solitary attribute – '*Find the X among an array of Ys*'. In this situation the number of distractors is largely irrelevant, and subjects describe the target as 'popping-out' from the array (see Fig. 9.3b). This process has been called 'pre-attentive', which is taken to mean that attention is not needed to find the target (although it is obviously invoked once the target has been found).

A similar attentional process can also be observed in studies of involuntary visual orienting (Posner & Cohen, 1984). In a typical experiment 'irrelevant' visual stimuli (such as brief light flashes) are presented to different locations in the visual field, interspersed with target stimuli to which the subject should respond. When a target stimulus falls in a similar location to a previous irrelevant light flash, reaction time to it is faster, indicating that the irrelevant stimulus somehow directed (researchers say 'primed') attentional mechanisms to that particular spatial location, albeit involuntarily. However, this effect is only observed if the interval between irrelevant and target stimuli is brief (less than 300 msec). With longer intervals the effect is reversed leading to slower reaction times. This paradoxical effect is known as 'inhibition of return' and serves a vital role in automatic visual orienting. If such a mechanism did not exist, we would probably find it difficult to attend voluntarily to anything for any period of time, being constantly distracted by new but irrelevant stimuli. The distinction between deliberate and incidental attentional processes appears critical, and I return to consider it again later in this chapter.

Space or object-based selection?

Visual search studies such as Treisman and Gelade's show that voluntary attention can operate effectively when it is directed to particular points in space. Posner (1980) reported a classic study illustrating the advantage of space-based attention. In this experiment, participants fixated on a central point on a computer screen with an empty box to the left and right of the fixation point. After a short delay, one of the two boxes became briefly illuminated. Then, after a further variable delay, a stimulus was presented either in the box that had been illuminated or the other box. Reaction times to the stimulus were consis-

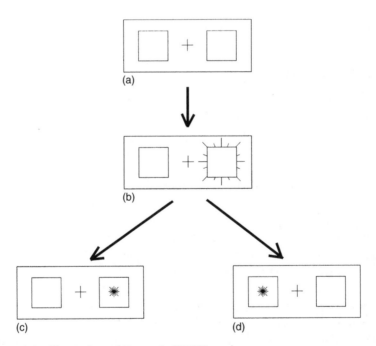

FIGURE 9.4 An illustration of Posner's (1980) study

A participant fixates his or her gaze on the cross in between the two squares. One of the boxes is then 'cued' (in this case by becoming more brightly illuminated) for a brief period. The respondent knows that the cue usually correctly predicts the subsequent presentation of a target stimulus (an asterisk). Response speeds (reaction times) are significantly faster when the cue correctly predicts the location of the stimulus (c) than when it predicts the incorrect location (d).

tently faster when it appeared in the 'cued' box than the 'non-cued' one; a finding interpreted as showing how shifting attention (from the expected cued box to the non-expected uncued one) takes time. It is important to note that in this paradigm, participants fixated gaze on the central point at all times, so covert mechanisms rather than overt eye movements were responsible for this voluntary orienting effect (see Fig. 9.4).

On the other hand, object-based attention can be illustrated in studies of negative priming (Tipper, Weaver, & Houghton, 1994). In one version of this paradigm, on each trial, the subject saw a display of two overlapping drawings; one green, the other blue. The subject's task was to respond to the green item. Then on the next trial, the item that had been ignored in the previous trial (the negative prime) now became the attended (green) item in another two-item display. In a control condition two new items would be presented. Results indicated that responses were slower in the negative priming condition; a finding which is usually explained in terms of the additional effort required to redirect attention to a previously ignored stimulus (object). Incidentally, this paradigm also reveals quite extensive processing of unattended stimuli. In fact, negative priming would not occur if this was not so!

Attention as a resource

Resource theory approaches to attention (Kahneman, 1973; Wickens, 1980) side-step many of the arguments introduced thus far by proposing that there is a finite central pool of information-processing capacity available to the individual, which is allocated according to demand. At one extreme, stimuli may be so simple or infrequent that only a fraction of the resource is 'used', and attention (as we have conceptualised it) is not really an issue, though vigilance may be. At the other extreme, tasks may be so complex or demanding that the entire resource is 'used up' by just part of the input invoking attention to this material at the expense of the remainder. Thus, the greater the effort needed to attend to target material, the less likely non-target material is to be processed. It follows that the greater the similarity between competing tasks (as in the dichotic listening studies) the greater the likelihood that such inputs will, by competing for the same resource, induce interference and errors.

A key question in this approach is whether the resource base is a single reservoir available to the individual irrespective of stimulus characteristics on a 'first-come', 'first-served' basis, or whether there are separate reservoirs set aside for different types of input. Wickens' model envisages three such resource domains with distinct pools: early versus late processing, verbal versus spatial processing, and auditory versus visual processing. It would be true to say that while this question has yet to be fully resolved, the experimental evidence tends to support separate pools. For example, in dual-task studies in which respondents try to complete two tasks simultaneously, there is less interference and hence fewer errors, when the tasks involve different stimulus modalities. (For example, try writing and singing at the same time – then try patting your head and rubbing your stomach with a circular motion at the same time!) Moreover, the ERP research (which I review below) shows that different brain regions seem to be involved in early and later stimulus processing.

The debate about shared or separate attentional resource pools is reminiscent of the one I touched on when reviewing the concept of working memory in Chapter 7. This coincidence has not escaped proponents of resource-based theories of attention who have argued that information-processing capacity limitations in attention *are determined* by working memory capacity limits. The overlap between attentional and working memory systems is the subject of current investigations, and I briefly revisit this issue when I review brain imaging studies of attention later in this chapter.

Interim comment

We know what we mean when we talk about attention, and there seem to be several ways of measuring it or invoking it. What we feel less sure about are its parameters – the extent to which it overlaps with consciousness or alertness for instance. The material introduced in the previous section amply illustrates *the absence* of a cohesive framework on which to build psychological models of attention. Studies of selective attention lead to the conclusion that unattended material is not so much 'filtered out', as 'attenuated'. In studies of visual search, attention may be 'location' or 'object' based, and we must also distinguish between voluntary and involuntary attentional mechanisms. Resource-based models raise the possibility that attentional mechanisms overlap closely with working memory systems.

The psychological approach seems to raise as many questions as it answers. It is of course essentially a 'top-down' approach; could a 'bottom-up' approach shed any more light on attention? In the next section I review some of the work examining brain regions that may be involved in attention.

Attention and the brain

Event-related potentials (ERPs) and attention

We can examine attentional processing in the nervous system by recording ERPs to attended and non-attended material. In a typical ERP study, the subject may be instructed to attend to inputs to one ear and ignore those to the other.

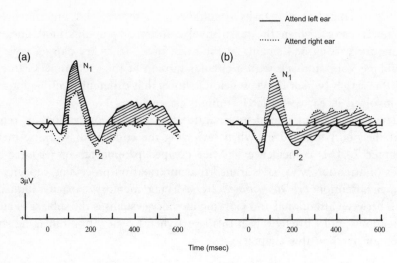

FIGURE 9.5 Auditory ERPs to attended and non-attended stimuli

(a)   The amplitude of the N1 peak of the ERP is greater to a tone presented to the left ear when the respondent is 'attending' to inputs to the left ear, than when the same tone is presented but the respondent is attending to inputs to the right ear.

(b)   This is not related to auditory acuity because the reverse effect can be observed if tones are now presented to the right ear. (Adapted from Andreassi, 1989.)

(At a later stage, the instructions can be reversed to avoid the possibility of differential ear sensitivity affecting results.) Typical findings from this type of study are illustrated in Fig. 9.5. They suggest that the ERP to the attended channel begins to differentiate itself from the ERP to the unattended channel about 80 msec after stimulus onset (Andreassi, 1989), as indicated by a markedly enhanced N1 wave. More recently, Woldorff and Hillyard (1991) found evidence of earlier cortical waveform changes in the 20 to 50 msec latency range. This means that attended material is being 'treated' differently by regions of sensory cortex very soon after stimulus presentation.

With ERP studies in the visual modality it becomes possible to investigate 'spatial' attention. In order to do this, researchers have adapted the paradigm developed by Posner, Snyder, and Davidson (1980) in which participants fixate on a central point but are cued to expect stimuli to the left or right of that point (see Fig. 9.4). The ERP wave shows characteristic changes in amplitude which start about 70–90 msec after stimulus presentation (known as the P100 wave) when the stimulus appears in the 'cued' location.

By combining ERP and ERF (event-related fields) procedures (see Chapter 2), Mangan, Hillyard, and Luck (1993) have confirmed that the enhanced ERP is cortical in origin. In other words, by voluntarily directing attention towards particular stimuli, changes in ERP wave form (reflecting enhanced cortical activity) can be seen well within one-tenth of a second. Interestingly, this technique can also be used to see if 'involuntary' shifts in attention activate the same mechanisms. Hopfinger and Mangan (1998) have shown that when an unexpected and irrelevant sensory cue (which draws attention to part of the visual field) precedes the target stimulus by up to 300 msec, the ERP to the target stimulus is enhanced, but with longer intervals between the cue and target the effect is reversed (see my earlier reference to 'inhibition of return'). This study strongly suggests that the attentional processes evoked by voluntary cues are also evoked by involuntary ones. It is also a reminder that any effective model (of attention) must accommodate both deliberate and incidental influences on the direction of attention. I return to this matter later.

A further component of the ERP has also interested researchers. The P300 is a positive wave occurring roughly 300 msec after stimulus presentation. This 'late' wave seems to be related to the meaning (relevance) of the stimulus, and shows that attention can modify the brain's response for some time after a stimulus has been presented. A typical P300 study might require the subject to listen out for infrequent high tones presented in a series with more frequent low tones. The ERP to the 'salient' high tones will show the typical positive shift (about one-third of a second after the stimulus is presented), while the nonsalient low tones will not evoke this response. One way of distinguishing between these two ERP components is to envisage the early negative changes in terms of physical relevance, and the later positive one as linked to semantic relevance (see Fig. 9.6).

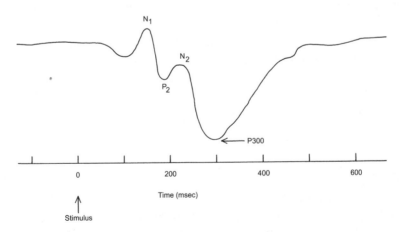

FIGURE 9.6 Early and late components of an auditory ERP

The early components (up to about 200 msec) are thought to reflect cortical processing of relatively simple stimulus attributes such as intensity or pitch. Later components such as the P300 wave vary in relation to 'significance' of stimuli and are thus thought to reflect higher level (semantic) processing of stimuli.

Brain structures and attention

There is no single attention 'centre' in the brain. Instead, several regions are thought to form a distributed neural network that is collectively responsible for the attributes of attention considered so far. The network comprises brainstem, midbrain and forebrain structures, and impaired attention may result from damage to any of these. However, as with most neural networks, it is also possible to predict the particular attentional dysfunction most directly linked to each component part of the system.

The ascending reticular activating system (ARAS)

This is a brain stem structure (actually a diffuse network itself) comprising neurons whose axons ascend through the midbrain to influence the cortex. The system was once thought to be unitary, but is now known to involve several distinct neurotransmitter systems (groups of neurons that release different chemical messengers to influence other neurons). It includes a cholinergic (acetyl-choline-releasing) pathway, a noradrenergic (noradrenaline-releasing) pathway, a dopaminergic (dopamine-releasing) pathway and a serotonergic (serotonin-releasing) pathway. The axons of most of these neurons divide many times on route to the cortex, and the upshot of this cortical innervation is that a relatively small number of brainstem and midbrain neurons can affect the excitability of virtually every cortical neuron. Not surprisingly, this system has long been implicated in arousal and the sleep–wake cycle. Damage to the ARAS will profoundly disrupt circadian rhythms and can result in coma, or chronic vegetative state. Stimulation of the ARAS will, conversely, quickly wake a sleeping animal. Moreover, drugs such as amphetamine, which are known to be CNS stimulants, are thought to have particular influences on the neurons in the ARAS and the pathway from it to the cortex. These findings suggest at least two roles for the ARAS in the control of attention. Tonic (background) influences will affect vigilance performance, while phasic (brief) changes will be important in orienting.

The superior colliculi

These are two modest bumps on the dorsal side of the brain stem in the midbrain region. They appear to play a key role in controlling a particular but vital type of eye movement in which objects initially in the peripheral field of vision 'draw' attention. Their role in visual attention is thus self-evident. The eye movements controlled by the superior colliculi are called express saccades – the eyes jump from their old focus of attention to a new one in one jerk rather than a smooth arc. Damage to these structures interferes with express saccades but not other slower eye movements. In **supra nuclear palsy**, a neuro-degenerative disorder that affects several subcortical regions including the superior colliculi, patients behave as if, in a sense, 'blind'. They fail to direct their gaze in the normal way, not looking at someone who is speaking or turning to greet an approaching friend. This deficit has been referred to as a loss of 'visual grasp', and a similar tempo-rary effect can be induced by local administration of drugs that block the action of neurotransmitters in the superior colliculi (Desimone et al., 1990). Incidentally, the inferior colliculi (two additional bumps just beneath the superior colliculi) are thought to play a similar role in orienting the individual towards 'salient' auditory stimuli.

The pulvinar region of the thalamus

This appears to play a vital role in filtering material to-be-attended-to from the vast amounts of sensory input that the brain actually receives. The thalamus as a whole acts as a relay station for almost all sensory inputs on route to the cortex, and is therefore ideally situated to serve as a filter. This idea was supported in a study by LaBerge and Buchsbaum (1990). In one condition, subjects had to attend to the presence/absence of a single letter. In a second condition, subjects had to 'look out' for the same letter embedded among other letters. The second task required more 'attention' than the first because there was now a requirement to filter or sift through the array to find the target letter. Sure enough, the second condition brought about greater PET activation of the pulvinar than the first, even when stimulus complexity was accounted for. The application of drugs that interfere with pulvinar functioning also disrupts shifts of attention (Petersen, Robinson, & Morris, 1985). Moreover, people with damage to this thalamic region are likely to have attentional difficulties involving the ability to filter stimuli; attending to one input and ignoring others. The pulv-inar receives an important input from the colliculi, and it is thought that the ability of incidental but salient visual stimuli to adjust the attentional spotlight alluded to earlier depends critically on this axis.

The cingulate gyrus

The cingulate gyrus (or just cingulate) is another cortical 'node' in the brain's attentional network. It appears to be involved in at least two separate atten-tional processes: on the one hand the cingulate as a whole provides an interface in which sensory inputs are linked to 'emotional tone' (was the movement in the periphery of your visual field a tree bending in the wind or a 'mugger'?). On the other, the anterior regions of this structure are critically involved in response selection (ignore the wind-blown tree, but escape ASAP from the mugger!). As I mention in Chapter 10, the anterior cingulate (AC) becomes active in circumstances in which appropriate 'correct' responses have to be selected in a deliberate (conscious) manner. PET studies of participants undertaking the Stroop test reinforce this role for the AC. In one variant of this test, respondents are presented with a list of words spelling different colours. Some of the words are printed in the same colour that they spell, but others are printed in a different colour. On some trials participants have to name the word irrespective of the colour it is printed in, and on other trials, they must name the colour irrespective of the word. The AC is much more active during colour naming than word naming (Pardo et al., 1990) because the former leads to a greater 'interference' effect. This is caused by the tendency to read the word even though this is not required! In Chapter 6 I also reported the increase in cingulate activity observed by Peterson et al. (1988) when subjects were required to generate appropriate verbs in response to nouns.

The parietal lobes

These are specialised for processing spatial relations and their role in attention is inferred from two independent research findings. First, parietal damage (on either side but especially the right) is associated with hemineglect, an attentional disorder in which half of the visual field is, effectively, ignored. (I discuss this condition later in this chapter.) Secondly, the P300 wave that I mentioned earlier is most marked in parietal regions. There is some debate about what exactly the P300 measures, but one idea is that it reflects 'attentional resource' allocated to a particular task. In other words, the more attention a person pays to particular stimuli, the larger the resultant P300. It is also noteworthy that individuals with damage to parieto-temporal regions no longer generate P300s.

The frontal lobes

These appear to be particularly important in influencing movement (motoric) aspects of attention. A form of neglect is seen in some individuals with frontal damage, although this is somewhat different from the classic hemineglect syndrome to be discussed later. In the frontal form, individuals seem disinterested in making movements towards the neglected side – a motor as opposed to a sensory neglect.

The frontal eye fields (located laterally in the frontal lobes) are also important attentional centres. These regions control voluntary gaze. This is important because we have already seen that the superior colliculi direct gaze in an involuntary manner towards unexpected stimuli. Clearly some mechanism is required to override this system, otherwise you would constantly be distracted by new stimuli, and this job is performed by the frontal eye fields. As you might expect, damage to this region brings about a form of distractibility in which the

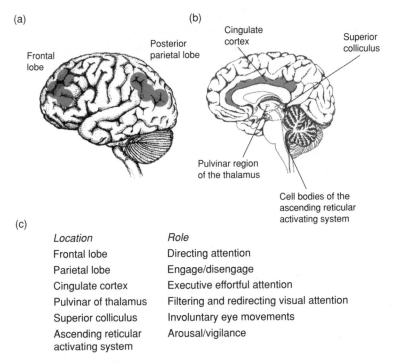

(a)

Frontal lobe

Posterior parietal lobe

(b)

Cingulate cortex

Superior colliculus

Pulvinar region of the thalamus

Cell bodies of the ascending reticular activating system

(c)

Location	Role
Frontal lobe	Directing attention
Parietal lobe	Engage/disengage
Cingulate cortex	Executive effortful attention
Pulvinar of thalamus	Filtering and redirecting visual attention
Superior colliculus	Involuntary eye movements
Ascending reticular activating system	Arousal/vigilance

FIGURE 9.7 Brain structures and attention

Figures (a) and (b) depict the principal structures involved in (some aspect of) attention. The possible role of each area is indicated in (c).

individual's visual attention is constantly drawn to irrelevant visual stimuli. The frontal lobes are also involved in attention to novel or unexpected stimuli. Earlier, I mentioned that the P300 wave was most marked in parietal regions. However, if a totally unexpected stimulus (rather than a rare but significant one) is presented, this induces a P300 that is maximal in frontal regions. Fig. 9.7 illustrates the brain regions I have identified, and their likely roles in attentional processes.

Neuropsychological models of attention

The brain regions I have described jibe quite well with Mesulam's (1981) distributed control model of attention, which is summarised in Box 9.1. This general model focuses on cortical mechanisms, proposing (in true neural network fashion) that the nodes (component structures) not only contribute to attention but to other independent processes as well. Moreover, damage to different components or connections in the network might bring about similar attentional deficits, and greater impairments (in attention) would be seen when more than one structure is damaged.

Box 9.1: Mesulam's model of attention

- Cortical inputs from the ARAS controls vigilance and arousal.
- The cingulate cortex imparts motivational significance to inputs/events.
- The posterior parietal lobes provide a sensory/spatial map of the world.
- The frontal lobes enable us to direct and redirect attention.

Posner and colleagues have proposed a somewhat different model specifically related to visual attention (Posner, Inhoff, Freidrich, & Cohen, 1987), which emphasises change and selection. These researchers argued that the redirection of attention must involve at least three elements: disengagement (from the present focus), redirection (to the new stimulus) and engagement (with the new stimulus). The three elements depend on the sequential interaction of different brain structures: the disengage process depends on intact parietal functioning, the redirect on the superior colliculi and the engage on the thalamus.

The evidence in support of this hypothesis is quite strong: patients with parietal damage find it difficult to disengage from an attended stimulus, and this problem is not related to engage deficits, which, under appropriate circumstances, can be shown to be normal. (See the later discussion of Balint's syndrome.) We noted earlier that patients with collicular damage such as that seen is supra nuclear palsy have difficulties redirecting gaze. Individuals with thalamic damage struggle to 'latch on' to new targets. This system, more recently referred to by Posner and others as a posterior attentional network, may be particularly important for (visual) spatial attention. Subsequently, Posner (1992) proposed a second anterior network that becomes active during semantic attentional processing, such as listening out for 'salient' target words, or evaluating the emotional importance of potentially threatening stimuli. This network comprises anterior cingulate and medial frontal regions, and clearly overlaps considerably with the component structures that contribute to the executive functions of the frontal lobes (discussed in Chapter 10). I will return to consider recent developments in the area of attentional networks after a brief review of neurological attentional disorders.

Interim comment

The ERP studies provide strong support for early selection models of attention because they indicate that cortical regions respond differently to target stimuli very quickly after stimulus presentation. Interestingly, the selective process seems to involve enhanced 'treatment' of the target rather than attenuation of the non-attended material.

The 'bottom-up' approach of trying to identify brain regions that may be involved in attentional systems has been helpful, but attempts to draw this information into a unified theory have not, so far, been wholly successful. It is of value to know about the cortical and subcortical structures that seem to be involved in various attentional tasks, and it seems likely that functional imaging techniques may soon shed more light on how these structures interact in situations requiring different types/amounts of attentional resource. However, progress is likely to remain slow unless and until researchers can agree on the parameters and categories of attention.

Neurological attentional disorders

Hemineglect

Hemineglect is a behavioural syndrome associated with parietal lobe damage. An individual with this condition effectively ignores (fails to pay attention to) one side of his or her visual space. This is usually identified with respect to the midline of the head or body, and I will concentrate on this classic form in this section. However, it should be noted that different types of neglect may involve different spatial referents such as left/right foreground and distance or even left/right upper and lower space (Behrmann, 2000).

The features of hemineglect depend on the extent of parietal damage, which usually results from a stroke. The region most frequently implicated is the supra-marginal gyrus and associated subcortical structures. Although hemineglect can occur to either the left or right side, it is far more common and severe for the left side of space, implying that the right parietal lobe is somehow more critically involved. One explanation for this finding is that whereas the left parietal lobe is only responsible for attention on the right side of space, the right parietal lobe has an 'executive' control for spatial attention on both sides. Thus, following right-sided damage, the left parietal lobe can still mediate attention to the right visual field, but attentional control of the left side is lost. Left-sided damage is typically less disabling because the intact right side can continue to exert some control over both sides (Weintraub & Mesulam, 1987). An alternative explanation invokes the differing processing styles of the left and right hemispheres that I introduced in Chapter 5. According to Robertson and Rafal (2000), the left parietal lobe is chiefly responsible for local shifts in attention whereas the right parietal lobe is involved in more global shifts in attention. Thus, following right hemisphere damage, the patient is limited to the local attentional shifts of his left hemisphere, leading to the fixation with local detail and the loss of effective disengagement.

The extent of hemineglect is variable, and may range from a general apparent indifference towards objects on the left side, to denial of the very existence of that side of the body. One of Sacks' patients (Sacks, 1985) famously called a nurse in the middle of the night to ask her to help him throw his own left leg out of bed, thinking that 'the alien leg' had been put there as a cruel joke by fellow patients! Less severely affected patients may simply ignore items in their left visual field, or to their left side generally.

It is important to note that hemineglect is not the result of any sensory impairment. In fact, under certain circumstances, patients can process items in the neglected visual field as effectively as normals. When, for example, identical objects are presented to both visual fields simultaneously, the 'neglect' patient usually fails to report the object in the left visual field. (This phenomenon, known as 'extinction', is used as a test of hemineglect. It is thought to reflect a failure in the 'disengage' process inherent in Posner's model of visual attention.) However, if different objects are presented one-at-a-time to each side, there will be near-normal recognition even on the 'neglected' side. The 'attentional' rather than 'sensory' nature of this condition is further illustrated by the observation of Mesulam (1985) that attention to objects on the neglected side can be improved by offering rewards for target detection on that side.

There is usually some degree of recovery in the months following injury/ damage and so typically the neglect is most marked early on, becoming less pronounced though never completely disappearing as recovery ensues. The late German artist Anton Raederscheidt suffered a right-sided stroke but continued to paint even though he had an initially severe form of hemineglect. In a famous

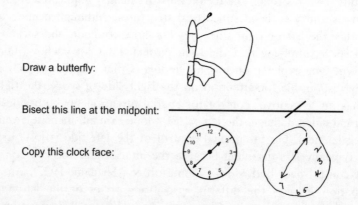

Draw a butterfly:

Bisect this line at the midpoint:

Copy this clock face:

FIGURE 9.8 Typical responses of hemineglect patients in drawing tasks

Hemineglect patients' drawings often reflect their indifference towards the left side of visual space. This is illustrated in the drawings of a butterfly and a clock, both of which substantially ignore the left side. When asked to bisect a line, hemineglect patients usually make a mark to the right of the true mid-point, once again highlighting their preference for the right side and indifference towards the left.

series of self-portraits it is possible to see the effects of the hemineglect and how this diminished over a period of months as he partially recovered after his stroke. In an interview his wife described how, in the early recovery period, she had to keep guiding him to the left side of the canvas, and it is clear from the paintings themselves that Raederscheidt's reconstruction of the left side of his visual space was a deliberate 'non-fluent' process.

The case of Anton Raederscheidt highlights an important subjective feature of hemineglect. The individual is not so much desperate to refind the missing half of their visual field, as utterly disinterested in it. It just doesn't exist as far as they are concerned, and in his case it had to be deliberately (and somewhat artificially) reconstructed. Fig. 9.8 illustrates some typical responses of hemineglect patients to simple requests to draw objects.

The idea that hemineglect results from a lack of awareness of the existence of one side of visual space seems alien to those of us with intact attentional mechanisms, but it is further demonstrated in the reports by Bisiach and Luzzatti (1978) of two hemineglect cases. The researchers asked their patients to imagine that they were standing in a famous Milanese square opposite the entrance to the cathedral, and to report the various buildings and other landmarks that came to mind. (Both knew this location well, having lived in the city for many years before their illnesses.) Later, the same respondents were asked to imagine themselves standing on the cathedral steps looking back to their initial vantage point, and now to report buildings and landmarks (again in their mind's eye so-to-speak) that they could see from this new vantage point. The results of this study are represented in Fig. 9.9. When the two patients imagined themselves standing opposite the cathedral, most of the identified landmarks were to the right. When they imagined themselves standing on the steps of the cathedral looking back, most of the identified landmarks were, once again, to the right! This simple case study reveals several important features of hemineglect. First, it does not relate to memory impairment because the total number of recalled landmarks was similar to the number generated by normal controls. Secondly, the attentional disturbance could not be caused by external cues because the entire test relied on imagery. The most parsimonious explanation of these findings is that the patients behaved as if they were missing the concept of one side of space – the left – even when they effectively rotated themselves through 180 degrees.

Balint's syndrome

This is a rare but very disabling condition in which the individual manifests a cluster of symptoms that could easily be mistaken for blindness for all but a very restricted area of the visual field. However, such individuals are not blind, and can actually 'see' objects anywhere in the visual field *if* they can direct attention to that location – and herein lies the problem. Balint's cases cannot point

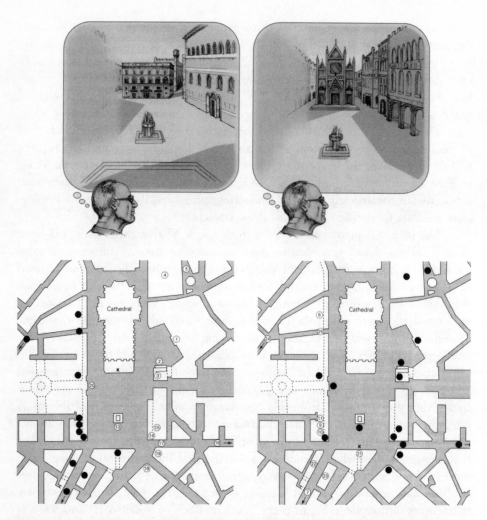

FIGURE 9.9 An illustration of the effects of hemineglect on spatial attention

In Bisiach and Luzzatti's classic study of hemineglect, when asked to imagine the view from the steps of the cathedral (marked 'x' on the left-hand map), both patients identified more landmarks and buildings to the right. When asked to imagine the view from the opposite end of the square (marked 'x' on the right-hand map) both patients once again identified many more landmarks and buildings to the right. Source: Bisiach, E., & Luzzatti, C. (1978). Unilateral neglect of representational space. *Cortex*, *14*, 129–133. As redrawn in *Cognitive Neuroscience: The Biology of the Mind* (Figure 6.38) by Michael S. Gazzaniga, Richard Ivry and George R. Mangun: Copyright © 1998 by W.W. Norton & Company, Inc. Reproduced by permission.

FIGURE 9.10 The sort of picture/story stimulus used by Farah

When Balint's patients view figures similar to the one shown here, their inability to voluntarily scan the entire figure and appreciate the 'story' that it depicts is apparent.

to a visual target; they cannot shift gaze voluntarily to a new target; and they cannot even perceive different objects in the same region of visual field presented simultaneously. The inability to redirect attention or to perceive different components of a single visual array is the one that defines Balint's syndrome as an attentional disorder (Damasio, 1985). When, for example, a crossed spoon and fork were held out in front of a Balint's patient, he reported only the presence of the spoon, and then later after a repeat presentation, the fork, yet the objects overlapped!

Farah (1990) further illustrated the attentional deficit seen in Balint's individuals. When shown a complex meaningful picture similar to that in Fig. 9.10, the patient could identify different elements of the picture as his attention switched involuntarily around the scene, but he could not grasp the full meaning of the picture because it was visually scanned in such a piecemeal way. So, although Balint's is an attentional disorder, the appreciation of spatial relationships is also compromised, which will influence the understanding and interpretation of visual displays (Robertson & Rafal, 2000). Balint's is almost always associated with bi-lateral damage to the occipital-parietal borders, and is also known as dorsal simultanagnosia.

Interim comment

Balint's syndrome and hemineglect demonstrate that our ability to construct a complete model of our visual world depends on being able to attend to different elements of it, to switch attention to new objects or new regions of space very quickly, and to use this specific information to build a relational map of the 'big picture'. In uni-lateral neglect, parietal damage means that this skill is lost (usually) for the contralateral visual field. As a result, attention appears to be focused on the remaining intact half. The person is not blind to the other half of the visual field, and can, under certain circumstances, see objects in it. But ordinarily, their attention is restricted to one half of the visual field, and they do not even seem to 'miss' the other half. Balint's syndrome is a more disabling condition in which attentional control, even to half the visual field, is lost. Instead, we see a sort of single object based attentional system operating without voluntary control. The experience of Balint's must be a little like only seeing visual stimuli from the end of a long tube, which roams around the visual field unpredictably.

Towards an integrated model of attention

For over 100 years psychologists have argued about whether selective attention occurs early or late in the information-processing stream, and whether attention is object-based or spatially-based. The evidence I have reviewed in this chapter suggests that both early and late selection can be observed in different experimental situations, and that attention may be object-based and spatially-based depending on the prevailing circumstances. We have also seen that attention can, at times, appear to be a deliberate process, as in the visual search for conjunctive stimuli. Yet at other times, as in the cocktail party phenomenon, attentional shifts occur despite best efforts to avoid distraction.

According to LaBerge (1995), the distinction between deliberate and incidental attention (top-down and bottom-up processes in his terminology) is critical, yet often overlooked. For him, attention comprises three elements: simple selection, preparation and maintenance. Simple selection is typically brief, and the goal is often the identification of the selected item itself. In preparatory and maintenance attention the aim is to sustain attention in a more deliberate way over a short (preparatory) or longer (maintenance) period of time. Posner's spatial cues would be a means of evoking preparatory attention. Completing the Stroop test would be an example of maintained attention.

At the cortical level, LaBerge envisages attention as enhanced (excitatory) activity in discreet cortical association areas. This, in turn, can be brought about by either top-down or bottom-up processes. Bottom-up control operates in two main ways: triggering shifts in attention, and directing attention to new locations. In each case, the processes are rapid and, effectively, involuntary. Attentional capture (the term used for this bottom-up process) encompasses those occasions when our attention is 'grabbed' by some salient but peripheral event or stimulus. According to LaBerge, it also accounts for the so-called pre-attentive visual search findings presented by Treisman and Gelade (1980) in which respondents report that distinct (non-conjunctive) targets almost 'pop out' from the array (see Fig. 9.3b). Of course, once detected, the target then directs attention to it, whereupon top-down influences 'decide' whether or not to maintain attention to that item. We know that this process is rapid and only short-lived because ERP enhancement to an unexpected salient cue in the same location as the target lasts only 250–300 msec (Hopfinger & Mangan, 1998). As I mentioned earlier, were this not the case, our attention would be subject to constant distraction by salient but irrelevant stimuli and we would find it very difficult to attend to anything in a deliberate way.

Top-down attentional control involves the frontal lobes, and almost certainly overlaps with (or shares) the same frontal structures (the dorso-lateral pre-frontal cortex [DLPFC] and the anterior cingulate in particular) that are involved in working memory and executive control (Chelazzi & Corbetta, 2000). Working memory must be involved if the subject seeks to keep 'in mind' information over a period of time that will guide his attention, as in the study by Posner et al. (1980) in which a directional cue appeared announcing the subsequent location of the target stimulus. (This would correspond to the preparatory component of LaBerge's model.) To underline the 'common ground' between attentional mechanisms and working memory PET and fMRI, studies by Jonides et al. (1993), Smith, Jonides, and Koeppe (1996) and Courtney et al. (1997) have demonstrated a significant degree of overlap in both right parietal and frontal regions of activation during tasks of spatial attention and spatial working memory. Sustained effortful attention over longer periods as required in the Stroop test (the maintenance component in LaBerge's model), engages medial frontal structures including the anterior cingulate and the frontal eye fields (Posner & DiGirolamo, 1998) in addition to DLPFC regions associated with the central executive control of working memory.

LaBerge has, effectively, adapted the earlier theories of Mesulam and Posner into his own 'triangular' model of attention (see Fig. 9.11). The three core components are the parietal lobe, the frontal lobe and the pulvinar of the thalamus, although the model also implicates the visual cortex and the superior colliculi. An abrupt visual stimulus induces brief parietal activity, either directly, or via the superior colliculi and thalamus. This is likened to a pre-attentive or orienting activation. The parietal lobe, which is assumed to be the anatomical location of spatial representations, has reciprocal (informational) connections with the

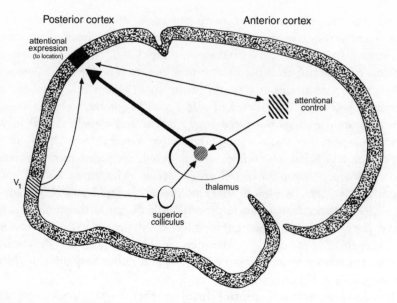

FIGURE 9.11 LaBerge's triangular circuit of attention

Following preliminary processing in area V1 of the occipital cortex, a new visual stimulus may induce some 'pre-attentive' registration in the parietal lobe, either by means of
a direct input or via the superior colliculus and pulvinar of the thalamus. Sustained attention engages regions of the frontal lobe. Continued attentional control can be achieved
by frontal output to the parietal lobe via the thalamus. (Adapted from LaBerge, 2000.)

frontal lobe. If the latter 'chooses' to sustain (or even initiate) activity in the
parietal lobe, it does so via the pulvinar, which can potentiate activity in particular cortical regions and inhibit it in others. The pathway from frontal lobe to
parietal lobe via the pulvinar is uni-directional, and is the means by which top-
down 'deliberate' control of attention can be effected.

Summary

Attentional mechanisms allow us to make the most of the cognitive limitations
of the brain, which has evolved to permit detailed processing of only a tiny
proportion of all the potential incoming sensory (and self-generated) material it
has access to. As psychologists have examined attentional processes it has become
clear that 'attention' is not a unitary phenomenon, and it probably needs to be
partitioned into a series of related but distinct domains. Researchers have made
progress in examining the processes involved in selective and sustained attention
and in distinguishing between pre-attentive processes and voluntary orienting in
different types of visual search.

ERP research has shown that 'top-down' (attentional) control processes can influence cortical processing within a very short period of time following stimulus onset, implying that selection of, and differential responding to, target stimuli occurs early in the processing stream. However, both the cocktail party phenomenon and the negative priming phenomenon remind us that certain non-attended material can also influence attention.

Several cortical and sub-cortical structures appear to be involved in mediating attentional processes. These were identified by Mesulam (1981) who proposed a neural network model of attention. Posner and colleagues have adapted elements of this model to describe a 'posterior' attentional network that is especially involved in visual selective attention. In this model, parietal regions facilitate disengagement, the superior colliculi contribute to the 'move' component, and the pulvinar of the thalamus redirects or 'engages' with a new focus. Posner has also proposed a frontal attentional system that is active when semantic or emotionally salient cues drive attention. This second system overlaps with the frontal regions that have been implicated in the coordination of certain executive functions. Posner's and Mesulam's theories have been further refined by LaBerge (1995; 2000) into a model that distinguishes between bottom-up (automatic/incidental/pre-attentive) and top-down (deliberate/executive) control.

Although we have still to delineate the parameters of attention, our consideration of relevant research has taken us into the domains of working memory, executive systems, consciousness and even pre-attentive (unconscious) processing. Such overlap is almost inevitable when the focus of our interest is sub-served by multiple brain regions collaborating in one or more attentional neural networks.

Chapter 10

Executive functions

■ **Introduction** 208

■ **Domains of executive dysfunction** 209

Impairments in action control 209

Impairments in abstract and conceptual
thinking 211

Impairments in goal-oriented behaviour 213

■ **The brain and executive function/
dysfunction** 216

Memory impairments 217

Inhibition and attention 218

A supervisory attentional system 220

The SAS and the anterior cingulate gyrus 221

■ **Executive dysfunction and psychiatric
disorders** 224

The rise and fall of frontal lobotomies 224

■ **Summary** 225

Introduction

The development of sophisticated neuropsychological testing techniques and the advent of in-vivo imaging have jointly led to increased interest in the role of cortical regions, particularly the frontal lobes, in what neuropsychologists call 'executive function(s)'. However, it is important at the outset to be clear about the term itself, and the relationship between executive functions and the frontal lobes. Executive functions refer to a raft of psychological attributes that are supervisory, controlling and organisational. Although these skills are all critical for normal everyday behaviour, their somewhat abstract nature means that routine psychological assessments such as IQ tests or measures of sensory perception may fail to detect any executive dysfunctions. They include the ability to plan, initiate and terminate actions, to think in abstract or conceptual terms, to adapt to changing circumstances and to respond in socially appropriate ways. It is therefore little wonder that individuals with impaired executive function show deficits in one or more of these domains. Baddeley (1986) has used the term 'dysexecutive syndrome' to identify these impairments.

At one time, psychologists used the terms 'executive' and 'frontal' in an almost interchangeable way because they believed that frontal lobe damage alone led to executive dysfunction. While this is often the case, we now need to qualify this relationship in two important though related ways. First, we should remember that the frontal lobes receive information from, and send information to, most other cortical regions and many subcortical systems (such as the basal ganglia, the limbic system and the cerebellum) as well. Secondly, and consistent with the idea of distributed control, we find that damage to regions other than the frontal lobes can sometimes lead to executive dysfunction, although it remains the case that frontal damage is most frequently associated with it.

A further point should be made before consideration of the nature and causes of executive dysfunction. That is, that in comparison with other psychological processes such as memory or perception, neuropsychologists are still, in a sense, at the stage of characterising the nature of the deficits associated with it. As yet, there is no clear agreement on the underlying causes of some of the executive deficits I will review, and therefore explanatory models of executive dysfunction (some of which I consider later in this chapter) may seem circular, overlapping, or of limited general application. Nevertheless, any comprehensive model of executive function must give due consideration to the range of psychological skills the frontal lobes and their connections sub-serve.

Domains of executive dysfunction

There remains considerable disagreement among researchers as to how to partition executive function (see for example Roberts, Robbins, & Weiskrantz, 1998). Historically, a sort of 'mass-action' approach to frontal lobe function has been favoured, with the region assumed to act as a unit in the coordination of executive functions. More recently though, neuropsychologists have made use of dissociations to tease apart apparently independent components of executive functions. Even so, it remains a matter of debate as to how many such components we need to consider. One way of looking at different aspects of executive dysfunction is to partition them into three domains, and I will consider:

- impairments in the initiation, maintenance and cessation of actions (action control);
- impairments in abstract and conceptual thinking; and
- impairments in the ability to organise behaviour towards a goal.

Readers should, however, note that these 'functional' domains do not map particularly well on to distinct 'structural' frontal regions, so further revision of the fractionation of executive functions is likely in the future.

Impairments in action control

People with frontal damage often display what neuropsychologists call psychological inertia (Lezak, 1983). Although this can take a variety of forms, there are two basic components. First, appropriate actions may not be initiated: an individual may, for example, neglect personal hygiene, or there may be a marked reduction in self-initiated speech, even with repeated prompting. The term 'couch-potato' to describe a slothful individual who does nothing but lounge around watching TV goes some way to characterising psychological inertia, except that our dysexecutive patient will probably not bother to switch the TV on in the first place. The individual seems indifferent to, and uninterested in, the world around them, and often (though not always) oblivious to their own indifference.

The second component of psychological inertia is characterised by difficulty in terminating or amending behaviour once started. It can be observed in the laboratory as well as social settings. The drawings in Fig. 10.1a illustrate the attempts of one 'frontal' patient to complete the 'memory for designs test' (Graham & Kendall, 1960) in which a set of simple geometric shapes are shown one at a time for a few seconds, and the respondent then has to draw each one as soon as the design is covered up. Although the actual designs vary considerably in their complexity and format, the drawings by the frontal patient all look

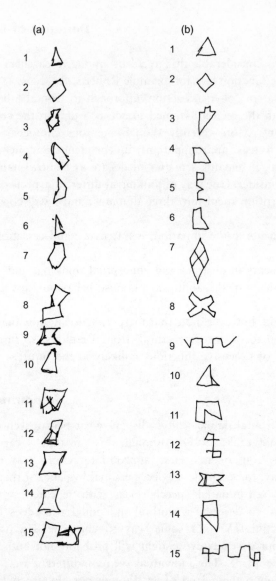

FIGURE 10.1 A control subject's and frontal patient's attempts at the memory for designs test

In the memory for designs test the respondent views a series of abstract figures one at a time for a few seconds each. Immediately after each presentation, they try to draw the design. A control participant's drawings are shown in the right column (b). Although they are not perfect, this person scored zero errors. The drawings of the same figures by a patient with frontal lobe damage are shown in the left column (a). The patient's drawings provide an indication of perseverative responding: each drawing looks similar to the previous one. The patient's error score was >20, which is indicative of marked damage.

very similar (in comparison with the drawings in Fig. 10.1b by a control subject), which is indicative of **perseverative** responding.

Both inertia and perseveration can also be seen in the pattern of responding of some individuals in tests of verbal fluency. When asked to name as many items as quickly as possible beginning with the letter 'F', a dysexecutive patient may first generate words comparatively slowly, and then get 'stuck in a rut' by generating only words that are interrelated; such as *'finger . . . , fingernail . . . , fingers . . .'* and so on. Sometimes, erroneous (but semantically related) intrusions such as *'ringfinger'* may slip in.

Another behavioural manifestation of executive dysfunction (which overlaps in some ways with the next category of disorder) has been described by L'hermitte (1983) and L'hermitte, Pillon, and Serdaru (1986). The environmental dependency syndrome (as it has come to be known) describes a pattern of behaviour in which environmental cues trigger responses irrespective of their appropriateness at the time. For example, when shown into a room in which there was a table with a hammer, nails and some pictures, one of L'hermitte's patients started hanging the pictures: another patient left to her own devices in a kitchen began washing the dirty dishes! This pattern of behaviour is sometimes referred to as 'stimulus-driven' or 'utilisation' behaviour, because the apparent impulsivity of such patients is influenced by immediate circumstances rather than the broader social context. Parents will recognise this as a common feature of child behaviour (perhaps not the washing-up!), and it is interesting to note that, in neuro-developmental terms, the frontal lobes are one of the last cortical regions to mature (in late adolescence). However, 'utilisation' can lead to embarrassingly inappropriate social behaviour in adults with frontal lobe damage, as happened when L'hermitte showed one of his patients a disposable cardboard bedpan, only for the patient to commence using it!

Impairments in abstract and conceptual thinking

A similar pattern of fixated or inflexible thinking is also seen in other manifestations of executive dysfunction. The Wisconsin card sort test (WCST) (see Chapter 2) was developed to examine concept formation and the ability of participants to overcome the tendency to perseverate. In this test the respondent must sort a pack of cards one card at a time so that each matches one of four 'key' cards in some way. Each card differs in three dimensions (see Fig. 2.5b and Fig. 10.2); the number of objects shown on the card (one, two, three or four), the shape of the objects (circles, triangles, squares or stars) and their colour (red, green, blue or yellow). So, for each card, the participant could match it according to shape, number or colour. As the participant places a card in a pile underneath one of the four key cards, they are told only whether or not the card matches according to the criterion the experimenter 'has in mind'. The idea is that by using this feedback,

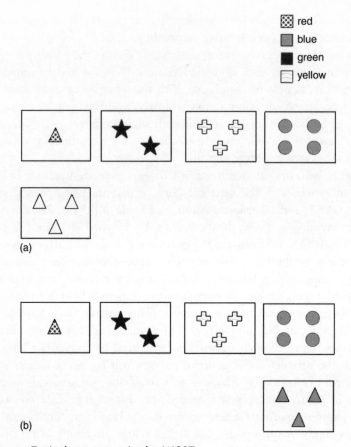

red
blue
green
yellow

FIGURE 10.2 Typical responses in the WCST

In (a) the unstated rule was 'sort by colour'. The subject's response is incorrect because they actually sort by shape.

In (b) the unstated rule is 'sort by colour', which the respondent does correctly even though the card differs from the matching cards both in respect of shape and number.

the individual will quite quickly learn (i.e. infer) the matching criterion, and sort subsequent cards according to it. After a number of correct sortings, the experimenter changes the matching criterion. (In some procedures, this is done without warning, but in the modified procedure [Nelson, 1976], the subject is explicitly told that the former matching rule no longer applies.)

People with frontal lobe damage generally learn to sort much more slowly than normal subjects, but, in particular, they make many more perseverative errors, meaning that they continue to sort according to the previous matching criterion even though it no longer applies. This is most obviously apparent in Nelson's modified procedure in which subjects are specifically told that the rule has changed (though not what it has changed to). Despite this instruction, some frontal patients will continue to sort according to the obsolete rule, showing an inability to think flexibly and change behaviour to adapt to the 'new situation'.

A recent variant of the WCST developed by Delis et al. (1992) required subjects to sort sets of six cards each showing an object/drawing/word into two equal piles. The cards could be sorted according to several criteria including shape, shading, category of word written on each and so on. Frontal patients struggled with this test in two characteristic ways. First, they were not very good at sorting the cards into meaningful groups at all, and secondly, even if they could sort as per the instructions, they struggled to describe the actual rule they were using.

Impairments in goal-oriented behaviour

Sequential planning

Research suggests that individuals with frontal lobe damage struggle with tasks that, for successful completion, must be broken down into a series of sub-routines to be completed in the right order. Problems may arise because of composite difficulties in sequential planning, memory, self-monitoring, and of course, not losing sight of the overall goal (see Box 10.1).

Box 10.1 'Tea for two'

Consider the executive components involved in making a cup of tea:

- First, there is, self-evidently, an overall goal that must be borne in mind as the tea-maker goes about their task.
- The task can be broken down into a number of sub-components. What materials and items will be needed, and where are they in the kitchen?
- What is the appropriate sequence of actions? The kettle must be filled, the tea should go in the pot, milk in the cups and so on.
- What about contingency plans? Perhaps the milk in the jug is sour? Is there more in the fridge? Is there any powdered milk? Did anyone want sugar? Are there any sweeteners instead?

The point of this example is to illustrate the range of psychological skills implicated in even this simple task: Our tea-maker has to have a strategy; they must sequence different elements of the task in the correct order; they must remember what has already been done, and what yet needs to be done; and finally they must be able to adapt the task to changing circumstances (if needs be) to fulfil the overall goal.

The example of making a cup of tea illustrates the vital importance of 'temporal' sequencing in planning many actions. A study by Milner (1982) neatly illustrates the particular difficulty some frontal patients have in distinguishing between more and less recent events. Subjects viewed a sequence of simple line drawings of objects one at a time. Every so often, a test card would be shown that had two objects on it. On recognition trials, the respondent had to decide which of the two objects had appeared in the preceding sequence (one had appeared but the other was new). In recency trials, the respondent had to decide which of the two objects had appeared most recently. The recognition rate of frontal patients was comparable with that of control participants, but recency judgements were significantly impaired. In other words, frontal patients could not remember the order in which the material was viewed. Incidentally, there was also a laterality effect evident in this study giving rise to a double dissociation. Patients with left frontal damage fared worse with verbal material than with drawings, and patients with right frontal damage did worse with drawings than words.

The previous study shows that frontal patients struggle to memorise sequence – but do they also struggle in planning sequential actions? Petrides and Milner (1982) developed a disarmingly simple procedure to test this. Respondents were required simply to point to any item in a 3×2 array that they had not pointed to before. The array always contained the same six items, but their location was changed on successive trials. Frontal patients made significantly more errors than controls, suggesting a marked impairment in planning of sequential actions. Of course, this task relies heavily on working memory (remembering what you have already pointed to in order to avoid doing it again), and we saw in Chapter 7 that central executive component of working memory is mediated by the dorso-lateral pre-frontal cortex (DLPFC).

Impaired planning of sequential action is also seen in tasks such as the 'Tower of London' puzzle (Shallice, 1982). In this test there are three coloured balls, and three prongs. One can hold three balls, the second two balls, and the third just one ball. On each trial the balls are placed in the standard starting position and the subject must move them to a different specified finishing position in the least possible number of moves. Some trials require only two moves, while others require ten or more to reach the final configuration. Frontal patients are worse than controls on both simple and complex trials, although the gap widens on complex trials. The behaviour of frontal patients seems aimless and devoid of strategy. Even when they do solve the puzzle, it is as if they have stumbled across the answer rather than thinking it through step-by-step (see Fig. 10.3).

Self-monitoring

When neuropsychologists refer to self-monitoring, they are really talking about the reflexive skill of self-inquiry: 'How am I getting along with this task?' 'What

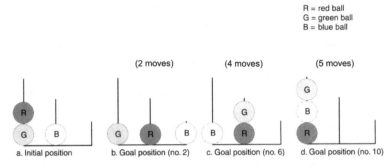

FIGURE 10.3 The 'Tower of London' test

In this test there are three coloured balls and three prongs, one of which can hold three balls, one two balls and the third just one ball. Respondents may only move one ball from the top of a prong at a time. From a standard starting position (a), the participant might be asked to rearrange the balls in various ways which require two, three or more moves. Patients with dorso-lateral pre-frontal damage struggle on this test because their ability to plan a sequence of actions is compromised.

was it I just did?' 'How close am I to successful completion?' Time and again, both anecdotal and experimental evidence points to frailties in this intrinsic ability in patients with frontal damage. Anecdotally, case reports frequently allude to the frontal patient's inability to 'keep on track' during prolonged tasks. When asked to copy one of several drawings on a page, they may start accurately, but then integrate material from one or more of the other drawings into their own.

In a classic 'real-life' study of the *derailment* that is seen in the goal-oriented behaviour of frontal patients, Shallice and Burgess (1991) set three patients a set of relatively simple tasks to complete. These included shopping for certain items, finding out some information about four queries (the price of a pack of tomatoes, etc.) and keeping an appointment. This was specifically not a memory test and respondents had a list of the tasks and instructions to follow. Nevertheless, each patient had difficulty completing the assignment. In one case an item could not be purchased because the shop did not stock the individual's favourite brand; in another, items were selected but not paid for; or worse still, an entire component of the assignment was ignored. This is a particularly good illustration of the problems frontal patients have in achieving goals. They start with the best intentions, but are easily distracted, and are unable to get back on track because of an apparent lack of awareness about being blown off-course.

Interim comment

In the previous section I described three principal domains of executive dysfunction. Individuals have difficulty initiating and terminating actions, and often seem indifferent to their own 'inertia'. Sometimes, their behaviour is guided more by immediate circumstances than any grand plan, and we see evidence of utilisation or stimulus-driven behaviour. Dysexecutive cases also have difficulties with tasks that demand flexibility and adaptation of behaviour, and, as a result, may show marked perseveration. Finally, they seem to have particular problems with complex tasks that need to be broken down into smaller sequential tasks in order to be completed successfully.

My list of executive dysfunctions is meant to be illustrative rather than comprehensive, and, even with my examples, it is possible to argue that the domains overlap. For instance, poor planning may be linked to a tendency to engage in stimulus-driven behaviour, and perseveration may be related to 'loss of goal' because both rely on impaired memory. Nevertheless, the overall impression of someone with executive dysfunction is of an individual whose thinking has undergone fundamental changes that may impact on almost every other aspect of behaviour; changes that go to the very roots of the cognitive processes that (we think) single out sentient humans from all other creatures. In the following sections I try to address these issues from a different 'bottom-up' perspective by considering in a little more detail what we know about the brain systems and regions that may be involved in executive function, and how damage or dysfunction to these areas is related to impaired executive function.

The brain and executive function/dysfunction

There are three reasonably well-established areas linking brain structure and executive function, and several other less well-developed ideas that go beyond the remit of this book. In each case, the 'primary' brain region of interest is, of course, within the frontal lobes, although as I mentioned in introducing this chapter, these regions collaborate with other cortical (or subcortical regions) to mediate overall control. A further point to mention is that each of the three approaches I consider can be regarded as offering ideas about frontal function that are complementary to one another rather than alternative and mutually exclusive. In the following sections I consider the potential importance of memory impairments, social and emotional integration through inhibition and the role of a supervisory attentional system in contributing to executive dysfunction.

Memory impairments

In Chapter 7 I reviewed the evidence that identifies an important role for the frontal lobes in working memory. Recall that imaging data from both animal and human research illustrates quite convincingly that the dorso-lateral pre-frontal cortex (DLPFC) is part of a network for holding 'on-line' either new information or information drawn from more posterior brain regions (where it is presumably permanently stored) for short-term processing. It is not difficult to imagine how impairments to working memory may account for some features of executive dysfunction. For example, inability to keep in mind 'overall goal' might lead to impaired goal-oriented behaviour. Failure to remember the rules of the WCST or keep 'on-line' the current matching criterion while ignoring previous matching criteria also both tap working memory function. Such failures could, in turn, account for perseveration and stimulus-driven behaviours. However, at least two other types of memory deficit that are not directly related to working memory are sometimes seen in executive dysfunction: namely, poor temporal memory and poor source memory.

Recall the study by Milner (1982) that I described earlier. It showed that people with surgical lesions of the frontal lobes had specific deficits in making recency judgements but no comparable problem with recognition judgements. The frontal region in question was area 46, which forms part of the region earlier implicated in mediating the central executive component of working memory (i.e. the DLPFC). Moreover, a control group comprising patients with lesions to their temporal lobes showed recency and recognition rates very similar to the control subjects.

Source memory also depends on frontal lobe function. This aspect of 'episodic' memory (see Chapter 7) is concerned less with memorising specific items than with remembering the context in which those items were learned. Janowsky, Shimamura, and Squire (1989) asked control subjects and frontal patients to learn a list of factual statements. About a week later, their memory was tested by assessing their ability to recall the original facts that were now jumbled up with some new and equally obscure factual statements. Whenever a subject made a correct recall, they were asked to say how they had learned the information. Was it from a newspaper, the TV, or perhaps the previous testing session? Frontal patients were almost as good as controls at recalling facts, but made many more errors in trying to identify how or when the fact had been acquired.

Interim comment

These studies show that frontal patients have memory impairments beyond those that are normally associated with working memory, and it is easy to see how these might contribute to the executive dysfunction syndrome. Failure to effectively add a temporal tag to a memorised item is likely to impact on any task that involves sequencing or temporal order. Deficits in source memory may contribute to impaired performance on goal-oriented tasks where the subject needs to keep track of what they themselves have already done at earlier stages of completing the task. However, some researchers have suggested an alternative interpretation of memory impairments in executive dysfunction. Perhaps, rather than the memory impairments themselves leading to dysexecutive features, both are linked by a more fundamental problem of impaired inhibition leading to difficulties with attention.

Inhibition and attention

There are good reasons stemming from electrophysiological research for thinking that frontal control operates on the basis of effective inhibition, and conversely, that frontal patients fail to engage in the appropriate inhibitory processes. One example will serve: Knight and Grabowecky (1995) employed a simple event-related potential (ERP) procedure to show that, in comparison with patients with temporal and parietal lesions, frontal patients showed an augmented P30 response to a series of auditory clicks, even though they required no response. This early 'non-signal' ERP component (occurring about 30 msec after the click) was 'inhibited' by controls but not by frontal patients.

Failure of inhibition could also account for some of the memory impairments identified earlier. In working memory tasks, good performance depends on avoiding distraction while keeping in mind whatever one wants to remember. One way to avoid distractions is to effectively inhibit them; to close your mind to them in order to attend to the task in hand (think of trying to hold in mind a telephone number while you wait for the phone to become available). Failure to inhibit will lead to poorer memory due to distraction or impaired attention.

Failure of inhibition also accounts well for other features of the dysexecutive syndrome. For example, it is easy to argue that perseveration results, in effect, from a failure to inhibit unwanted responses. However, one of the clearest examples of impaired inhibitory processing is seen in the Stroop test. As I described in the previous chapter, in one version of this test subjects must read different coloured words aloud from a computer screen. The words are colour names, and sometimes the colour name is congruent with the colour of the word, but on other 'incongruent' trials the word 'pink' may be shown in 'green ink', and so on. Although all subjects are slower (and make more errors) for incongruent stimuli, this distraction effect of naming the colour when the word name is different to it is particularly marked in frontal patients (Perret, 1974). Brain-imaging studies have shown that tests like the Stroop activate several regions in the frontal cortex. However, when brain activation from the congruent stimuli is subtracted from brain activation for incongruent stimuli, the anterior cingulate gyrus region seems to be most active. Perhaps this region is important in the selection of appropriate responses and the inhibition of inappropriate ones in this and similar domains of behaviour.

The Hayling test (Burgess & Shallice, 1996) also reveals the difficulties that frontal patients have both initiating and inhibiting responses. In this test, participants must complete sentences by 'generating' the final missing word. In half the trials respondents are instructed to generate a 'congruent' word (i.e. one appropriate to the rest of the sentence). In the remaining trials, the word should be 'incongruent' and make no sense in relation to the rest of the sentence. Burgess and Shallice reported that frontal patients are poor at both tasks, being slower at congruent response initiation, and both slower and more error prone for incongruent word generation. Interestingly, individuals did not necessarily perform at a similar level on the two tasks (i.e. the correlation between congruent and incongruent test performance within subjects was low), suggesting that they may well depend on different frontal processes (and regions).

Failure of inhibitory processes may also account for the utilisation behaviour described by L'hermitte, which I summarised earlier in this chapter. His frontal patients engaged in stimulus-driven acts because they were unable to muster the inhibitory forces to prevent themselves. In the literature of frontal lobe dysfunction the seminal case is, of course, Phineas Gage (see Gazzaniga et al., 1998). He was a railway worker and his job was to ram explosives into bore holes using a tamping iron (about 2 cms wide and 100 cms long). One day, explosives in the hole 'shot' the tamping iron through his brain, injuring but not killing him. One of the most marked changes seen in Gage after his accident was to his personality. After recovery he was described as irreverent, impatient and fitful. The inhibitory processes that had hitherto kept these tendencies in check were now lost and his behaviour became 'disinhibited'.

The damage to Gage's brain was to orbital and medial regions rather than dorso-lateral regions of the frontal lobe, and other evidence identifies these regions as critical for mediation of inhibition in the social domain. For example, one of Damasio's patients underwent surgery for a tumour that had invaded medial orbital regions bi-laterally (Damasio, 1994). After recovery, he continued to demonstrate above-average performance on working memory tests and even on the WCST, but his social functioning unravelled. Having previously been measured, cautious and thorough, he now struggled to initiate activities, he became immersed in trivial matters at the expense of more important ones, and he began to take business risks that eventually led to his bankruptcy.

Loss of goal and behavioural inertia are familiar features of the dysexecutive syndrome, but psychologists have speculated that the loss of social competence seen both in Gage and in Damasio's patient is particularly related to discon-nection between orbito-medial frontal regions and the limbic system. Loss of this input means that the frontal lobes no longer receive information about emotional processing that may occur in limbic structures such as the hippocampus and amygdala. Impulses now are acted upon without consideration of their social consequences, giving rise to a form of emotional detachment that psychiatrists and neurologists have referred to as pseudo-psychopathy (Benson & Stuss, 1989).

A supervisory attentional system

A third approach to understanding frontal lobe function (and, *inter alia*, the dysexecutive syndrome) has been suggested by Norman and Shallice (1986). Their 'information-processing' model was initially developed to explain goal-oriented behaviour where attainment depended on successful orderly completion of several sub-goals (see Box 10.1). Consider now the intention to decorate a room. In order to achieve this 'goal', the task must be broken down into a series of smaller sub-routines that should be undertaken in a quite strict order. For example, there

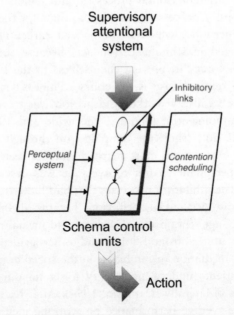

FIGURE 10.4 Norman and Shallice's supervisory attentional system

In Norman and Shallice's model, certain components within an overall plan of action are mutually inhibitory (you cannot stir the tea without already having picked up the spoon, for example). This relatively passive organisational process is known as contention sched-uling. However, it can be 'overridden' by a supervisory attentional process if required (if, for example, your guest advises you that he or she has recently adopted a preference for sweeteners or skimmed milk).

is no point in removing the carpet *after* you have painted the ceiling. According to the model (which is illustrated in Fig. 10.4) response selection is a competitive process: even an amateur decorator probably has stored memories of each of the component tasks that must be enacted to achieve the goal – how to strip wallpaper, how to roll the carpet, how to fill cracks and so on. Of course, these will probably be stored along with representations of hundreds if not thousands of other learned actions or responses that are nothing to do with decorating. The decorator must inhibit these unwanted actions, and correctly order the required actions. Norman and Shallice called these memory representations schema control units.

For a professional decorator, experience may mean that ordering the subgoals becomes a semi-automatic process, although even for the amateur, some of the component schema control units effectively inhibit others: wallpaper cannot be hung without already having mixed the paste, it cannot be painted until it has been hung, and so on. Norman and Shallice called this somewhat passive process 'contention scheduling'.

However for the amateur decorator, in addition to contention scheduling, the entire process is likely to require planning at a higher 'supervisory' level, which Norman and Shallice suggest depends on a supervisory attentional system (or SAS). The SAS can override the semi-automatic process of contention scheduling, bringing order (and the potential for flexibility) to the task in hand. After all, even the experienced decorator must engage his SAS when some exceptional circumstance requiring hitherto unanticipated action arises, such as the discovery of exposed electrical cables or an area of perished plaster. From this illustration it is easy to see how some of the features of executive dysfunction may come about if the SAS is unable to override contention scheduling. Behaviour will lose flexibility and will be stimulus-driven. There may be perseveration, and there will be poor goal-oriented behaviour.

The SAS and the anterior cingulate gyrus

In the past few years, there has been increased interest in trying to identify the anatomical substrate of the SAS, and the spotlight has fallen on the anterior cingulate gyrus, which for many years was more closely linked with the limbic system. At present, the evidence implicating the anterior cingulate is circumstantial rather than direct, but it still merits consideration.

Recall from the previous passage that we might expect the SAS to be most active under the circumstances identified in Box 10.2. In-vivo imaging studies have shed considerable light on activity levels in the anterior cingulate in many of these circumstances. Using PET, Corbetta et al. (1991) illustrated that when subjects had to focus attention on a particular stimulus parameter (such as shape, colour or movement), most PET activation was observed in posterior cortical

---

Box 10.2: Situations prompting activation of the SAS

- Requirement of a novel or flexible response.
- Overriding a well-learned (but inappropriate) response.
- When there is potential danger or significant risk.
- When careful planning is required.
- When decisions must be made.

---

regions associated with visual processing of those features. However, when attentional demand was increased by requiring subjects to monitor changes in all three parameters concurrently, the most marked activation was recorded in the anterior cingulate.

A second illustration comes from the study of Peterson et al. (1988), which I described in Chapter 6. In their PET study of language, you may recall that various experimental conditions were included in which subjects listened to (or viewed) words passively, repeated them aloud, or generated associated verbs. Compared with the other conditions, the 'generate' condition led to most activation in the DLPFC and the anterior cingulate. But if the 'generate' condition was repeated, the anterior cingulate activation diminished. Subjects tended to 'recall' the same verb as on the first trial, making the repeat condition more of a memory task. However, this was clearly not just an **habituation** effect because anterior cingulate activation returned when new words were presented.

Temporal resolution of PET is relatively poor, but an ERP study by Snyder et al. (1995) has confirmed the temporal sequencing of events in Peterson et al.'s task. The first activation does indeed occur in the anterior cingulate about 200 msec after presentation of the noun. This is followed about 30 msec later by an activation in the DLPFC and a further 500 msec later by left temporal activation. The most compelling explanation of this sequence is that the anterior cingulate activation represents executive attentional focusing. It, in turn, activates the working memory system in the DLPFC to hold the stimulus word in mind, and then to recruit a related verb from semantic store (in the left temporal lobe).

Finally, an elegantly simple PET study by Frith et al. (1991) implicated the anterior cingulate in 'willed' decision making. Participants were scanned while they made very simple movements with one of two fingers. In one control condition, they had to move a 'stimulated' finger (the finger was gently pushed from underneath by a lever). In a second control condition they had to move the non-stimulated finger, and in the experimental condition they had to decide for themselves which finger to move, in a random pattern. In comparison with the two control conditions, the 'free-will' condition led to greater anterior cingulate activation.

Interim comment

Norman and Shallice's model provides a framework for understanding the processes involved in the allocation of attentional resources, the selection of appropriate responses and the capacity to override more automatically generated responses when the need arises. It has the added advantage of seeming to tally with personal experience of how attention and response selection operate for an individual at certain times or in a particular situation, such as those listed in Box 10.2. Imaging and ERP studies have implicated the anterior cingulate as a key component in this model, and it is known that it has major reciprocal links with the DLPFC.

However, the recent enthusiasm for thinking of the anterior cingulate as *the* anatomical substrate of the SAS needs to be weighed against the fairly well-established observation that damage to this structure does not necessarily induce a lasting dysexecutive syndrome. The evidence is patchy, but there are at least a handful of people who have incurred damage to the anterior cingulate, or had it surgically removed for various reasons, yet who showed only partial or transient features of dysfunction.

The links between frontal regions and different features of executive function are summarised in Box 10.3.

Box 10.3: Summary of frontal regions implicated in different aspects of executive functioning

Dorso-lateral pre-frontal area
Working memory, temporal and source memory, planning actions and concept formation.

Medial-frontal region
Perceptions are given 'emotional' tone via direct links with the limbic system.

Anterior cingulate
Focusing and supervision of attention to external events and internal thoughts/plans, and selection of appropriate responses.

Orbital region
Inhibition of inappropriate responses especially in the social domain and inertia in social behaviour.

Executive dysfunction and psychiatric disorders

The rise and fall of frontal lobotomies

In view of what has been said so far about damage to the frontal lobes and associated impaired function, it is both ironic and (for psychiatry) somewhat embarrassing to record that some of the earliest attempts to modify presumed brain disorder among psychiatric patients involved wholesale removal (or isolation) of frontal tissue. The development of the procedure that came to be known as the frontal lobotomy or leucotomy represents one of the darkest times in the history of psychiatry, yet merits retelling if only to serve as a reminder to avoid making the same sort of mistake ever again.

The procedure itself was introduced in the early 1930s by the respected Portuguese neurologist Egas Moniz. Of course at this time there were no effective treatments for any of the major psychiatric disorders, and in Moniz's defence, it must be said that clinicians were desperate for access to any therapeutic procedures that offered hope of favourable outcome, or even a measure of effective control. Moniz heard of the work by two American researchers who reported a change to the 'personality' of a chimpanzee whose frontal lobes they had removed. From being uncooperative and aggressive, the chimp became docile and pliant after surgery. Moniz reasoned that the same effect may offer relief for severely agitated mental patients. However, he was uneasy about operating on the whole of the frontal lobes so modified the procedure to encompass only the pre-frontal areas.

Moniz eventually settled on a surgical procedure in which a hole was drilled in the side of the patient's forehead, and a probe with a retractable blade (a leucotome) inserted and moved through an arc, lesioning all the tissue it encountered. After World War II, the technique was adopted (and simplified) by Freeman in the United States. The 'lobotomy' (as it now came to be known) could be administered (under anaesthesia) in a doctor's surgery in a matter of minutes. Over the next few years thousands of lobotomies were carried out using Freeman's procedure, and, to compound insult with injury, Moniz received the Nobel prize for physiology and medicine in 1949.

It is, of course, easy to be wise after the event. Records show that a small number of aggressive agitated patients did become more cooperative and manageable after surgery. Some depressed and extremely anxious patients also showed a reduction in their symptoms, but often exchanged these for the behavioural inertia that I described earlier. Proper clinical trials were never instigated even though the procedure itself was used on an ever-wider cross-section of psychiatric patients. It was, for example, used extensively for a period as a treatment for schizophrenia, yet no formal evaluative study of its effectiveness for such patients was ever conducted, and so far as we can tell anecdotally, it seemed to do little good and clearly made symptoms worse for some schizophrenic patients.

The procedure eventually fell out of favour, largely because of the development in the early 1950s of effective drugs for schizophrenia, and then later for depression and the anxiety disorders. Today psycho-surgical procedures are still occasionally carried out as a last-ditch treatment for intractable depression or drug-resistant obsessive-compulsive disorder. Interestingly, the surgery is in the frontal lobes, although it is usually restricted to severing pathways connecting them to the striatum (see Chapter 5).

Earlier I mentioned pseudo-psychopathy as a term 'coined' to identify some of the disinhibited features, especially in the social domain, that frontal patients may exhibit. A second syndrome, called pseudo-depression, was also characterised by Blumer and Benson (1975) to encompass the apathy, indifference, withdrawal and loss of initiative seen in some frontal patients. These descriptors are, of course, also applicable to many people with chronic schizophrenia, and subsequent research has confirmed that people with this diagnosis often have functional abnormalities indicative of frontal impairment (Stirling, Hellewell, & Quraishi, 1998). Underactivation of the frontal lobes (during the completion of tasks that lead to activation in control respondents) is now a relatively robust finding in schizophrenia and seems most closely linked to the presence of negative symptoms. These symptoms predominate in the sub-type that Liddle (1987, 1993) has called psychomotor poverty, and converging evidence points to functional disturbances involving the neurotransmitters dopamine and glutamate in the DLPFC (Mitchell, Elliott, & Woodruff, 2001). In the case of clinical depression, as with schizophrenia, functional changes are apparent in the frontal lobes but the picture is more complicated than first thought (Drevets et al., 1997).

Summary

The raft of well-documented dysexecutive impairments can be categorised in a variety of ways. Nevertheless, the list will include problems in the initiation and cessation of actions, impaired strategy formation, and loss of goal-oriented behaviour.

No single theory of frontal lobe impairment can currently account for the range of dysfunctions associated with them. Instead, three reasonably well-established approaches have been described. In the first, there is an emphasis on the impaired memory function commonly observed in frontal patients, which encompasses source and temporal memory as well as working memory. Damage to the DLPFC is most frequently associated with these types of memory deficit. In the second, it is argued that there is a general failure to recruit inhibitory processes appropriately. This may lead to many of the features of the dysexecutive syndrome (and account for some forms of memory impairment as well). Disinhibited behaviour is more likely to be associated with damage to orbito-medial frontal regions. Where there is a social component to the disinhibition, the focus has been on the connections between the limbic system (especially the hippocampus and amygdala) and these orbito-medial regions. The third approach, initially developed to explain how complex tasks could be completed successfully, proposes the existence of a supervisory attentional system that can, if necessary, override and amend the component behaviours routinely driven by schema control units. The idea here is that even complex behaviour can result from relatively automatic control processes that may be stimulus-driven or may control one another through contention scheduling. However, the SAS can over-ride these processes (just as a pilot may take control of a plane by cancelling auto-pilot) to bring about appropriate adaptive flexible strategic behaviour. In-vivo imaging research has identified the anterior cingulate as a possible substrate for the SAS.

Surgical lesioning of frontal regions of the brain was introduced as a treatment for severe mental illness in the 1930s. Although no properly controlled evaluation studies of the procedure were ever conducted, the lobotomy continued to be employed until the mid-1950s. More recently it has become apparent that a significant proportion of people meeting diagnostic criteria for schizophrenia show an unusual pattern of hypo-activation when required to undertake tests that normally 'tap' frontal lobe function. This has prompted some researchers to propose that schizophrenics whose illness takes a chronic course and who have a preponderance of negative signs actually have a severe executive dysfunction.

Chapter 11

Summary and concluding thoughts

■ Two broad approaches   228

■ Localisation/modularity   228

■ Laterality/plasticity   229

■ Integrity of brain function   229

■ Links to consciousness   230

■ Future directions   232

THE PRECEDING 10 CHAPTERS HAVE, I hope, given you some insight into the core subject matter of neuropsychology. In this final chapter I want to take the opportunity to stand back from the research and case studies that I have described, and give brief consideration to the main ideas that emerge from our review of the material, the current direction of research, and issues that neuropsychology will have to address in the future.

Two broad approaches

As we saw in Chapter 1, neuropsychology is an evolving subject area that can confidently draw on at least 100 years' worth of reasonably sound scientific research, and double that if the (more dubious) enterprises of writers and researchers from the 19th century are included. Neuropsychology is not a unitary discipline, and I also reviewed the differing approaches of cognitive and clinical neuropsychologists. I stated at the time that both approaches merited our attention and I hope that I have, by now, persuaded you that this is indeed the case.

Localisation/modularity

Early in the book I also introduced the 'localisation of function' debate, which neuropsychology has grappled with (yet never fully resolved) throughout its existence. No sooner do we think we have identified the anatomical location(s) of a particular psychological function than a case study or imaging project is published throwing the issue into doubt once again. A heuristic answer can be found in Fodor's concept of modularity, exploited so effectively by cognitive neuropsychologists in their attempts to understand (for example) anomia, which I reviewed in Chapter 6. Modularity is ultimately an endorsement of localisation, but 'function' now means something quite different to the 'faculties' of the phrenologists, or even the psychological functions that interested Lashley. Modules are 'dedicated' to dealing with a very specific type of information in a slavish (and probably) fixed manner. Thus many modules collaborate even in an apparently simple process such as naming a *viewed* object, and different modules will be involved in identifying and naming the same object if it is *described in speech*.

I have presented quite detailed evidence in support of modularity in Chapters 6, 7 and 8, and further support can be garnered from the various examples I provide of the selective effects (on psychological functions) of localised brain damage. Even so, the available evidence sometimes seems to undermine unconditional support for it. For example, the precise location (or boundaries) of Wernicke's area are still a matter of some debate (see Chapter 6), and some neuropsychologists have questioned the validity of assuming that specific modules can (ever) be anatomically localised (e.g. Caramazza, 1984), or at least need occupy identical locations in different individuals.

Laterality/plasticity

To muddy the waters still further, the work on lateralisation (Chapter 3) raises the possibility that the left and right hemispheres may be functionally organised along rather different lines – the left hemisphere operating in a predominantly analytic (modular) way and the right operating in a more holistic way. All these ideas must be tempered by observations of individuals who have incurred extensive brain damage, especially early in life. Studies of cortical plasticity (introduced in Chapter 4) show that a significant amount of cortical rewiring may take place following localised damage or if the patterns of sensory input change for some reason (such as limb amputation). The literature also reveals several case studies of children who have had large areas of cortex removed, either in order to remove diseased tissue, or as a result of trauma or accident, and who, after a suitable period of convalescence and rehabilitation, seem to have regained much (or all) lost function.

Such plastic changes are not, however, restricted to children (although scope for change may be greatest here). Functional cortical rewiring can also be observed in adult humans, as I described in Chapter 4. It may also be worth recalling at this point the case of the adult split-brain patient described by Gazzaniga (see Chapter 3), who developed the ability to speak simple words 'with his right hemisphere' 13 years after split-brain surgery.

Integrity of brain function

In Chapter 5 I reviewed the role of different brain regions in movement. Detailed coverage of this material is, I think, important in view of the fact that almost all 'behaviour' involves movement, and even thinking passively about possible future actions activates many of the cortical regions that become active prior to and during actual movement. Brain control of movement is complicated, but our understanding of it continues to develop rapidly.

Chapter 5 illustrates a theme that, I hope, also permeates other parts of the book: namely the *integrity* or *coherence* of brain function. For instance, whereas earlier neuropsychologists drew a sharp distinction between pyramidal and extra-pyramidal motor systems, present understanding shows how 'integrated' the two actually are – how they collaborate (to the point at which the names seem almost irrelevant) to bring about the apparently effortless skills of the touch typist or Olympic gymnast. If further evidence of the integrity of brain function were required, then you need look no further than the split-brain studies reported in Chapter 3. Even when the corpus callosum is completely lesioned, split-brain patients do not routinely report being troubled by competing influences of their two hemispheres (although anecdotal reports sometimes hint at this).

Chapter 5 also undermines a key idea about motor function, sometimes attributed to the famous Russian neuropsychologist Luria, that cortical control of movement is solely the domain of the frontal lobes ('the motor unit' to borrow Luria's own term). Not only do a proportion of pyramidal neurons controlling motor output emanate from the parietal lobes rather than the motor strip, but we can also associate at least one form of the movement disorder, apraxia (the ideational form), with damage to the left parietal lobe, where, it has been suggested, memories for particular motor routines may be stored, and, in the case of this disorder, become lost, corrupted or inaccessible.

The integrity and coherence of brain function is, I hope, further illustrated in Chapters 6, 7 and 8. Although psycholinguistics has, to some extent, followed its own agenda, memory and perception have long held centre stage for cognitive psychologists, and in these chapters I have tried to show how our understanding of these domains can be positively enhanced by an appreciation of parallel neuropsychological research – especially that involving clinical cases of brain damage, and, more recently, the application of in-vivo scanning procedures to normal individuals. (These techniques were covered in some detail in Chapter 2.) Neuropsychological research, for example, generally supports the psychological approaches to subdividing different types of memory, and it strongly endorses modularity in both language and visual perception. On the other hand, 'coherence' is exemplified by the strong 'intuitive' sense that memory, perception and language work as integrated systems. Their 'modularity' only becomes apparent when specific parts of the system are damaged or disordered.

Links to consciousness

Chapters 9 and 10 take us on to higher ground. Attention and executive function are both somewhat abstract concepts and therefore harder to define than memory or language. Both, as it turns out, are also inextricably linked, though in different ways, to consciousness. A detailed review of this concept is beyond the remit of an introductory text in neuropsychology. However, one cannot help but feel that neuropsychology has much to offer in the quest to unravel the structure of consciousness, if only through consideration of neurological disorders that impair its normal operations. In Chapter 9 I tried to show how attentional mechanisms can operate at both conscious and unconscious levels, and that (in large part) similar brain regions are involved, except that for conscious attentional control the pathway between the frontal cortex and thalamus comes into play. I also tried to show how cortical damage in the parietal lobes can affect our ability to redirect attention. With uni-lateral damage (particularly on the right) the neglect syndrome is sometimes seen. The individual with uni-lateral neglect is not blind for half of their visual field, just indifferent to it, typically failing to redirect attention to it. With bi-lateral parietal damage, Balint's syndrome, an even more severe form of attentional disorder may develop. The Balint's patient has lost the ability to redirect their attention to any part of their visual field voluntarily, seeming to fixate on particular discrete components of a visual display in an involuntary manner. In each condition, conscious experience is profoundly compromised (in different ways) as a result of parietal damage.

In the same chapter, I also tried to emphasise the overlap between 'deliberate' (sustained) attentional processes and the central executive component of working memory. The anatomical location of this is known to be in the dorsolateral pre-frontal cortex (DLPFC), and I concluded the chapter with a synopsis of Laberge's model, which, you might recall, also implicates these same frontal regions as necessary in directing sustained attention to visual stimuli. However, even when our 'attentional spotlight' is directed towards one particular 'thing' (such as an object in, or area of, our visual field), personal experience attests to the ease with which we can be distracted by other stimuli/events, and I used the term 'attentional capture' in Chapter 9 to describe this process. It reminds us that the 'grip' that consciousness can impose is relative rather than absolute.

In Chapter 10 I described the brain's involvement in three different aspects of executive function. Again, the pivotal role of different regions of the frontal lobes in coordinating executive control is apparent. In addition to the DLPFC's contribution to various aspects of memory and attention, the medial and orbital regions seem to play critical roles in the regulation of socially appropriate and emotionally driven behaviour, especially through the process of inhibiting inappropriate actions. Damage to these regions appears somehow to impair conscious control processes and decision making, giving rise to various characteristic features of the 'dysexecutive' syndrome. The inability to keep a goal in mind, stimulus-driven behaviour, perseveration, in addition to various manifestations of short-term memory impairment, may all be apparent.

Several lines of evidence implicate the anterior cingulate (and its connections with other frontal areas including the DLPFC) in situations where some sort of 'override' command is required to bring about appropriate behaviour. In 'tick-over' mode this executive system may be quiet, with well-learned behavioural routines being run off sequentially as per Norman and Shallice's 'contention scheduling' and 'schema control units' (see my example of decorating in Chapter 10). The supervisory attentional system need only come into play if there is a need to interrupt the ongoing activities for some reason. That we all occasionally suffer lapses in our SAS is illustrated by the common experience of setting out along a familiar route knowing that on this particular occasion we intend to break our journey mid-way for some purpose, and then only realising as we get to our ultimate destination that we entirely forgot to make the mid-way detour that we had planned! This manifestation of 'inattention' is an occasional experience for most of us, but becomes commonplace in people with frontal damage. Incidentally, it is also seen in some individuals carrying a diagnosis of schizophrenia. Other examples of neuropsychological phenomena that may, in due course, inform our understanding of consciousness include anterograde amnesia, agnosia and Capgras syndrome.

Another 'take-home' message of this book is that a great deal of information processing takes place without conscious awareness, or, perhaps I had better say, without troubling the highest 'executive' processing components of consciousness. This realisation often comes as something of a surprise to us, inclined as we are to think of ourselves as 'sentient' beings with free will and our actions shaped by conscious rational decisions. The reality may be rather different, as we have seen throughout the book. Consider for instance movement control: clearly choice of action *can* be deliberate (as in my conscious decision to get out of my seat and look out of my office window), but it very often is not. Indeed, many skilled actions can be performed too quickly for conscious control to be involved. These are routines, in effect, 'run off' by what we used to call the extra-pyramidal system and in particular the cerebellum and PMC. When there is damage to these structures and true conscious control has to take over, we see how behaviourally impaired individuals are (see Chapter 5). The same point can be made in respect of spoken language (see Chapter 6). The ability to correct (so rapidly) errors that occur in speech is a further indication of the subtle and complex information processing that takes place without troubling conscious processes. I have provided further examples of non-conscious information processing in my consideration of research on selective attention, priming and implicit memory.

Future directions

What then lies ahead for students of neuropsychology? As we have seen, an ongoing development is in-vivo imaging, but these procedures are currently quite restrictive (see Chapter 2). In the future, greater flexibility, perhaps through telemetry (i.e. remote recording as a person walks around rather than as they lie prone in a scanner) may be possible. A greater use of combined procedures

– for example, fMRI with ERP – also offers significant advantages (some of which we saw in Chapters 9 and 10). In the clinical domain, we will see much more work on recovery of function, either through a greater understanding of the mechanisms of neuronal plasticity (and how we can influence it), or through the development of mechanical or computational aids that 'interact' with the nervous system to bring about a functional recovery following damage or disease. This work is ongoing, and is likely, in due course, to lead to effective treatments for various diseases of the nervous system, such as dementia, vascular disease and so on, which are currently often untreatable and invariably incurable.

However, the greatest challenge for neuropsychology is to continue to make meaningful contributions towards unravelling brain-behaviour relations. It has made excellent progress so far, and the future looks every bit as promising.

A primer of nervous system structure and function

■ Introduction   236

■ Neurons and glia   237
  Nerve impulses and synaptic transmission   238
  Developmental and ageing aspects   242

■ Dividing up the nervous system   243

■ The central nervous system   244
  The spinal cord   244
  The brainstem   244
  The midbrain   245
  The basal ganglia and limbic system   246

■ The cortex   246
  Sensory, motor and association cortex   249

■ The lobes of the cortex   249
  Frontal lobes   249
  Parietal lobes   250
  Occipital lobes   250
  Temporal lobes   250

■ Summary   251

Introduction

Almost all the textbooks mentioned in the Preface (and listed in the 'Further reading' section after this Appendix), and many others besides, provide detailed illustrated accounts of the 'workings' of the mammalian nervous system. Rather than reiterate this material in full here, I aim to provide the minimum grounding to help contextualise the material covered in the preceding 11 chapters, and I have pitched this appendix at a level to suit readers not already familiar with nervous system structure and function. If what follows whets your appetite to learn more about the brain, spinal cord and other components of the nervous system, so much the better. If, on the other hand, you are approaching this appendix with some trepidation, having read the Preface and promptly by-passed Chapters 1 to 11, remember that many important ideas in neuropsychology pre-date our current level of understanding of brain physiology. Thus, an encyclopaedic knowledge of the nervous system is not a prerequisite for the neuropsychologist, although a basic understanding probably is.

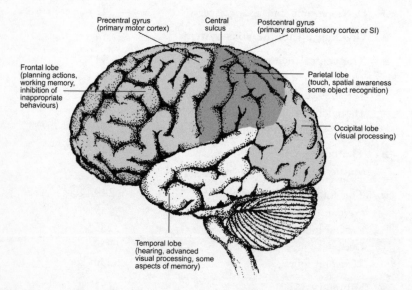

FIGURE A1 The lobes of the cortex

The anatomical locations (and some functional specialisms) of the four cortical lobes are indicated.

We know that, like other parts of the nervous system, the brain and spinal cord are made up of different types of component nerve cell, so a starting point is to learn how these work and communicate with each other. Knowing some of the basic terminology about the layout of the nervous system will also be advantageous. Inevitably, our prime interest is the brain; a structure that has been described as the most complicated known to man! It therefore makes sense to divide it up into separate regions, each of which will be briefly considered in turn. Since neuropsychology is usually concerned with functions and operations that have cortical origins, the cortex clearly deserves special consideration. This structure is the outer surface of the brain, and, in evolutionary terms, the most recently developed region. It too is usually divided up, first, in terms of left or right side, and then, in relation to the bones of the skull, into lobes. As you will see, cortical lobes can also be distinguished in terms of the psychological functions they mediate (see Fig. A1).

Neurons and glia

Our entire nervous system is made up of two fundamentally different classes of cell; neurons and glial cells (see Fig. A2). Neurons are responsible for conveying nerve impulses around the nervous system, and communicating, via synaptic transmission, with other neurons, or in the periphery, with muscles. Neurons themselves do not move, but they can convey nerve impulses along their length very efficiently and quickly (see Fig. A3).

Although no one has ever actually counted them, it is estimated that the adult human brain contains at least 10,000,000,000,000 neurons, and glial cells (sometimes called neuroglia, or just glia) are thought to outnumber neurons 10-to-1! They play a range of vital supporting roles but are not directly involved in either conveying nerve impulses or in synaptic transmission. For example, in the central nervous system one type of glial cell (known as an oligodendrocyte) literally wraps itself around the 'cable' part of a neuron (the axon), rather like a carpet is wrapped round a central cardboard tube, to provide a form of insulation known as a myelin sheath. (Schwann cells do a similar job in the peripheral nervous system.) Another type of glial cell (known as microglia) *can* move around the nervous system, and they act rather like vacuum cleaners, removing (and digesting) dead or damaged tissue, and filling what would otherwise be empty space with scar tissue. Astrocytes surround blood vessels in the brain, and are involved in regulating the transfer of substances (glucose, oxygen, hormones and potentially harmful toxins) between blood and brain.

As with glial cells, there are a variety of different types of neuron, some of which are found throughout the nervous system, and others that are only found in very discrete locations. For example, amacrine cells are found only in

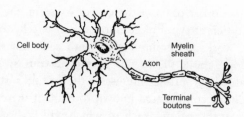

a) The principal structures or regions of a motor neuron

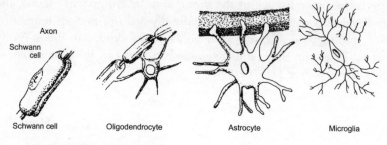

b) A Schwann cell & three types of glial cell

FIGURE A2   A neuron (a) and glia (b)

Not all neurons look like the one shown (a), but all have a cell body, an axon (that usually branches) and terminal boutons. This neuron is myelinated, and several dendrites are apparent as processes (outgrowths) of the cell body. A Schwann cell and three types of glial cell are illustrated. See the text for an explanation of their principal functions.

the retina, whereas interneurons are widespread throughout the brain and spinal cord. However, because most neurons carry nerve impulses and engage in synaptic transmission, it is helpful (though not entirely accurate) to think of them as all working in the same way.

Nerve impulses and synaptic transmission

Most of the physiological psychology textbooks mentioned in general further reading include elegant descriptions of these processes, and the interested reader should consult these sources for detailed information. However, the points summarised in Boxes A1 and A2 may help provide a clearer idea of the basics of both 'within' and 'between' neuron communication. When considering these points remember that nerve impulses can travel the length of your body (2 metres or so) within about 20 msec, and that synaptic transmission can occur in an even shorter period of time. So, although my account of the processes may seem long-winded, they actually happen incredibly quickly. Remember too that scientists estimate that

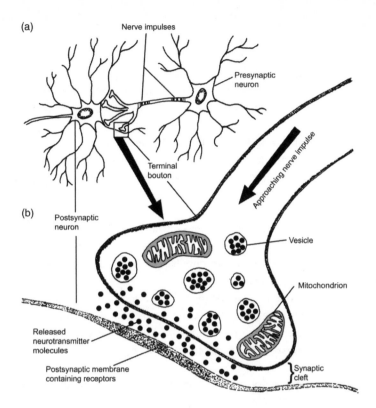

FIGURE A3 A neuron conveying a volley of nerve impulses, and a schematic synapse

(a) You wouldn't actually 'see' the nerve impulses but they could be detected with the appropriate recording equipment.

(b) When nerve impulses arrive in the terminal bouton region, a sequence of events is triggered culminating in the release of neurotransmitter into the synaptic cleft.

the average central nervous system neuron (not that any such thing really exists) probably receives several thousand converging inputs, and can in turn influence about the same number of neurons (i.e. several thousand) via its dividing axon (**divergence**). For some neurons whose role is to control the activity levels of others, the degree of divergence is such that a single neuron may synaptically influence at least 0.25 million other neurons!

See Fig. A3 for an illustration of an active neuron and a schematic synapse, and Fig. A4 for an illustration of 'summation' of excitatory and inhibitory influences on a receiving (post-synaptic) neuron.

Box A1: Nerve impulses

- Think of nerve impulses as tiny electrical 'blips' that travel along the surface of the cable part (the axon) of neurons. Most are formed at the axon hillock – a region where the cell body 'becomes' the axon.

- A neuron is able to generate its own nerve impulses (when stimulated), and once they are formed they travel at a fixed speed and amplitude (size) in a given neuron, though speed and size of nerve impulse may vary between neurons.

- In the human nervous system, large myelinated neurons can convey nerve impulses at over 100 metres per second; small diameter non-myelinated neurons may propagate nerve impulses at less than 1 metre per second.

- Nerve impulses tend to occur in volleys (bursts) rather than alone. Thus a few nerve impulses may indicate a weak stimulus; more will signal a strong stimulus. Frequency coding, as this is known, appears to be a general feature of nervous system functioning.

- Nerve impulses conform to the 'all or none' law, meaning they either occur fully or not at all. You cannot have a partial action potential.

- When a nerve impulse is at a particular point along an axon, its presence 'excites' the region of axon just in front of it, effectively causing the impulse to move on to the next region of axon. This is analogous to a 'domino' effect where a falling domino in one position causes the domino next to it to fall, and so on. The main difference is that, in neurons, 'fallen' dominoes quickly pick themselves up ready to be knocked down again by the next passing nerve impulse!

- A variety of factors can influence a neuron and determine whether or not it produces nerve impulses, but in the brain and spinal cord the most likely influence is from other neurons via synaptic transmission.

Box A2: Synaptic transmission

- Action potentials arriving at the terminal bouton region of a neuron induce the neuron to discharge chemical messengers (called neuro-transmitters) into the space between it and the 'receiving' neuron. This narrow gap is called the synaptic cleft, and it contains extra-cellular fluid (water with ions and enzymes).

- Neurotransmitters are stored ready for release in tiny sacks called vesicles, present in the terminal bouton region of neurons. Neurons manufacture their own neurotransmitters from the breakdown products of food.

- There are many different neurotransmitters but the vast majority of synapses are mediated by one (or more) of a core group of about 10, which includes acetylcholine (ACH), noradrenaline (NA), serotonin (5HT), dopamine (DA), gamma amino butyric acid (GABA) and glutamate (GLU).

- Some released molecules of neurotransmitter find their way to particular receptor sites on the surface of the receiving neuron into which they fit (like a key in a lock).

- Their presence in the receptor can cause the receiving neuron to become excited, making it more likely to generate its own nerve impulses (an excitatory synapse).

- At other synapses, a neurotransmitter may have the opposite effect, causing the receiving neuron to become less excited, reducing the like-lihood of it producing action potentials (an inhibitory synapse).

- Some neurotransmitters (such as GLU) are exclusively excitatory. Others such as GABA are exclusively inhibitory (see Fig. A4).

- Some neurotransmitters can be excitatory at certain synapses and inhibitory at others. Such opposite effects are possible because there are different receptor types for some neurotransmitters. For example, ACH has an excitatory influence at so-called nicotinic ACH receptors and an inhibitory influence at muscarinic ACH receptors.

- The action of a neurotransmitter is quickly terminated either by it being broken down by enzymes present in the cleft, or by being pumped back into the terminal bouton of the sending neuron (a process called re-uptake).

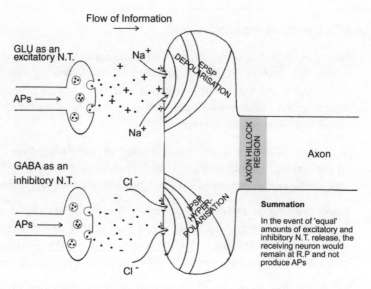

FIGURE A4 The convergence of an excitatory and inhibitory input on to a receiving neuron

A grossly simplified illustration of this fundamental nervous system process. Two neurons converge on a single 'receiving' neuron. One releases the excitatory neurotransmitter (GLU) the other releases the inhibitory neurotransmitter (GABA). Whether or not the receiving neuron fires will depend on the relative influencing of the two competing inputs.

Developmental and ageing aspects

Where do neurons and glia come from and how do they end up where they are? The answer to the first question is straightforward. Like all cells in our body, neurons and glia are the products of cell division, ultimately traceable back to the single fertilised egg which begins to divide shortly after conception. The second part of the question is, with a few exceptions, currently unanswerable, except that, during development, cells migrate (move), divide, and in certain cases selectively die. The neurons and glia remaining are our nervous system!

One thing we can be sure of is that the maximum number of neurons an individual ever has reaches a peak relatively early in life, and there is little evidence of further neuron proliferation after the age of two. The fact that many neurons are already present explains (in part) why a new-born baby's head is large in comparison with the rest of its body.

The number of neurons remains static throughout childhood then begins to decline in adolescence. It has been estimated that from the age of 15 or so onwards, humans lose about 15,000 neurons every day, which are not replaced! This works out to about 600 per hour or 10 per minute! This apparently alarming figure must be set alongside the vast number we start off with. If you consider a lifespan of 75 years, and use the figures I have given, you will find that the loss of neurons at age 75 is no more than 3% of the total, assuming a normal healthy life. Accelerated cell loss is, of course, a feature of several neurological disorders including Alzheimer's and Parkinson's diseases.

Unlike neurons, glial cells do increase in number throughout childhood and adolescence, and even in adulthood. In the corpus callosum (a structure in the middle of the brain that I discuss in Chapter 3), the amount of myelination increases (i.e. more oligodendrocytes form myelin sheaths) annually, with the structure only reaching full maturity at about 18 years. Incidentally, on a more sinister note, most brain tumours arise as a result of uncontrolled division of glial cells, not neurons.

Before we leave the issue of lifespan changes, it is important to realise that for a nervous system to work effectively, it is not just the number of neurons that is important, but how they interconnect with each other. We know that neurons communicate through (predominantly) chemical synapses. Although the absolute number of neurons declines with age from adolescence onwards, the number of connections or synapses between neurons *can* increase, and certainly does not necessarily follow the declining neuron count. When there is brain damage, loss of cells may be compensated for by the formation of new synapses (called synaptogenesis). In Parkinson's disease (discussed in Chapter 5), there is progressive loss of a particular type of neuron, but it is not until about three-quarters of these cells have died that the characteristic symptoms of tremor and rigidity appear. Researchers think that in the period of disease prior to symptom onset, the remaining healthy cells continually form new synapses on to target cells, in effect replacing the inputs from the neurons that have died.

Dividing up the nervous system

Because the nervous system stretches from the top of your head to the tip of your toes, it makes sense to divide it up into more manageable chunks. One important distinction is between the central (CNS) and peripheral nervous system (PNS). For mammals, the CNS is the brain and spinal cord, and the PNS is everything else. Sometimes it is useful to further subdivide the peripheral nervous system into the branch in which neurons carry nerve impulses to voluntary muscles (i.e. ones you can consciously control), and the branch carrying nerve impulses to muscles such as the heart and gut, which are not under voluntary control. The former is referred to as the skeletal nervous system and the latter as the autonomic nervous system (ANS).

Another way of subdividing the nervous system is to take into account the direction of nerve impulses conveyed along particular neurons. Afferent (or sensory) neurons carry nerve impulses towards the brain. Efferent (or motor) neurons carry impulses from the brain outward towards muscles.

A further useful distinction differentiates neurons with and without myelin sheaths. The sheath (which actually only covers the axon part of the neuron), dramatically improves speed of conduction, and the myelin gives these neurons a characteristic pinky-white appearance; hence the term white matter. Unmyelinated neurons convey action potentials much more slowly, and have a pinky-grey appearance. So too do cell bodies, giving rise to the term grey matter.

Quite often, cell bodies of neurons will be clumped together in one location. (They don't actually touch one another but lie in close proximity to each other.) These clumps are known as ganglia or nuclei. Similarly, the cable parts of neurons (the axons) often run side-by-side from one part of the nervous system to another. Once again, they don't actually merge into a single structure, but they do lie next to each other. Bundles of axons are known as tracts or nerves. It is important to remember just how small and densely packed axons can be. The human optic nerve is made up exclusively of myelinated axons, being about the same diameter as a piece of cooked spaghetti. Yet it comprises axons of over 2 million individual retinal cells conveying information in the form of nerve impulses from the retina into the brain.

The central nervous system

In mammals, the central nervous system (CNS) includes all nerve tissue that is encased in bone. Although neuropsychology is often preoccupied with the cortex and its functions, it is important to realise that the cortex itself is only one part of the brain, and many other brain structures in addition to 'medial' cortex are highlighted in Fig. A5. We will consider the cortex shortly, but for completeness, we will briefly consider other elements of the CNS too.

The spinal cord

The spinal cord nestles within the vertebrae, and is made up of both grey and white matter. The grey matter comprises, for the most part, unmyelinated interneurons. The white matter surrounds the central grey matter, and comprises vast tracts of myelinated axons conveying both afferent and efferent information. Some of these run the entire length of the spinal cord although any given neuron only carries information in one direction.

The brainstem

This comprises the medulla, pons and cerebellum. The medulla is the lowest region of the brain, and, in addition to the pathways from the spinal cord,

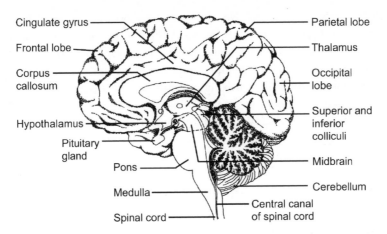

FIGURE A5 A medial sagittal view of the adult human brain

The dotted lines represent the anatomical positions of the notional divisions between the hindbrain, midbrain and forebrain. Clearly, the latter has evolved at the expense of the former two regions. (See text for detailed information.)

contains a series of regions that control basic vegetative processes such as respiration, heart rate and certain reflexes. Brain death is assessed by the absence of electrical activity in this lowest region of the brain.

The pons lies just above the medulla on the front of the brainstem. It is the main link between the cerebellum and the rest of the brain. It also has a role in certain aspects of both visual and auditory processing, and, among other things, helps to coordinate eye movements in relation to balance.

The cerebellum is the large 'walnut' like structure on the back part of the brainstem roughly at the level of the ears. Amongst other functions, this structure is concerned with the learning and control of skilled movements, particularly those 'enacted' through time: in other words, skills such as playing a piano, or performing some complex gymnastic routine, in which the sequence of controlling muscles has to be precisely coordinated. People who have incurred damage to their cerebellum often appear drunk, even to the point of slurring their speech, which after all, depends on the coordination (in time) of muscles in the throat and mouth (see Chapter 5).

The midbrain

Here, we find the thalamus, the hypothalamus, and four little bumps on the back of the brain stem above the cerebellum. The bottom two (the inferior colliculi) are concerned with auditory processing, and especially in turning the head towards an auditory stimulus. The top two (the superior colliculi) do a similar job, but for visual processing (see Chapter 9).

The hypothalamus is involved in controlling behaviours that help the body maintain an equilibrium or satisfy its needs. It will be no surprise to learn that it is the nerve centre (no pun intended) for the control of eating, drinking and temperature regulation. It also includes control regions for the autonomic nervous system, and, in collaboration with the pituitary gland, helps to coordinate much of the endocrine (hormone) system.

The thalamus is a relay station for sensory information coming into the brain, and for much motor output leaving it. By relay station, I mean that sensory information (from a particular modality such as vision) enters the thalamus, or more specifically a particular nucleus of it, where it may undergo some processing, before being sent on to the cortex for further detailed analysis.

The basal ganglia and limbic system

Two other systems of neurons need mention at this point. The basal ganglia (see Chapter 5) comprise not one but several interconnected structures (the caudate, putamen, globus pallidus and substantia nigra). While it is not necessary to remember their names, it is helpful to have an idea of how this network of structures collectively helps to control movement. The basal ganglia do not, for example, initiate or terminate movement in isolation: rather, in combination with the motor cortex, they determine which possible actions actually get put into effect, by permitting some and inhibiting others. Researchers now think that the basal ganglia serve as a sort of gatekeeper for motor plans that originate in the cortex, and damage to any of the component structures (or the pathways that interconnect them) will impair the coordination or control of movement.

The limbic system also comprises several different interconnected structures, including the hippocampus, amygdala, septum and hypothalamus. It is, in certain respects, the *emotional* equivalent of the *motor* basal ganglia: in other words, activity in the limbic system adds emotional tone (fear, anger, pleasure) to behaviour. Like the basal ganglia, the limbic system seems not to work in isolation, but rather in collaboration with both lower (brainstem) and higher (cortical) brain centres. Damage or abnormal functioning in the limbic system is associated with inappropriate emotional responding, and may be related to certain psychiatric disorders including schizophrenia, depression and anxiety. Both of these systems are conventionally regarded as forebrain structures.

The cortex

When you look at an intact human brain, you can see the brain stem, the cerebellum and cortex. The cortex seems to cover much of the rest of the brain, although it is actually a forebrain (front) structure. It has a bumpy, folded appearance. The bumps are called gyri (singular: gyrus), and the folds or indents are called sulci (singular: sulcus). Gyri and sulci dramatically increase the surface area of the cortex. In fact, about two-thirds of cortical tissue is hidden in these folds. If you could flatten out the human cortex, it would cover a square measuring about 50 cm × 50 cm.

Cortex means bark and it is a very apt term in this case, for the cortex is only a few millimetres thick. Its pinky grey appearance tells us that it is made up primarily of cell bodies (remember cell bodies do not have myelin sheaths), which are usually arranged in a series of between four and six layers parallel to the surface. Immediately underneath, the appearance changes to white, indicating vast tracts of myelinated neuron axons conveying information to and from the cortex (via the thalamus), and between one cortical region and another.

Like many other brain structures the cortex is often described as being 'bi-laterally symmetrical', which means that the left and right sides are like mirror images of each other. However, as I mention in Chapter 3, this is only approx-imately true, and several important anatomical distinctions between left and right side are apparent on closer inspection. The two sides of the cortex are some-times referred to as hemispheres, and again the term is apt: taken as a whole, the cortex looks a little like a partly inflated ball. However, it is important to

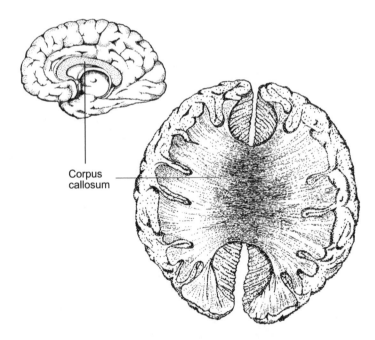

Corpus
callosum

FIGURE A6 The corpus callosum
(See text for details.)

note that strictly speaking each hemisphere actually contains many subcortical structures as well.

The hemispheres are connected to each other by a number of pathways, of which the largest by far is the corpus callosum (see Fig. A6). This structure is actually a massive band of axons running from one side of the cortex to the other. Although it is only about 10 cm long and no more than 1 cm in thickness, it comprises well over 200,000,000 myelinated axons. The relative isolation of the two hemispheres is best demonstrated by the observation that it is possible to insert a thin probe at any point along the longitudinal fissure (which separates them) and the first thing you would touch is the corpus callosum about 2 to 3 cm down.

I mentioned earlier that the cortex itself is made up primarily of cell bodies, and one of the largest and most prominent types of cortical cell is the so-called pyramidal cell (see Fig. A7). This type of neuron has a very extensive branch-like structure. The branches are known as dendrites, and are the part of the neuron most likely to receive inputs from other neurons. Under a microscope

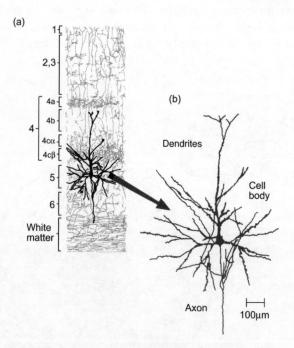

FIGURE A7 The layers of the cortex and a pyramidal neuron

Most regions of cortex are laminated perpendicular to the surface. Neuroanatomists identify six layers. In this figure, one pyramidal neuron has been highlighted. It has an extensive dendritic structure that permeates several cortical layers, a centrally located cell body, and an axon, which descends and ultimately leaves the cortex via layer six. (Adapted from Rosenzweig et al., 1999.)

these pyramidal cells look a little like Christmas trees, with the top branches corresponding to dendrites, and the lower broader part comprising a cell body and further sideways pointing dendrites. The stem and roots of the tree would be the axon, which leaves the cortex to form a strand of white matter. Pyramidal cells are oriented at 90 degrees to the surface of the cortex, and clusters of these cells are sometimes called columns. Indeed, a regular feature of cortical organisation is its 'so-called' column structure.

Sensory, motor and association cortex

Another way of distinguishing between different parts of the cortex has, historically, been according to function. Some (discrete) cortical regions clearly have primary sensory or motor responsibilities (for example Brodmann's areas 1, 2, 3a and b constitute the primary somatosensory cortex (see Chapter 4), and Brodmann's area 4 is the primary motor strip (see Chapter 5)). Other (more extensive) regions don't have primary sensory or motor responsibilities, and the term 'association cortex' has been used for many years as a 'catch-all' for these cortical areas. Yet research shows that relatively little associating (or combining) of sensory input actually takes place here. Rather, much association cortex is involved in what amounts to a more elaborate (or 'higher-order') processing of information. For example, the primary visual cortex deals with sensory registration, while regions of visual association cortex are concerned (among other things) with colour perception, object recognition and movement (see Chapter 8).

The lobes of the cortex

Another way of identifying cortical regions is in relation to the skull bones that they lie under. We differentiate between four lobes, or eight if you include both hemispheres (see Fig. A1). Not only can the lobes be distinguished by their anatomical location, they also separate to some extent in terms of the psychological processes that they are concerned with.

Frontal lobes

If you think of the human brain as looking a little like a boxing glove from the side, then the frontal lobes comprise the part of the glove that the fingers would occupy. They comprise more than 30% of the entire complement of cortical brain cells, and are the part of the cortex that is more highly developed in humans than other primates. At one time, the main function of these lobes was thought to be that of controlling movement. However, as we have learned more about them it has become clear that, in addition to their key role in movement, they are also involved in planning, generating ideas, language, working memory and personality (see Chapter 10). I describe the role of the frontal lobes in movement in Chapter 5.

Parietal lobes

The parietal lobes are located immediately behind the frontal lobes, and are separated from them by the central sulcus, which is a deep groove running across the top of the brain (roughly from ear to ear but by no means in a straight line). These lobes have important sensory functions, especially in relation to touch and vision, which I describe in some detail in Chapters 4 and 8, and they are also critical for attention (see Chapter 9).

The first strip of parietal lobe (the furthest forward gyrus) is the primary somatosensory cortex (see above). Neurons here respond to touch sensation from very distinct body regions, and the entire body is 'mapped' on to this cortical strip. For example, touch receptors in your right hand will send nerve impulses that end up in your left primary somatosensory strip. Different adjacent columns of neurons here will respond to input from each finger (and each part of each finger!). Further back (i.e. further away from the central sulcus), more posterior regions of parietal lobe are involved in more 'integrative' sensory functions, linking, for example, touch with visual information or with memory. Damage here can lead to a disorder known as astereognosis, which is marked by the inability to recognise objects by touch. The parietal lobes are also involved in visuo-spatial processing, some aspects of language and attention.

Occipital lobes

The left and right occipital lobes are tucked behind and underneath the parietal lobes at the back of the cortex and they deal with visual input. Some areas are concerned with the perception of form, others with movement and still others with colour. I describe some of these functions in Chapter 8. Damage here almost always results in some impairment to vision, and can lead to cortical blindness. For example, extensive damage to just the right occipital lobe will result in blindness in the left visual field (everything to the left of centre as you look straight ahead).

Temporal lobes

In my boxing glove analogy, the temporal lobe would be the thumb (except you have one on each side). The front part of this lobe is separated from the frontal lobe (which it lies to the side of), but the rear (posterior) sections are bounded by the parietal and occipital lobes, and the actual boundaries are not clearly defined by sulci.

The upper region of the temporal lobe is the primary auditory cortex (Heschl's gyrus), input coming mainly from the ear on the opposite side of the body. On the left side, adjacent regions, especially behind the primary auditory cortex, are involved in the recognition of language sounds. On the right side, the equivalent regions are involved in interpreting non-verbal speech sounds such as tone, rhythm and emotion.

However, the temporal lobes are not just concerned with auditory processing. Lower (inferior) regions for example are involved in visual object recognition. In general, cells towards the front of the temporal lobes respond only to very specific visual stimuli such as faces, or types of animal, suggesting that stored representations (memories) of items may be located here. I consider some of the evidence in support of this idea in Chapter 8.

Summary

The brain, like other parts of the nervous system, is made up of neurons and glial cells, although neurons alone carry nerve impulses around the nervous system. To begin to understand how the brain works, it makes sense to divide it up, and the principal component parts of the hindbrain, midbrain and forebrain have been introduced. It is also helpful to divide up the cortex in terms of both the anatomical location of the lobes and their diverse functions.

No matter how many times I describe the brain to students, I still marvel at the sheer complexity of it, and I hope you share my sense of wonder. I am also amazed that such a complicated structure goes wrong so infrequently. However, when brain damage, disorder or disease does occur, it can sometimes shed considerable light on the functioning of the normal intact brain.

Further reading

Chapter 1: The beginnings of neuropsychology

Fischbach, G.D. (1992). Mind and brain. *Scientific American*, *267(3)*, 48–57.
Fodor, J.A. (1985). Precis of the modularity of mind (with commentaries). *Behavioural and Brain Sciences*, 8, 1–42.

Chapter 2: Methods in neuropsychology

Raichle, M.E. (1994). Visualising the mind. *Scientific American*, *270*, 58–64.
Wickelgren, I. (1997). Getting a grasp on working memory. *Science*, 275, 1580–1582.

Chapter 3: Lateralisation

Gazzaniga, M.S. (1995). Principles of human brain organisation derived from split-brain studies. *Neuron*, *14*, 217–228.
Hellige, J.B. (1990). Hemispheric asymmetry. *Annual Review of Psychology*, *41*, 55–80.

Chapter 4: Somatosensation

Mogilner, A., et al. (1993). Somatosensory cortical plasticity in adult humans revealed by magnetoencephalography. *Proceedings of National Academy of Science*, 90, 3593–3597.

Weinberger, N.M. (1995). Dynamic regulation of receptive fields and maps in the adult sensory cortex. *Annual Review of Neuroscience*, 18, 129–158.

Chapter 5: Motor control and movement disorders

Catalan, M.J., Honda, M., Weekes, R.A., Cohen, L.G., & Hallet, M. (1998). The functional neuroanatomy of simple and complex sequential finger movements: A PET study. *Brain*, 121, 253–264.

Saxena, S., Brody, A.L., Schwartz, J.M., & Baxter, L.R. (1998). Neuro-imaging and frontal subcortical circuitry in obsessive-compulsive disorder. *British Journal of Psychiatry*, 173 (suppl. 35), 26–37.

Wichmann, T., & Delong, M.R. (1996). Functional and pathophysiological models of the basal ganglia. *Current Opinion in Neurobiology*, 6, 751–758.

Youdim, M.B.H., & Riederer, P. (1997). Understanding Parkinson's disease. *Scientific American*, 276, 52–59.

Chapter 6: Language and the brain

Binder, J.R., Frost, J.A., Hammeke, T.A., Cox, R.M., Rao, S.M., & Prieto, T. (1997). Human brain language areas identified by functional magnetic resonance imaging. *Journal of Neuroscience*, 17, 353–362.

Chertkow, H., & Murtha, S. (1997). PET activation and language. *Clinical Neuroscience*, 4, 78–86.

Dronkers, N.F., Redfern, B.B., & Knight, R.T. (2000). The neural architecture of language disorders. In M.S. Gazzaniga (Ed.), *The new cognitive neurosciences*. Cambridge, MA: MIT Press.

Chapter 7: Memory and amnesia

Braver, T.S., Cohen, J.D., Nystrom, L.E., Jonides, J., Smith, E.E., & Noll, D.C. (1997). A parametric study of pre-frontal cortex involvement in human working memory. *Neuroimage*, 5, 49–62.

Cohen, M.J. (1997). Memory. In M.T. Banich (Ed.), *Neuropsychology: The neural bases of mental function*. Boston, MA: Houghton-Mifflin.

Wickelgren, I. (1997). Getting a grasp on working memory. *Science*, 275, 1580–1582.

Chapter 8: Visual object recognition and spatial processing

Clarke, S., Assal, G. & DeTribolet, N. (1993). Left hemisphere strategies in visual recognition, topographical orientation and time planning. *Neuropsychologia, 31,* 99–113.

DeRenzi, E., Perani, D., Carlesimo, G.A., Silveri, M.C., & Fazio, F. (1994). Prosopagnosia can be associated with damage confined to the right hemisphere: An MRI and PET study and a review of the literature. *Neuropsychologia, 32,* 893–902.

Haxby, J.V., Ungerleider, L.G., Horwitz, B., Masiog, J.M., Rapaport, S.I., & Grady, C.L. (1996). Face encoding and recognition in the human brain. *Proceedings of the National Academy of Science, 93,* 922–927.

Ramachandran, V.S. (1998). Consciousness and body image: Lessons from phantom limbs, Capgras syndrome and pain asymbolia. *Philosophical Transactions of the Royal Society of London, 353,* 1851–1859.

Chapter 9: Attention

LaBerge, D. (2000). Attentional networks. In M.S. Gazzaniga (Ed.), *The new cognitive neurosciences.* Cambridge, MA: MIT Press.

Mesulam, M.M. (1998). From sensation to cognition. *Brain, 121,* 1013–1052.

Robertson, L.C., & Rafal, R. (2000). Disorders of visual attention. In M.S Gazzaniga (Ed.), *The new cognitive neurosciences.* Cambridge, MA: MIT Press.

Chapter 10: Executive functions

Goldman-Rakic, P.S. (1996). Regional and cellular fractionation of working memory. *Proceedings of the National Academy of Science, 93,* 13473–13480.

Mitchell, R., Elliott, R., & Woodruf, P. (2001). fMRI and cognitive dysfunction in schizophrenia. *Trends in Cognitive Sciences, 5(2),* 71–81.

Norman, D.A., & Shallice, T. (1986). Attention to action: Willed and automatic control of behaviour. In R.J. Davidson et al. (Eds.), *Consciousness and self-regulation, vol. 4* (pp. 1–18). New York: Plenum Press.

General further reading

Banich, M. (1997). *Neuropsychology: The neural bases of mental function.* Boston, MA: Houghton-Mifflin.

Bradshaw, J.L., & Mattingley, J.B. (1995). *Clinical neuropsychology.* London: Academic Press.

Carter, R. (1998). *Mapping the mind.* London: Weidenfeld & Nicolson.

Ellis, A.W., & Young, A.W. (1996). *Human cognitive neuropsychology.* Hove, UK: Psychology Press.

Gazzaniga, M.S. (Ed.) (2000). *Cognitive neuroscience: A reader*. Oxford: Blackwell Publishers.

Gazzaniga, M.S. (Ed.) (2000). *The new cognitive neurosciences*. Cambridge, MA: MIT Press.

Gazzaniga, M.S., Ivry, R.B., & Mangun, G.R. (1998). *Cognitive neuroscience: The biology of the mind*. London: Norton.

Kolb, B., & Whishaw, I.Q. (1996). *Fundamentals of human neuropsychology (4th edition)*. New York: Freeman & Co.

Rozenzweig, M.R., Leiman, A.L. & Breedlove, S.M. (1999). *Biological psychology* (second edition). Sunderland, MA: Sinauer Associates Inc.

Springer, S.P., & Deutsch, G. (1993). *Left brain, right brain (4th edition)*. New York: Freeman & Co.

Temple, C. (1993). *The brain*. London: Penguin.

Selected neuropsychology web sites

http://www.neuroguide.com
A links page with a comprehensive search facility, table of contents and opportunities to sign up for newsletters.

http://neuropsychologycentral.com
Mainly links, but the site also offers an in-house and web search facility.

http://home.epix.net/~tcannon1/Neuropsychology.htm
Professor Cannon's homepage with lots of links to journals, other neuropsychology information pages, and links and information on specific brain disorders.

http://www.lib.uiowa.edu/hardin/md/neuro.html
A links page to many other neuropsychology sites regularly updated by staff at the Hardin Library, University of Iowa.

http://lbc.nimh.nih.gov
The website of the laboratory of brain cognition, National Institute for Mental Health (NIMH), with lots on functional neuro-imaging, and other neuroscience material.

http://www.brainsource.com
A web site prepared by neuropsychologist Denis Swiercinsky, offering numerous links. Particularly good for information on neuropsychological testing.

http://faculty.washington.edu/chudler/neurok.html
Don't be put off because this page claims to be aimed at kids. Lots to do, some useful links, and a chance to learn the words and music to *The Dendrite Song*!

Glossary

Ablation. The surgical removal of brain tissue.

Alexia/acquired alexia. Inability to read/loss of the ability to read following an accident or brain damage.

Alzheimer's disease. A form of dementia involving progressive loss of psychological functions as a result of widespread loss of cortical and subcortical neurons.

Amnesia. General term for loss of memory. Anterograde amnesia is loss of memory following some trauma. Retrograde amnesia is loss of memory for a period of time prior to trauma.

Amnesics. Collective name for people suffering from amnesia.

Analgesia. Pain relief.

Aneurysm. A form of stroke caused by a blood vessel in the brain suddenly expanding then bursting.

Angular gyrus. A region of cortex on the temporal/parietal border roughly equivalent to Brodmann's area 39. The left side is probably involved in reading (sentences).

Anomia. Inability to name objects or items.

Anterior cingulate. A mid-line frontal lobe structure implicated in attention, response inhibition, and emotional response (especially to pain).

Anterior commissure. A set of axons that connect the left and right frontal brain regions (smaller than the corpus callosum).

Aphasia. Deficit in some aspect of language comprehension or expression.

259

Apraxia. The inability to carry out certain motor acts on instruction without evident loss of muscle tone (acts may be performed spontaneously for example).

Aspiration pneumonia. Bronchial infection and congestion that affects ability to breathe and can lead to death.

Astereognosis. An agnosic condition in which objects cannot be recognised by touch alone.

Autism. A developmental disorder characterised by aloofness, automaticity and aphasia.

Behaviourism. The school of psychology founded by Thorndike and popularised by Skinner, which places emphasis on the acquisition of behaviour through learning and reinforcement.

Biopsy. The removal of tissue (in a living individual) for analysis.

Clot. A solid deposit in the blood that may block a narrow blood vessel leading to a form of stroke.

Conduction aphasia. An aphasic condition in which the principal deficit is the inability to repeat spoken language.

Convergence. In the nervous system, the process of many (converging) inputs influencing one component (for example, a neuron).

Coronal. (As in section.) The orientation of a brain slice if you were looking 'face on' and the brain was sliced vertically.

Cortex. The outer surface of the brain, having, in the higher mammals, a bumpy creased appearance.

D1 receptors. A class of dopamine receptor found particularly in the frontal lobes and striatum.

D2 receptors. Another class of dopamine receptor found particularly in the striatum and pituitary.

Dementia pugilistica. The medical term for 'punch-drunk'.

Descartes. The French philosopher famous for his ideas about the separate identities of mind and body.

Digit span. A measure of short-term memory based on the average number of digits a person can correctly memorise after a single brief presentation (typically in the order of 6–8).

Disconnection. The general term for a group of disorders thought to be caused by damage to a pathway between two undamaged regions (e.g. the split brain syndrome).

Distal. Far away, as opposed to proximal, meaning near to.

Divergence. In the nervous system, the principle that, because axons may branch many times, a single neuron can influence a large number of targets (usually other neurons).

Dopamine. A catecholamine neurotransmitter found in the brain.

Dyslexia. A specific reading difficulty found in a person with otherwise normal intelligence.

Echoic trace. A form of very short-term auditory memory (a sort of acoustic after image) thought to last no more than 1 or 2 seconds.

End-stage illness. The chronic features of illness or disease prior to death.

Epilepsy. The term for a group of neurological disorders characterised by synchronised but excessive neuronal activity.

Equipotentiality. The term associated with Lashley, broadly meaning that any region of cortex can assume responsibility for a given function (memory being the function of interest for Lashley).

Famous faces recognition test. A test comprising photographs of famous people drawn from various walks of life over the preceding several decades.

Figure. (As in figure and ground.) The figure is the prominent or core feature of an array.

Finger maze. A piece of apparatus in which the (usually blindfolded) respondent must negotiate a route from A to B. Typically the maze comprises a grooved piece of wood with one correct route and a series of blind alleys. The respondent pushes their finger along the 'correct' path.

Fluent aphasia. Another name for Wernicke's aphasia. Language is 'fluent' but nonsensical.

Ground. (As in figure and ground.) The ground is the background or peripheral element of an array.

Gyrus. An elongated bump (convexity) in the cortex. (Plural: gyri.)

Habituation. The process of becoming used to an event or stimulus and no longer attending or responding to it.

Haemorrhage. A general term for bleeding. In the brain, this may occur following an aneurysm, or other damage to a blood vessel.

Hallucinations. Perceptual experiences unrelated to physical sensation. They may occur in any sensory modality, and are often associated with mental illness.

Hemiparesis. Partial or complete loss of movement in one side of the body.

Hemiplegia. Loss of sensory awareness from, and muscle control of, one side of the body.

Hemispheres. A term for the two sides of the cortex (which may include subcortical tissue as well).

Herpes simplex infection. Infection with this virus can affect brain function, leading to permanent damage.

Hippocampal commissure. Another fibre bundle (axons) connecting the two halves of the brain.

Huntington's chorea. A rare, genetically determined, neurological disorder causing dementia and death due to progressive loss of neurons in the striatum.

Huntington's disease. (See above.)

Hyperactivity. In neurological terms, excess functional activity. In behavioural terms, a developmental disorder marked by excess excitability, inattentiveness, restlessness and recklesss/antisocial behaviour.

Ictal focus. The point of origin of epileptic activity, often a discrete region of damaged cortical tissue.

Interneurons. The name for neurons that receive input from neurons and send their output to other neurons, found throughout the CNS.

In-vivo techniques. A range of imaging/recording techniques to assess structure and/or function in living subjects.

Ipsilateral. Same-sided. An unusual anatomical 'wiring' arrangement in which brain function is linked to behaviour function on the same side (the norm being contralateral or opposite side control).

Kinaesthetic. Anything related to the sensation of body movement/location. Sensory information about the status of joints and muscles.

Lateral inhibition. A relatively common feature of nervous system 'wiring' in which active neurons tend to suppress activity of adjacent neurons.

Lesion. A cut (or severing) of brain tissue. This may occur as a result of an accident, or be done as a surgical procedure.

Lexicon. Loosely equates to stored vocabulary; that is one's long-term memory of native tongue words (estimated to be about 50,000 for English speakers).

Lobectomy. Surgical removal of all or part of a cortical lobe (as in temporal lobectomy for removal of the temporal lobe).

Long-term potentiation. The enduring increase in functional activity (at synapses) that may be related to memory storage in the brain.

Mass-action. The principle (alongside equipotentiality) that cortical regions of the brain are inherently non-specialised, and have the capacity to engage in any psychological function.

Meta-analysis. A research technique in which data from similar but separate projects is pooled into a single data set to increase statistical power.

Mid-line. Anatomically, in mammals, the imaginary line separating the left from the right side.

Mnemonics. Deliberate (conscious) aids to memory: 'Richard of York gave battle in vain' for the colours of the visible spectrum for example.

Modularity. The idea (attributed to Fodor) that psychological functions such as language and perception can be broken down into multiple components that may, in turn, depend on the effective processing of discrete brain regions.

Module. A core unit in an integral modular system (see above).

Myelin sheath. A wrapping of insulation found on axons of many neurons giving a characteristic white appearance and leading to faster nerve impulse propagation.

Myelination. The developmental process of laying down (forming) a myelin sheath, brought about by Schwann cells or oligodendrocytes wrapping themselves around neurons' axons.

Nerves. The technical name for a bundle of axons running alongside one another (e.g. the optic nerve).

Neurons. The cell type that conveys nerve impulses around the nervous system and interacts synaptically with other neurons or muscles.

Neurotransmitters. A heterogeneous group of chemical messengers usually manufactured by, stored in, and released by neurons that can influence the excitability of other neurons (or muscles).

Open head injury. A head injury involving damage to the cranium, so that the brain is 'exposed' (visible). Often compared with a 'closed head' injury in which brain damage has occurred although the cranium has not been penetrated: for example, dementia pugilistica (brain damage associated with boxing).

Orienting response. The characteristic 'alerting' response seen in animals presented with a novel stimulus or situation.

Paralysis. Loss of movement in a body region (such as a limb).

Parkinsonism. Signs and symptoms that resemble Parkinson's disease. Certain drugs (such as neuroleptics) can induce these as a side effect.

Parkinson's disease. A neurological disorder in which movements become slowed or are lost altogether. Rigidity and tremor are also found. Associated with loss of cells in and around the basal ganglia.

Pathology. In neuropsychology, usually the underlying physical signs or features of a disease.

Percept. The 'whole' that is perceived by putting together the constituent parts.

Perseveration. The tendency to repeat the same (or similar) response despite it no longer being appropriate.

Perseverative. (See above.) A response may be perseverative in the sense of being an unnecessary or inappropriate regurgitation of an earlier response.

Poly-sensory. Responsive to input from several modalities.

Priming. The (possibly sub-conscious) influence of some preliminary event or stimulus on subsequent responding.

Prosodic. An adjective to describe emotionally intoned language. (Aprosodic speech is devoid of emotional intonation, or monotone.)

Prosodic speech. Speech which, through tone, pitch, or emphasis carries emotional meaning/significance.

Psychoanalysis. The school of psychology initiated by Freud that emphasises the role(s) of unresolved subconscious conflicts in psychological disorder.

Psychogenic amnesia. Loss of memory linked to psychological trauma (such as child abuse).

Receptive fields. The area of external influence on any given internal sensory element. Typically, for example, cells in your fovea (central field of vision) have much smaller receptive fields than those in the periphery.

Receptor sites. Molecular structures on (or in) the membranes of neurons that neurotransmitter substances (and hormones) can 'influence' when they occupy them, usually by making the neuron more or less excited.

Reinforcement. Typically some form of reward (positive reinforcement) or punishment (negative reinforcement) that affects the likelihood of a response being repeated.

Sagittal. Sideways, as in sagittal brain scans taken from the side of the head.

Sensory nerves. Nerves carrying action potentials from sensory receptors towards the CNS (e.g. the optic nerve).

Signs. The indications of some abnormality or disturbance that are apparent to the trained clinician/observer (as opposed to symptoms, which are things an individual describes/complains of).

Speech apraxia. A characteristic sign of Broca's aphasia in which articulatory problems are apparent and speech is peppered with neologisms or paraphasias.

Striatum. A collective name for the caudate and putamen; key input regions in the basal ganglia.

Stroke. A catch-all term for severe disturbances in the blood supply to the brain. Most commonly, strokes are caused by obstruction to, or rupture of, blood vessels in the brain.

Substantia nigra. Another component of the basal ganglia. Neurons originating in the substantia nigra terminate in the striatum, where they release the neurotransmitter dopamine.

Sulci. The smaller folds or indents on the surface of the cortex (singular: sulcus). Larger ones are called fissures.

Supra nuclear palsy. One of the so-called subcortical dementias in which there is progressive tissue loss in the basal ganglia and midbrain structures such as the superior and inferior colliculi.

Symptoms. (See signs above.) Symptoms are the features of a disorder or disease that the individual reports/complains of.

Synapses. The tiny fluid-filled gaps between neurons where synaptic transmission (see below) may occur. Typically 20–30 nanometres (millionths of a millimetre wide).

Synaptic transmission. The chemically (or occasionally electrically) mediated communication between one neuron and another, or between a neuron and muscle.

Syndromal. A feature of a syndrome. The latter being a term for a disorder or condition (such as split-brain syndrome) characterised by a cluster of interrelated signs and symptoms rather than one defining feature.

Tachistoscope. An item of psychological equipment via which visual material can be presented to respondents for very brief exposure times (these days replaced by digital computers).

Telegraphic speech. A name to describe the non-fluent 'stop-start' agrammatic speech associated with Broca's aphasia.

Temporal lobe. The region of cortex (on both sides of the brain) running forward horizontally above and in front of the ear, known to be involved in language, memory and visual processing.

Ultra-sound. An anti-natal procedure for generating images of unborn children.

Voluntary gaze. Intentional adjustments of eyes in the deliberate process of attending to a feature in the visual field.

Wada test. A test that involves the administration of a fast-acting barbiturate (via the carotid artery) to one hemisphere at a time, to determine, among other things, the hemisphere that is dominant for language.

Working memory. A form of short-term memory, first characterised by Alan Baddeley, which allows a person to hold 'on-line' (and manipulate) a certain amount of information for a few seconds after it has been presented. For example, keeping a phone number in mind until you have dialled it.

References

Albuquerque, E.X., Hudson, C.S., Mayer, R.F., & Satterfield, J.R. (1976). Studies of human myasthenia gravis: Electrophysiological and ultrastructural evidence compatible with antibody attachment to acetylcholine receptor complex. *Proceedings of the National Academy of Sciences, 73,* 4584–4588.

Andreassi, J.L. (1989). *Psychophysiology: Human behaviour and physiological response* (second edition). Hillsdale, NJ: Lawrence Erlbaum Associates Inc.

Annett, M. (1985). *Left, right, hand and brain.* London: Lawrence Erlbaum Associates Ltd.

Assal, G., Favre, C., & Anders, J.P. (1984). Non-reconnaissance d'animaux familiers chez un paysan: Zooagnosie ou prosopagnosie pour les animaux. *Revue Neurologique, 140,* 580–584.

Atkinson, R.C., & Shiffrin, R.M. (1968). Human memory: A proposed system and its control processes. In K.W. Spence and J.T. Spence (Eds.), *The psychology of learning and motivation, 2.* New York: Academic Press.

Baddeley, A.D. (1986). *Working memory.* Oxford: Clarendon Press.

Baddeley, A.D. (1997). *Human memory: Theory and practice.* Hove, UK: Psychology Press.

Baddeley, A.D., & Hitch, G. (1974). Working memory. In G.H. Bower (Ed.), *The psychology of learning and motivation, 8* (pp. 47–90). New York: Academic Press.

Baddeley, A.D., Thomson, N., & Buchanan, M. (1975). Word length and the structure of short-term memory. *Journal of Verbal Learning and Verbal Behaviour*, *14*, 575–589.

Basbaum, A., & Fields, H.L. (1984). Endogenous pain control systems: brainstem spinal pathways and endorphin circuitry. *Annual Review of Neuroscience*, 7, 309–339.

Bavelier, D., Corina, D., Jezzard, P., Padmanabhan, S., Clark, V.P., Karni, A., Prinster, A., Braun, A., Lalwani, A., Rauschecker, J.P., Turner, R., & Neville, H. (1997). Sentence reading: a functional MRI study at 4 tesla. *Journal of Cognitive Neuroscience*, *9(5)* 664–686.

Bay, E. (1953). Disturbances of visual perception and their examination. *Brain*, *76*, 515–551.

Baylis, G.C., Rolls, E.T., & Leonard, C.M. (1985). Selectivity between faces in the responses of a population of neurons in the cortex in the superior temporal sulcus of the monkey. *Brain Research*, *342*, 91–102.

Behrens, S. (1988). The role of the right hemisphere in the production of linguistic stress. *Brain and Language*, *33*, 104–107.

Behrmann, M. (2000). Spatial reference frames and hemispatial neglect. In M.S. Gazzaniga (Ed.), *The new cognitive neurosciences* (pp. 651–666). Cambridge, MA: MIT Press.

Bennett, E.L., Diamond, M.L., Krech, D., & Rosenzweig, M.R. (1964). Chemical and anatomical plasticity of brain. *Science*, *146*, 610–619.

Benson, D.F., & Greenberg, J.P. (1969). Visual form agnosia. *Archives of Neurology*, *20*, 82–89.

Benson, D.F., & Stuss, D.T. (1989). Theories of frontal lobe function. In D. Mueller (Ed.), *Neurology and psychiatry: A meeting of minds* (pp. 266–283). Basel: Karger.

Benton, A.L. (1967). Constructional apraxia and the minor hemisphere. *Confina Neurologica*, *29*, 1–16.

Benton, A.L., Hannay, H.J., & Varney, N.R. (1975). Visual perception of line direction in patients with unilateral brain disease. *Neurology*, *25*, 907–910.

Benton, A.L., & Hecaen, H. (1970). Stereoscopic vision in patients with unilateral cerebral disease. *Neurology*, *20*, 1084–1088.

Best, C.T., Hoffman, H., & Glanville, B.B. (1982). Development of infant ear asymmetries for speech and music. *Perception and Psychophysics*, *31*, 75–85.

Binder, J.R., Frost, J.A., Hammeke, T.A., Cox, R.M., Rao, S.M., & Prieto, T. (1997). Human brain language areas identified by functional magnetic resonance imaging. *Journal of Neuroscience*, *17*, 353–362.

Bisiach, E., & Luzzatti, C. (1978). Unilateral neglect of representational space. *Cortex*, *14*, 129–133.

Blumer, D., & Benson, D.F. (1975). Personality changes with frontal and temporal lobe lesions. In D.F. Benson and D. Blumer (Eds.), *Psychiatric aspects of neurological disease* (pp. 151–170). New York: Grune and Stratton.

Bodamer, J. (1947). Die prosopagnosie. *Archiv fur Psychiatrie und Nervenkrankheiten*, *179*, 6–53.

Boussaoud, D., Ungerleider, L.G., & Desimone, R. (1990). Pathways for motion analysis: cortical connections of the medial superior temporal and fundus of the superior temporal visual areas in the macaque. *Journal of Comparative Neurology*, *296*, 462–495.

Bradshaw, J.L., & Mattingley, J.B. (1995). *Clinical neuropsychology: Behavioural and brain science.* Academic Press: London

Braver, T.S., Cohen, J.D., Nystrom, L.E., Jonides, J., Smith, E.E., & Noll, D.C. (1997). A parametric study of pre-frontal cortex involvement in human working memory. *Neuroimage, 5,* 49–62.

Breiter, H.C., Rauch, S.L., Kwong, K.K., Baker, J.R., Weiskoff, R.M., Kennedy, D.N., Kendrick, A.D., Davis, A.D., Jiang, T.L., Cohen, A.P., Stern, M.S., Belliveau, J.W., Baer, L., O'Sullivan, R.L., Savage, C.R., Jenike, M.A., & Rosen, B.R. (1996). Functional magnetic resonance imaging of symptom provocation in obsessive compulsive disorder. *Archives of General Psychiatry, 53,* 595–606.

Broadbent, D.A. (1958). *Perception and communication.* Oxford: Pergamon Press.

Broadbent, D.A. (1970). Stimulus set and response set: Two kinds of selective attention. In D.I. Motofsky (Ed.), *Attention: Contemporary theory and analysis* (pp. 51–60). New York: Appleton Century Crofts.

Broca, P. (1861). Remarques sur la siege de la facultie du language articule. *Bulletin de la Société Anatomique de Paris, 16,* 343–357.

Brodmann, K. (1909). Vergleichende Lokalisationslehreder grosshirnrinde in ihren prinzipien dargestellt auf grund des zellenbaues. Leipzig: J.A. Barth. In G. von Bonin (Ed.), *Some papers on the cerebral cortex* (pp. 201–230). Springfield IL: Charles C. Thomas (1960).

Brown, J. (1958). Some tests of the decay theory of immediate memory. *Quarterly Journal of Experimental Psychology, 10,* 12–21.

Brownell, H. (1988). Appreciation of metaphoric and connotative word meaning by brain-damaged patients. In C. Chiarello (Ed.), *Right hemisphere contributions to lexical semantics* (pp. 19–31). Springer-Verlag: New York.

Bruyer, R., Laterre, C., Seron, X., Feyereisen, P., Strypstein, E., Pierrard, E., & Rectem, D. (1983). A case of prosopagnosia with some preserved covert remembrance of familiar faces. *Brain and Cognition, 2,* 257–284.

Burgess, P.W., & Shallice, T. (1996). Response suppression, initiation, and strategy use following frontal lobe lesions. *Neuropsychologia, 34,* 263–276.

Caplan, D. (1992). *Language: Structure, processing and disorders.* Cambridge, MA: MIT Press.

Caramazza, A. (1984). The logic of neuropsychological research and the problem of patient classification in aphasia. *Brain and Language, 21,* 9–20.

Catalan, M.J., Honda, M., Weekes, R.A., Cohen, L.G., & Hallet, M. (1998). The functional neuroanatomy of simple and complex sequential finger movements: A PET study. *Brain, 121,* 253–264.

Chang, F.L., & Greenhough, W.T. (1982). Lateralised effects of monocular training on dendritic branching in adult split-brain rats. *Brain Research, 232,* 283–292.

Chelazzi, L., & Corbetta, M. (2000). Cortical mechanisms of visuospatial attention in the primate brain In M.S. Gazzaniga (Ed.), *The new cognitive neurosciences* (pp. 667–686). Cambridge, MA: MIT Press.

Cherry, E.C. (1953). Some experiments on the recognition of speech with one or two ears. *Journal of the Acoustic Society of America, 25,* 975–979.

Chertkow, H. & Murtha, S. (1997). PET activation and language. *Clinical Neuroscience, 4,* 78–86.

Clarke, S., Assal, G., & DeTribolet, N. (1993). Left-hemisphere strategies in visual recognition, topographical orientation and time planning. *Neuropsychologia, 31*, 99–113.

Cohen, N.J. (1997). Memory. In M.T. Banich (Ed.), *Neuropsychology; the neural bases of mental function* (pp. 314–367). Boston, MA: Houghton Mifflin.

Cohen, N.J., & Squire, L.R. (1980). Preserved learning and retention of pattern analysing skill in amnesia: Dissociation of knowing how and knowing that. *Science, 210*, 207–210.

Corballis, M.C. (1991). *The lop-sided ape: Evolution of the generative mind*. Oxford: Oxford University Press.

Corbetta, M., Miezen, F.M., Dobmeyer, S., Shulman, G.L., & Petersen, S.E. (1991). Selective and divided attention during visual discriminations of shape, colour and speed: Functional anatomy by PET. *Journal of Neuroscience, 11*, 2383–2402.

Corsi, P.M. (1972). *Human memory and the medial temporal region of the brain*. PhD dissertation. Montreal: McGill University.

Courtney, S.M., Ungerleider, L.G., Keil, K., & Haxby, J.V. (1997). Transient and sustained activity in a distributed neural system for human working memory. *Nature, 386*, 608–611.

Craig, A.D., Reiman, E.M., Evans, A., & Bushnell, M.C. (1996). Functional imaging of an illusion of pain. *Nature, 384*, 258–260.

Crow, T.J. (1998). Nuclear schizophrenic symptoms as a window on the relationship between thought and speech. *British Journal of Psychiatry, 173*, 303–309.

Damasio, A.R. (1985). Disorders of complex visual processing: agnosia, achromatopsia, Balint's syndrome, and related difficulties of orientation and construction. In M.M. Mesulam (Ed.), *Principles of behavioural neurology* (pp. 259–288). Philadelphia: F.A. Davis.

Damasio, A.R. (1994). *Descartes error: Emotion, reason and the human brain*. New York: Putnam.

Damasio, H., & Damasio, A.R. (1989). *Lesion analysis in neuropsychology*. New York: Oxford University Press.

Danta, G., Hilton, R.C., & O'Boyle, D.J. (1978). Hemisphere function and binocular depth perception, *Brain, 101*, 569–590.

Dejerine, J. (1892). Contribution a l'étude anatomo-pathologique et clinique des différentes variétés de cécite verbale. *Comptes Rendus des Seances de la Société de Biologie et de ses Filiales, 4*, 61–90.

Delis, D.C., Robertson, L.C., & Efron, R. (1986). Hemispheric specialisation of memory for visual hierarchical stimuli. *Neuropsychologia, 24(2)*, 205–216.

Delis, D.C., Squire, L.R., Bihrle, A., & Massman, P. (1992). Componential analysis of problem solving ability: Performance of patients with frontal lobe damage and amnesiac patients on a new sorting test. *Neuropsychologia, 30*, 683–697.

DeLong, M.R. (1993). Overview of basal ganglia function. In N. Mamo, I. Hamada and R. DeLong (Eds.), *Role of the cerebellum and basal ganglia in voluntary movement* (pp. 65–70). Amsterdam: Elsevier.

Dennis, M., & Kohn, B. (1975). Comprehension of syntax in infantile hemiplegics after cerebral hemidecortication: Left hemisphere superiority. *Brain and Language, 2*, 472–482.

DeRenzi, E., & Nichelli, P. (1975). Verbal and non-verbal short-term memory impairment following hemispheric damage. *Cortex, 11*, 341–354.

DeRenzi, E., Perani, D., Carlesimo, G.A., Silveri, M.C., & Fazio, F. (1994). Prosopagnosia can be associated with damage confined to the right hemisphere: an MRI and PET study and a review of the literature. *Neuropsychologia, 32*, 893–902.

DeRenzi, E., & Vignolo, L.A. (1962). The token test: A sensitive test to detect disturbances in aphasics. *Brain, 85*, 665–678.

Descartes, R. (1664). *Traite del'homme*. Paris: Angot.

Desimone, R., & Gross, C.G. (1979). Visual areas in the temporal cortex of the macaque. *Brain Research, 178*, 363–380.

Desimone, R., Wessinger, M., Thomas, L., & Schneider, W. (1990). Attentional control of visual perception: cortical and sub-cortical mechanisms. *Cold Spring Harbour Symposia on Quantitative Biology, 55*, 963–971.

Deutsch, G., Bourbon, W., Papanicolaou, A., & Eisenberg, H. (1988). Visuo-spatial tasks compared during activation of regional cerebral blood flow. *Neuropsychologia, 26*, 445–452.

Doyon, J., Gaudreau, D., LeForce, R., & Castonguay, M. (1997). Role of striatum, cerebellum, and frontal lobes in the learning of a visuo-motor sequence. *Brain and Cognition, 34(2)*, 218–245.

Drevets, W.C., Price, J.L., Simpson, J.R., Todd, R.D., Reich, T., Vannier, M., & Raiche, M.E. (1997). Subgenual prefrontal cortex abnormalities in mood disorders. *Nature, 386*, 824–827.

Dronkers, N.F., Redfern, B.B., & Knight, R.T. (2000). The neural architecture of language disorders. In M.S. Gazzaniga (Ed.), *The new cognitive neurosciences* (pp. 949–958). Cambridge, MA: MIT Press.

Dronkers, N.F., Redfern, B.B., & Ludy, C.A. (1995). Lesion localisation in chronic Wernicke's aphasia. *Brain and Language, 51(1)*, 62–65.

Dronkers, N.F., Redfern, B.B., Ludy, C., & Baldo, J. (1998). Brain regions associated with conduction aphasia and echoic rehearsal. *Journal of the International Neuropsychology Society, 4(1)*, 23–24.

Dronkers, N.F., Shapiro, J.K., Redfern, B., & Knight, R.T. (1992). The role of Broca's area in Broca's aphasia. *Journal of Clinical and Experimental Neuropsychology, 14*, 52–53.

Ellis, A.W., & Young, A.W. (1996). *Human cognitive neuropsychology: A textbook with readings*. Hove, UK: Psychology Press.

Ellis, A.W., Miller, D., & Sin, G. (1983). Wernicke's aphasia and normal language processing: A case study in cognitive neuropsychology. *Cognition, 15*, 111–144.

Engel, A.G. (1984). Myasthenia gravis and myasthenic syndromes. *Annals of Neurology, 16*, 519–535.

Farah, M.J. (1988). Is visual imagery really visual? Overlooked evidence from neuropsychology. *Psychological Review, 95*, 307–317.

Farah, M.J. (1990). *Visual agnosia: Disorders of object recognition and what they tell us about normal vision*. Cambridge, MA: MIT Press.

Fischbach, G.D. (1992). Mind and Brain. *Scientific American, 267(3)*, 48–57.

Flament, D., Ellerman, J.M., Kim, S.G., Ugurbil, K., & Ebner, T.J. (1996). Functional magnetic resonance imaging of cerebella activation during the learning of a visuo-motor dissociation task. *Human Brain Mapping, 4*, 210–226.

Flourens, M.J.P. (1824). *Recherches expérimentales sur les propriétés et les functiones du système nerveux dans le animaux vertebres*. Paris: Balliere.

Fodor, J.A. (1983). *The modularity of mind*. Cambridge, MA: MIT Press.

Fodor, J.A. (1985). Précis of the modularity of mind (with commentaries). *Behavioural and Brain Sciences, 8*, 1–42.

Franco, L., & Sperry, R.W. (1977). Hemisphere lateralisation for cognitive processing of geometry. *Neuropsychologia, 15*, 107–114.

Freed, C.R., Greene, P.E., Breeze, R.E., Tsai, W.Y., DuMouchel, W., Kao, R., Dillon, S., Winfield, H., Culver, S., Trojanowski, J.O.Q., Eidelberg, D., & Fahn, S. (2001). Transplantation of embryonic dopamine neurons for severe Parkinson's disease. *New England Journal of Medicine, 344*, 710–719.

Freund, H. (1984). Pre-motor areas in man. *Trends in Neurosciences, 7*, 481–483.

Frith, C.D., Friston, K., Liddle, P.F., & Frackowiak, R.S. (1991). Willed action and the prefrontal cortex in man: a study with PET. *Proceedings of the Royal Society of London; Biological Sciences, 244*, 241–246.

Fritsch, G., & Hitzig, E. (1870). On the electrical excitability of the cerebrum. In G. VonBonin (Ed.), *The cerebral cortex*. (1960) Springfield IL: C.C. Thomas.

Gabrieli, J.D., Cohen, N.J., & Corkin, S. (1988). The impaired learning of semantic knowledge following bilateral medial temporal lobe resection. *Brain and Cognition, 7(2)*, 57–177.

Gabrieli, J.D., Fleischman, D., Keane, M., Reminger, S., & Morell, F. (1995). Double dissociation between memory systems underlying explicit and implicit memory in the human brain. *Psychological Science, 6*, 76–82.

Gall, F.J., & Spurzheim, J. (1810–1819). *Anatomie et physiologie du système nerveux en général, et du cerveau particulier*. Paris: Schoell.

Gazzaniga, M.S. (1995). Principles of human brain organisation derived from split-brain studies. *Neuron, 14*, 217–228.

Gazzaniga, M.S., & Hillyard, S.A. (1971). Language and spatial capacity of the right hemisphere. *Neuropsychologia, 9*, 273–280.

Gazzaniga, M.S., Ivry, R.B., & Mangun, G.R. (1998). *Cognitive neuroscience: The biology of the mind*. New York: W.W. Norton.

Geffen, G., & Butterworth, P. (1992). Born with a split brain: The 15-year development of a case of congenital absence of the corpus callosum. In S. Schwartz (Ed.), *Case Studies in Abnormal Psychology* (pp. 113–117). New York: John Wiley.

Georgopoulos, A.P., Taira, M., & Lukashin, A. (1993). Cognitive neurophysiology of the motor cortex. *Science, 260*, 47–52.

Geschwind, N. (1965). Disconnexion syndromes in animals and man. *Brain, 88*, 237–294.

Geschwind, N. (1967). The varieties of naming errors. *Cortex, 3*, 97–112.

Geschwind, N. (1972). Language and the brain. *Scientific American, 226(4)*, 76–83.

Glanzer, M., & Cunitz, A.R. (1966). Two storage mechanisms in free recall. *Journal of Verbal Learning and Verbal Behaviour, 5*, 351–360.

Goldman-Rakic, P.S. (1992). Working memory and the mind. *Scientific American, 267(3)*, 111–117.

Goldman-Rakic, P.S. (1996). Regional and cellular fractionation of working memory. *Proceedings of the National Academy of Science, 93*, 13473–13480.

Goldman-Rakic, P.S., Chafee, M., & Friedman, H. (1993). Allocation of function in distributed circuits. In T. Onon, L.R. Squire, M.E. Raichle, D.I. Perrett, and M. Fukuda (Eds.), *Brain mechanisms of perception and memory: From neuron to behaviour.* Oxford: Oxford University Press.

Golgi, C. (1875). *Opera omnia, vols 1 and 2.* Milan: Hoepli.

Gollin, E.S. (1960). Developmental studies of visual recognition of incomplete objects. *Perceptual and Motor Skills, 11,* 289–298.

Goodale, M.A., & Milner, A.D. (1992). Separate visual pathways for perception and action. *Trends in Neurosciences, 15,* 22–25.

Graf, P., Squire, L.R., & Mandler, G. (1984). The information that amnesiac patients do not forget. *Journal of Experimental Psychology, 10(1),* 164–168.

Grafton, S.T., Mazziotta, J.C., Presty, S., Friston, K.J., Frackowiak, R.S., & Phelps, M.E. (1992). Functional anatomy of human procedural learning determined with regional cerebral blood flow and PET. *Journal of Neuroscience, 12,* 2542–2548.

Graham, F.K., & Kendall, B.S. (1960). Memory for designs test. *Perceptual and Motor Skills, 11,* 147–188.

Groeger, J. (1997). *Memory and remembering: Everyday memory in context.* Harlow: Longman.

Groome, D. (1999). *An introduction to cognitive psychology: Processes and disorders.* Hove, UK: Psychology Press.

Gross, C.G., Rocha-Miranda, C.E., & Bender, D.B. (1972). Visual properties of neurons in inferotemporal cortex of the macaque. *Journal of Neurophysiology, 35,* 96–111.

Gusella, J.F., & MacDonald, M.E. (1994). Hunting for Huntington's Disease. *Molecular Genetic Medicine, 3,* 139–158.

Hardyck, C., & Petrinovich, L.F. (1977). Left-handedness. *Psychological Bulletin, 84,* 383–404.

Hart, J., Berndt, R.S., & Caramazza, A. (1985). Category specific naming deficit following cerebral infarction. *Nature, 316,* 439–440.

Haxby, J.V., Ungerleider, L.G., Horwitz, B., Masiog, J.M., Rapaport, S.I., & Grady, C.L. (1996). Face encoding and recognition in the human brain. *Proceedings of the National Academy of Science, 93,* 922–927.

Hebb, D.O. (1949). *The organisation of behaviour: A neuropsychological theory.* New York: Wiley.

Heilman, K.M., & Rothi, L.J. (1993). Apraxia. In K.M. Heilman and E. Valenstein (Eds.), *Clinical Neuropsychology, 3rd edition* (pp. 141–164). Oxford: Oxford University Press.

Hellige, J.B. (1990). Hemispheric asymmetry. *Annual Review of Psychology, 41,* 55–80.

Hepper, P.G., McCartney, G.R., & Alyson, S.E. (1998). Lateralised behaviour in first trimester human foetuses. *Neuropsychologia, 36(2),* 531–534.

Hepper, P.G., Shalidullah, S., & White, R. (1991). Handedness in the human foetus. *Neuropsychologia, 29(11),* 1107–1111.

Hiscock, M., Israelian, M., Inch, R., Jacek, C., & Hiscock-Kalil, C. (1994). Is there a sex difference in human laterality? I. An exhaustive survey of visual laterality studies from six neuropsychology journals. *Journal of Clinical and Experimental Neuropsychology, 16,* 423–435.

REFERENCES

Hiscock, M., Israelian, M., Inch, R., Jacek, C., & Hiscock-Kalil, C. (1995). Is there a sex difference in human laterality? II. An exhaustive survey of visual laterality studies from six neuropsychology journals. *Journal of Clinical and Experimental Neuropsychology, 17, 590–610.*

Hopfinger, J.B., & Mangan, G.R. (1998). Reflexive attention modulates processing of visual stimuli in human extra-striate cortex. *Psychological Science, 9, 441–447.*

Hornykiewicz, O. (1966). Dopamine (3-hydroxytyramine) and brain functions. *Pharmacological Review, 18, 925–964.*

Howard, D., & Orchard-Lisle, V. (1984). On the origin of semantic errors in naming: Evidence from the case of a global aphasic. *Cognitive Neuropsychology, 1, 163–190.*

Hubel, D., & Weisel, T. (1968). Receptive fields and functional architecture of monkey striate cortex. *Journal of Physiology, 195, 215–243.*

Humphreys, G.W., & Riddoch, M.J. (1984). Routes to object constancy: implications for neurological impairments of object constancy. *Quarterly Journal of Experimental Psychology, 36A, 385–415.*

Humphreys, G.W., & Riddoch, M.J. (1987). *To see but not to see: A case study of visual agnosia.* Hove, UK: Lawrence Erlbaum Associates.

Hyde, J.S., Fennema, E., & Lamon, S.J. (1990). Gender differences in mathematics performance: A meta-analysis. *Psychological Bulletin, 107(2), 139–155.*

Indefrey, P., & Levelt, W.J. (2000). The neural correlates of language production. In M.S. Gazzaniga (Ed.), *The new cognitive neurosciences (2nd edn),* London: MIT Press.

James, W. (1890/1950). *The principles of psychology.* New York: Dover Publications.

Janowsky, J.S., Shimamura, A.P., & Squire, L.R. (1989). Source memory impairment in patients with frontal lobe lesions. *Neuropsychologia, 27, 1043–1056.*

Jeeves, M.A., & Temple, C.M. (1987). A further study of language function in callosal agenesis. *Brain and Language, 32, 325–335.*

Jenkins, I.H., Brooks, D.J., Nixon, P.D., Frackowiak, R.S., & Passingham, R.E. (1994). Motor sequence learning: A study with positron emission tomography. *Journal of Neuroscience, 14, 3775–3790.*

Jonides, J., Smith, E.E., Koeppe, R.A., Awh, E., Minoshima, S., & Mintun, M.A. (1993). Spatial working memory in humans as revealed by PET. *Nature, 363, 623–625.*

Kaas, J.H. (1983). What if anything is S1? Organisation of first somatosensory area of cortex. *Physiological Reviews, 63, 206–231.*

Kahneman, D. (1973). *Attention and effort.* Englewood Cliffs, NJ: Prentice Hall.

Kandel, E., Schwartz, J.H. & Jessell, T.M. (Eds.) (1991). *Principles of neural science* (third edition). New York: Elsevier.

Kaplan, J.A., Fein, D., Morris, R., & Delis, D.C. (1990). The effects of right hemisphere damage on pragmatic interpretation of conversational remarks. *Brain and Language, 38, 315–333.*

Kay, J., & Ellis, A.W. (1987). A cognitive neuropsychological case study of anomia: implications for psychological models of word retrieval. *Brain, 110, 613–629.*

Kimura, D. (1973). The asymmetry of the human brain. *Scientific American, 228, 70–78.*

Kimura, D. (1992). Sex differences in the brain. *Scientific American, 267(3) 118–125.*

Kimura, D., & Hampson, E. (1994). Cognitive pattern in men and women is influenced by fluctuations in sex hormones. *Current Directions in Psychological Science, 3, 57–61.*

Knight, R.T., & Grabowecky, M. (1995). Escape from linear time: pre-frontal cortex and conscious experience. In M.S. Gazzaniga, (Ed.) *The cognitive neurosciences* (pp. 1357–1371). Cambridge MA: MIT Press.

Kolb, B., & Whishaw, I.Q. (1980). *Fundamentals of human neuropsychology* (first edition). New York: Freeman and Co.

Kolb, B., & Whishaw, I.Q. (1996). *Fundamentals of human neuropsychology* (fourth edition). New York: Freeman and Co.

Korsakoff, S. (1889). Étude medico-psychologique sur une form des maladies de la mémoire. *Review Philosophique, 28,* 501–530.

Kosslyn, S.M. (1987). Seeing and imagining in the cerebral hemispheres: A computational approach. *Psychological Review, 94,* 148–175.

Kosslyn, S., & Anderson, R. (1992). *Frontiers in cognitive neuroscience.* Cambridge, MA: MIT Press.

Kurlan, R., Como, P.G., Deeley, C., & McDermott, M. (1993). A pilot controlled study of fluoxetine for obsessive-compulsive symptoms in children with Tourette syndrome. *Clinical Neuropharmacology, 16(2),* 167–172.

Kuypers, H.G. (1981). Anatomy of descending pathways. In V.B. Brooks (Ed.), *Handbook of physiology, Vol. 7: The nervous system* (pp. 579–666). Bethesda, MD: American Physiology Society.

L'hermitte, F. (1983). Utilisation behaviour and its relation to lesions of the frontal lobes. *Brain, 106,* 237–255.

L'hermitte, F., Pillon, B., & Serdaru, M. (1986). Human autonomy and the frontal lobes. Part 1: Imitation and utilisation behaviour: a neuropsychological study of 75 patients. *Annals of Neurology, 19,* 326–334.

LaBerge, D. (1990). Thalamic and cortical mechanisms of attention suggested by recent positron emission tomographic experiments. *Journal of Cognitive Neuroscience, 2,* 358–372.

LaBerge, D. (1995). *Attentional processing: The brain's art of mindfulness.* Cambridge, MA: Harvard University Press.

LaBerge, D. (2000). Attentional networks. In M.S. Gazzaniga (Ed.), *The new cognitive neurosciences* (pp. 711–724). Cambridge, MA: MIT Press.

LaBerge, D., & Buchsbaum, M.S. (1990). Positron emission tomographic measurements of pulvinar activity during an attention task. *Journal of Neuroscience, 10,* 613–619.

Lashley, K.S. (1930). Basic neural mechanisms in behaviour. *The Psychological Review, 37,* 1–24.

Lechevalier, B., Petit, M.C., Eustache, F., Lambert, J., Chapon, F., & Vaider, F. (1989). Regional cerebral blood flow during comprehension and speech (in cerebrally healthy subjects). *Brain and Language, 37,* 1–11.

Lepage, M., Habib, R., & Tulving, E. (1998). Hippocampal PET activations of memory encoding and retrieval: the HIPER model. *Hippocampus, 8,* 313–322.

Levelt, W.J., Roelofs, A., & Meyer, A.S. (1999). A theory of lexical access in speech production. *Behavioural and Brain Sciences, 22,* 1–38.

Levine, S.C., Banich, M.T., & Koch-Weser, M. (1988). Face recognition: a general or specific right hemisphere capacity? *Brain and Cognition, 8,* 303–325.

Levy, J. (1969). Possible basis for the evolution of lateral specialisation of the human brain. *Nature, 224,* 614–615.

Levy, J., & Trevarthen, C.W. (1976). Metacontrol of hemisphere function in human split brain patients. *Journal of Experimental Psychology: Human Perception and Performance, 2,* 299–312.

Levy, J., Trevarthen, C.W., & Sperry, R.W. (1972). Perception of bilateral chimeric figures following 'hemispheric deconnection'. *Brain, 95,* 61–78.

Lezak, M.D. (1983). *Neuropsychological assessment.* New York: Oxford University Press.

Lichtheim, L. (1885). On aphasia. *Brain, 7,* 433–484.

Liddle, P.F. (1987). The symptoms of chronic schizophrenia: A re-examination of the positive–negative dichotomy. *British Journal of Psychiatry, 151,* 145–151.

Liddle, P.F. (1993). The psychomotor disorders: Disorders of the supervisory mental processes. *Behavioural Neurology, 6(5),* 5–14.

Linebarger, M.C., Schwarz, M.F., & Saffran, E.M. (1983). Sensitivity to grammatical structure in so-called agrammatical aphasics. *Cognition, 13,* 361–392.

Lissauer, H. (1890). Ein fall von seelenblindheit nebst einem Beitrage zur Theorie derselben. *Archiv fur Psychiatrie und Nervenkrankheiten, 21,* 222–270.

Logan, C.G., & Grafton, S.T. (1995). Functional anatomy of human eyeblink conditioning determined with regional cerebral glucose metabolism and positron emission tomography. *Proceedings of the National Academy of Sciences, 92,* 7500–7504.

Luria, A.R. (1966). *Higher cortical functions in man.* New York: Basic Books.

Luria, A.R. (1973). *The working brain: An introduction to neuropsychology.* Harmondsworth: Penguin Books.

MacCoby, E., & Jacklin, C. (1974). *The psychology of sex differences.* Stanford, CA: Stanford University Press.

Mandler, G. (1989). Memory: conscious and unconscious. In P.R. Soloman, G.R. Goethals, C.M. Kelley and B.R. Stephens (Eds.), *Memory: Interdisciplinary approaches* (pp. 170–192). New York: Springer-Verlag.

Mangan, G.R., Hillyard, S., & Luck, S. (1993). Electrocortical substrates of visual selective attention. In D.E. Meyer and S. Kornblum (Eds.), *Attention and performance (XIV): Synergies in experimental psychology, artificial intelligence and cognitive neuroscience* (pp. 219–242). Cambridge, MA: MIT Press.

Marr, D. (1982). *Vision: A computational investigation into the human representation and processing of visual information.* San Francisco: Freeman.

Martin, W.R., & Hayden, M.R. (1987). Cerebral glucose and dopa metabolism in movement disorders. *Canadian Journal of Neurological Sciences, 14,* 448–451.

Martuza, R.L., Chiocca, E.A., Jenike, M.A., Giriunuas, I.E., & Ballantine, H.T. (1990). Stereotactic radiofrequency thermal cingulectomy for obsessive compulsive disorder. *Journal of Neuropsychiatry and Clinical Neurosciences, 2,* 331–336.

Mazoyer, B.M., Tzourio, N., Frak, V., Syrota, A., Murayama, N., Levrier, O., Salamon, G., Dehaene, S., Cohen, L., & Mehler, J. (1993). The cortical representation of speech. *Journal of Cognitive Neuroscience, 5,* 467–479.

McCarthy, G., Blamire, A.M., Puce, A., Nobe, A.C., Bloch, G., Goldman-Rakic, P., & Shulman, R.G. (1994). Functional magnetic resonance imaging of human pre-frontal cortex activation during a spatial working memory task. *Proceedings of the National Academy of Sciences, 91,* 8690–8694.

McGlone, J. (1980). Sex differences in human brain asymmetry: A critical survey. *Behavioural and Brain Sciences, 3(2),* 215–263.

McNeil, J.E., & Warrington, E.K. (1993). Prosopagnosia: A face specific disorder. *Quarterly Journal of Experimental Psychology, 46(a),* 1–10.

Melzak, R. (1992). Phantom limbs. *Scientific American, 266(4),* 120–126.

Melzak, R., & Wall, P.D. (1965). Pain mechanisms: A new theory. *Science, 150,* 971–979.

Merzenich, M., & Jenkins, W.M. (1995). Cortical plasticity, learning and learning dysfunction. In B. Julesz and I. Kovacs (Eds.), *Maturational windows and adult cortical plasticity* (pp. 2–24). Reading, MA: Addison-Wesley.

Merzenich, M.M., & Kaas, J.H. (1980). Principles of organisation of sensory-perceptual systems in mammals. In J.M. Sprague and A.N. Epstein (Eds.), *Progress in psychobiology and physiological psychology, 9,* New York: Academic Press.

Mesulam, M.M. (1981). A cortical network for directed attention and unilateral neglect. *Annals of Neurology, 10,* 309–325.

Mesulam, M.M. (Ed.) (1985). *Principles of behavioural neurology.* Philadelphia: F.A. Davis.

Mesulam. M.M. (1998). From sensation to cognition. *Brain, 121,* 1013–1052.

Milner, B. (1962). Les troubles de la memoire accompagnat des lesions hippocampiques bilaterales. In P. Passouant (Ed.), *Physiologie delhippocampe.* Paris: Centre National de la Recherche Scientifique.

Milner, B. (1965). Visually guided maze learning in man: Effects of bilateral hippocampal, bilateral frontal and unilateral cerebral brain lesions. *Neuropsychologia, 3,* 317–338.

Milner, B. (1966). Amnesia following operation on the temporal lobes. In C.W. Whitty and O.L. Zangwill (Eds.), *Amnesia* (pp. 109–133). London: Butterworth.

Milner, B. (1982). Some cognitive effects of frontal lobe lesions in man. *Philosophical Transactions of the Royal Society of London, 298,* 211–226.

Mitchell, R.L., Elliott, R., & Woodruff, P.W. (2001). fMRI and cognitive dysfunction in schizophrenia. *Trends in Cognitive Sciences, 5(2),* 71–81.

Mogilner, A., Grossman, J.A., Ribary, U., Joliot, M., Volkman, J., Rapaport, D., Beasley, R.W., & Llinas, R.R. (1993). Somatosensory cortical plasticity in adult humans revealed by magnetoencephalography. *Proceedings of the National Academy of Sciences, 90,* 3593–3597.

Money, J.A. (1976). *A standardised road map test of directional sense: Manual.* San Rafael, CA: Academic Therapy Publications.

Moray, N. (1959). Attention in dichotic listening: Effective cues and the influence of instructions. *Quarterly Journal of Experimental Psychology, 9,* 56–60.

Moriarty, J., Campos-Costa, D., Schmitz, B., Trimble, M.R., Ell, P.J., & Robertson, M. (1995). Brain perfusion abnormalities in Gilles de la Tourettes syndrome. *British Journal of Psychiatry, 167,* 249–254.

Moscovitch, M. (1989). Confabulation and the frontal system: Strategic versus associative retrieval in neuropsychological theories of memory. In H.L. Roediger and F.I.M. Craik (Eds.), *Variety of memory and consciousness: Essays in honour of Endel Tulving.* Hillsdale, NJ: Laurence Earlbaum Associates Inc.

Motter, B.C., & Mountcastle, V.B. (1981). The functional properties of light sensitive neurons of the posterior parietal cortex studied in waking animals. *Journal of Neuroscience, 1,* 3–36.

Naeser, M.A., & Hayward, R.W. (1978). Lesion localisation in aphasia with cranial computed tomography and the Boston Diagnostic Aphasia Exam. *Neurology, 28,* 545–551.

Nelson, H.E. (1976). A modified card sorting test sensitive to frontal lobe defects. *Cortex, 12,* 313–324.

Nelson, H.E. (1982). *National Adult Reading Test: Test manual.* Windsor: NFER-Nelson.

Norman, D.A., & Shallice, T. (1980). Attention to action: Willed and automatic control of behaviour. *Centre for Human Information Processing Report 99.* La Jolla, CA: UCSD.

Norman, D.A., & Shallice, T. (1986). Attention to action: Willed and automatic control of behaviour. In R.J. Davidson, et al. (Eds.), *Consciousness and self-regulation, 4* (pp. 1–18). New York: Plenum Press.

Nyberg, L., McIntosh, A., Cabeza, R., Habib, R., Houle, S., & Tulving, E. (1996). General and specific brain regions involved in encoding and retrieval of events: What, where and when. *Proceedings of the National Academy of Sciences, 93,* 11280–11285.

O'Keefe, J.A., & Speakman, A. (1987). Single unit activity in the rat hippocampus during a spatial memory task. *Experimental Brain Research, 68,* 1–27.

Olanow, C.W., Kordower, J.H., & Freeman, T.B. (1996). Fetal nigral transplantation as a therapy for Parkinson's disease. *Trends in Neurosciences, 19(3),* 102–109.

Pardo, J.V., Pardo P.J., Janer, K.W., & Raichle, M.E. (1990). The anterior cingulate cortex mediates processing selection in the Stroop attentional conflict paradigm. *Proceedings of the National Academy of Science, USA, 87,* 256–259.

Penfield, W., & Boldrey, E. (1958). Somatic motor and sensory representation in the cerebral cortex as studied by electrical stimulation. *Brain, 60,* 389–443.

Perret, E. (1974). The left frontal lobe of man and the suppression of habitual responses in verbal categorical behaviour. *Neuropsychologia, 12,* 323–330.

Petersen, L.R., & Petersen, M.R. (1959). Short-term retention of individual verbal items. *Journal of Experimental Psychology, 58,* 193–198.

Petersen, S.E., & Fiez, J.A. (1993). The processing of single words studied with positron emission tomography. *Annual Review of Neuroscience, 16,* 509–530.

Petersen, S.E., Fox, P.T., Posner, M.I., Mintun, M., & Raichle, M.E. (1988). Positron emission tomographic studies of the cortical anatomy of single word processing. *Nature, 331,* 585–589.

Petersen, S.E., Robinson, D.L., & Morris, J.D. (1985). Pulvinar nuclei of the behaving rhesus monkey: visual responses and their modulation. *Journal of Neurophysiology, 54,* 867–886.

Petrides, M. (1996). Specialised systems for the processing of mnemonic information within the primate frontal cortex. *Philosophical Transactions of the Royal Society, 351,* 1455–1462.

Petrides, M., & Milner, B (1982). Deficits on subject-ordered tasks after frontal and temporal lobe lesions in man. *Neuropsychologia, 20,* 249–262.

Pohl, W. (1973). Dissociation of spatial discrimination deficits following frontal and parietal lesions in monkeys. *Journal of Comparative and Physiological Psychology, 82,* 227–239.

Posner, M.I. (1980). Orienting of attention. *Quarterly Journal of Experimental Psychology, 32,* 3–25.

Posner, M.I. (1992). Attention as a cognitive and neural system. *Current Directions in Psychological Science*, *1*, 11–14.

Posner, M.I., & Cohen, Y. (1984). Components of visual orienting. In H. Bouma and D. Bowhuis (Eds.), *Attention and Performance X* (pp. 531–556). Hillsdale, NJ: Lawrence Erlbaum Associates Inc.

Posner, M.I., & DiGirolamo, G.J. (1998). Executive attention: conflict, target detection and cognitive control. In R. Parasuraman (Ed.), *The Attentive Brain*. Cambridge, MA: MIT Press.

Posner, M.I., Inhoff, A.W., Freidrich, F.J., & Cohen, A. (1987). Isolating attentional systems: A cognitive anatomical analysis. *Psychobiology*, *15*, 107–121.

Posner, M.I., Snyder, C.R., & Davidson, J. (1980). Attention and the detection of signals. *Journal of Experimental Psychology*, *109*, 160–174.

Previc, F.H. (1991). A general theory concerning the prenatal origins of cerebral lateralisation in humans. *Psychological Review*, *98*, 299–334.

Raichle, M.E. (1994). Visualising the mind. *Scientific American*, *269(1)*, 36–42.

Ramachandran, V.S. (1994). Phantom limbs, neglect syndromes and Freudian psychology. *Review of Neurobiology*, *37*, 291–333.

Ramachandran, V.S. (1998). Consciousness and body image: Lessons from phantom limbs, Capgras' syndrome and pain asymbolia. *Philosophical Transactions of the Royal Society of London*, *353*, 1851–1859.

Ramon y Cajal, S. (1989). *Recollections of my life*. Cambridge, MA: MIT Press.

Rapoport, J.L. (1990). Obsessive compulsive disorder and basal ganglia dysfunction. *Psychological Medicine*, *20*, 465–469.

Rasmussen, T., & Milner, B. (1977). The role of early left brain injury in determining lateralisation of cerebral speech function. *Annals of the New York Academy of Sciences*, *299*, 355–369.

Ratcliff, G., & Newcombe, F. (1973). Spatial orientation in man: Effects of left, right and bi-lateral posterior cerebral lesions. *Journal of Neurology, Neurosurgery and Psychiatry*, *36*, 448–454.

Ratcliff, G., & Newcombe, F. (1982). Object recognition: Some deductions from the clinical evidence. In A.W. Ellis (Ed.), *Normality and pathology in cognitive functions* (pp. 147–171). London: Academic Press.

Regard, M., & Landis, T. (1984). Transient global amnesia: Neuropsychological dysfunction during attack and recovery of two pure cases. *Journal of Neurology, Neurosurgery, and Psychiatry*, *47*, 668–672.

Reitan, R.M., & Wolfson, D. (1993). *The Halstead-Reitan Neuropsychological test battery: Theory and clinical interpretation*. Tucson AZ: Neuropsychology Press.

Renner, M.J., & Rosensweig, M.R. (1987). *Enriched and impoverished environments: Effects on brain and behaviour*. New York: Springer-Verlag.

Roberts, A.C., Robbins, T.W., & Weiskrantz, L. (1998). *The pre-frontal cortex*. Oxford: Oxford University Press.

Robertson, L.C. and Rafal, R. (2000). Disorders of visual attention. In M.S. Gazzaniga (Ed.), *The new cognitive neurosciences* (pp. 633–650). Cambridge, MA: MIT Press.

Roland, P.E. (1993). *Brain activation*. New York: Wiley-Liss.

REFERENCES

Roland, P.E., Larson, B., Lassen, N.A., & Skinhoje, E. (1980). Supplementary motor area and other cortical areas in organisation of voluntary movements in man. *Journal of Neurophysiology, 43,* 118–136.

Rosenzweig, M.R., Leiman, A.L., & Breedlove, S.M. (1996). *Biological psychology.* Sunderland, MA: Sinauer Associates Inc.

Sacks, O. (1985). *The man who mistook his wife for a hat.* New York: Summit Books.

Saxena, S., Brody, A.L., Schwartz, J.M., & Baxter, L.R. (1998). Neuro-imaging and frontal-subcortical circuitry in obsessive-compulsive disorder. *British Journal of Psychiatry, 173 (suppl. 35),* 26–37.

Schacter, D., Alpert, N., Savage, C., & Rauch, S. (1996). Conscious recollection and the human hippocampal formation: Evidence from PET. *Proceedings of the National Academy of Sciences, 93,* 321–325.

Schneiderman, E.I., Murasugi, K.G., & Saddy, J.D. (1992). Story arrangement ability in right brain damaged patients. *Brain and Language, 43,* 107–120.

Semmes, J., Weinstein, S., Ghent, L., & Teuber, H.L. (1955). Spatial orientation: Analysis of locus of lesion. *Journal of Psychology, 39,* 227–244.

Semmes, J., Weinstein, S., Ghent, L., & Teuber, H.L. (1963). Impaired orientation in personal and extra-personal space. *Brain, 86,* 747–772.

Sergent, J. (1982). The cerebral balance of power: Confrontation or cooperation? *Journal of Experimental Psychology: Human Perception and Performance, 8,* 252–272.

Sergent, J. (1990). Further incursions into bicameral minds. *Brain, 113,* 537–568.

Sergent, J., & Signoret, J.L. (1992). Functional and anatomical decomposition of face processing: Evidence from prosopagnosia and PET study of normal individuals. *Philosophical Transactions of the Royal Society of London, B335,* 55–62.

Sergent, J., Ohta, S., & MacDonald, B. (1992). Functional neuroanatomy of face and object processing. *Brain, 115,* 15–36.

Shallice, T. (1982). Specific impairments in planning. *Philosophical Transactions of the Royal Society of London, 298,* 199–209.

Shallice, T., & Burgess, W. (1991). Deficits in strategy and application following frontal lobe damage in man. *Brain, 114,* 727–741.

Shallice, T., & Warrington, E. (1969). Independent functioning of verbal memory stores: A neuropsychological study. *Quarterly Journal of Experimental Psychology, 22,* 261–273.

Shergill, S.S., Brammer, M.J., Williams, S.C., Murray, R.M., & McGuire, P.K. (2000). Mapping auditory hallucinations in schizophrenia using functional magnetic resonance imaging. *Archives of General Psychiatry, 57 (11),* 1033–1038.

Silbersweig, D.A., Stern, E., Frith, C., Cahill, C., Holmes, A., Grootoonk, S., Seaward, J., McKenna, P., Chua, S.E., Schnorr, L., Jones, T., & Frackowiak, R.S.J. (1995). A functional neuroanatomy of hallucinations in schizophrenia. *Nature, 378,* 176–179.

Smith, E.E., & Jonides, J. (1994). Working memory in humans: Neuropsychological evidence. In M.S. Gazzaniga (Ed.), *The cognitive neurosciences* (pp. 1009–1020). Cambridge, MA: MIT Press.

Smith, E.E., Jonides, J., & Koeppe, R.A. (1996). Dissociating verbal and spatial working memory using PET. *Cerebral Cortex, 6,* 11–20.

Snyder, A.Z., Abdullaev, Y.G., Posner, M.I., & Raichle, M.E. (1995). Scalp electrical potentials reflect regional cerebral blood flow responses during processing of written words. *Proceedings of the National Academy of Sciences, 92*, 1689–1693.

Sperry, R.W. (1968). Hemisphere deconnection and unity of conscious awareness. *American Psychologist, 23*, 723–733.

Sperry, R.W., Gazzaniga, M.S., & Bogen, J.E. (1969). Inter-hemispheric relationships: The neocortical commissures; syndromes of hemisphere disconnection. In P.J. Vinken and G.W. Bruyn (Eds.), *Handbook of clinical neurology, 4* (273–290). New York: John Wiley and Sons.

Springer, S.P., & Deutsch, G. (1993). *Left Brain–Right Brain*. New York: Freeman and Co.

Squire, L.R. (1992). Comparisons between forms of amnesia: Some deficits are unique to Korsakoff's syndrome. *Journal of Experimental Psychology: Learning, Memory and Cognition, 8(6)*, 560–571.

Squire, L.R., Ojemann, J.G., Miezen, F.M., Petersen, S.E., Videen, T.O., & Raichle, M. (1992). Activation of the hippocampus in normal humans: A functional anatomical study of memory. *Proceedings of the National Academy of Sciences, 89*, 1837–1841.

Squire, L.R., Slater, P.C., & Miller, P.L. (1981). Retrograde amnesia and bilateral electroconvulsive therapy. *Archives of General Psychiatry, 38*, 89–95.

Steg, G., & Johnels, B. (1993). Physiological mechanisms and assessment of motor disorders in Parkinson's disease. In H. Narabayashi, T. Nagatsu, N. Yanagisawa and Y. Mizuno (Eds.), *Advances in neurology*, New York: Raven Press.

Stirling, J. (1999). *Cortical functions*, London: Routledge.

Stirling, J.D., Cavill, J., & Wilkinson, A. (2000). Dichotically presented emotionally intoned words produce laterality differences as a function of localisation task. *Laterality, 5(4)*, 363–371.

Stirling, J.D., Hellewell, J.S., & Quraishi, N. (1998). Self-monitoring and the schizophrenic symptoms of alien control. *Psychological Medicine, 28*, 675–683.

Taddese, A., Nah, S.Y., & McClesky, E.W. (1995). Selective opioid inhibition of small nociceptive neurons. *Science, 270*, 1366–1369.

Tang, N.G., Dong, H.W., Wang, X.M., Tsui, Z.C., & Han, J.S. (1997). Cholycystokinin antisense RNA increases the analgesic effect induced by electro-acupuncture or low dose morphine: Conversion of low responder rats into high responders. *Pain, 71*, 71–80.

Taylor, L.B. (1969). Localisation of cerebral lesions by psychological testing. *Clinical Neurosurgery, 16*, 269–287.

Temple, C. (1993). *The brain*. Harmondsworth, Middlesex: Penguin Books.

Temple, C.N., & Ilsley, J. (1993). Phonemic discrimination in callosal agenesis. *Cortex, 29(2)*, 341–348.

Tipper, S.P., Weaver, B., & Houghton, G. (1994). Behavioural goals determine inhibitory mechanisms of selective attention. *Quarterly Journal of Experimental Psychology, 47(a)* 809–840.

Treisman, A.M. (1964). Verbal cues, language and meaning in selective attention. *American Journal of Psychology, 77*, 206–219.

Treisman, A., & Gelade, G. (1980). A feature-integration theory of attention. *Cognitive Psychology, 12,* 97–136.

Tulving, E. (1972). Episodic and semantic memory. In E. Tulving and W. Donaldson (Eds), *Organisation of memory* (pp. 382–402). New York: Academic Press.

Tulving, E. (1985). How many memory systems are there? *American Psychologist, 40,* 385–398.

Tulving, E. (1989). Memory: Performance, knowledge and experience. *The European Journal of Cognitive Psychology, 1,* 3–26.

Tulving, E., Schacter, D.L., & Stark, H.A. (1982). Priming effects in word fragment completion are independent of recognition memory. *Journal of Experimental Psychology: Learning, Memory and Cognition, 17,* 595–617.

Turner, A.M., & Greenhough, W.T. (1985). Differential rearing effects on rat visual cortex synapses: I. Synaptic and neuronal density and synapses per neuron. *Brain Research, 329,* 195–203.

Tyszka, J.M., Grafton, S.T., Chew, W., Woods, R.P., & Colletti, P.M. (1994). Parcelling of mesial frontal motor areas during ideation and movement using functional resonance imaging at 1.5 tesla. *Annals of Neurology, 35,* 746–749.

Ungerleider, L.G., & Mishkin, M. (1982). Two cortical visual systems. In D.J. Ingle, M.A. Goodale and R.J.W. Mansfield (Eds.), *Analysis of visual behaviour* (pp. 549–586). Cambridge, MA: MIT Press.

Wada, J., & Rasmusssen, T. (1960). Intracarotid injection of sodium amytal for the lateralisation of cerebral speech dominance. *Journal of Neurosurgery, 17,* 266–282.

Wallesch, C.W., Henriksen, L., Kornhuber, H.H., & Paulson, O.B. (1985). Observations on regional cerebral blood flow in cortical and sub-cortical structures during language production in normal man. *Brain and Language, 25,* 224–233.

Warren, E.W., & Groome, D.H. (1984). Memory test performance under three different waveforms of ECT for depression. *British Journal of Psychiatry, 144,* 370–375.

Warrington, E.K. (1975). The selective impairment of semantic memory. *Quarterly Journal of Experimental Psychology, 27,* 187–199.

Warrington, E.K. (1982). Neuropsychological studies of object recognition. *Philosophical Transactions of the Royal Society of London, B298,* 15–33.

Warrington, E.K., & McCarthy, R.A. (1994). Multiple meaning systems in the brain: A case for visual semantics. *Neuropsychologia, 32,* 1465–1473.

Warrington, E.K., & Shallice, T. (1984). Category specific semantic impairments. *Brain, 107,* 829–854.

Warrington, E.K., & Taylor, A.M. (1973). The contribution of the right parietal lobe to object recognition. *Cortex, 9,* 152–164.

Warrington, E.K., & Taylor, A.M. (1978). Two categorical stages of object recognition. *Perception, 7,* 695–705.

Warrington, E.K., & Weiskrantz, L. (1970). Amnesic syndrome: Consolidation or retrieval? *Nature, 228,* 628–630.

Weintraub, S., & Mesulam, M.M. (1987). Right cerebral dominance in spatial attention. *Archives of Neurology, 44,* 621–625.

Wernicke, C. (1874). *Der Aphasische Symptomenkomplexe.* Breslau, Poland: Cohn and Weigert.

Weschler, D. (1981). *Manual for the Wechsler Adult Intelligence Scale–revised.* San Antonio, TX: Psychological Corporation.

Whitlow, S.D., Althoff, R.R., & Cohen, N.J. (1995). Deficit in relational (declarative) memory in amnesia. *Society for Neuroscience Abstracts, 21,* 754.

Wichmann, T., & Delong, M.R. (1996). Functional and pathophysiological models of the basal ganglia. *Current Opinion in Neurobiology, 6,* 751–758.

Wickelgren, I. (1997). Getting a grasp on working memory. *Science, 275,* 1580–1582.

Wickens, C.D. (1980). The structure of attentional resources. In R. Nickerson and R. Pew (Eds.), *Attention and performance VIII* (pp. 87–113). Hillsdale, NJ: Lawrence Erlbaum and Associates Inc.

Wilson, B.A., & Wearing, D. (1995). Amnesia in a musician. In R. Campbell and M. Conway (Eds.), *Broken memories* (pp. 67–84). Oxford: Blackwell.

Wise, R., Chollet, E., Hadar, U., Friston, K., Hoffner, E., & Frackowiak, R. (1991). Distribution of cortical neural networks involved in word comprehension and word retrieval. *Brain, 114,* 1803–1817.

Woldorff, M.G., & Hillyard, S.A. (1991). Modulation of early auditory processing during selective listening to rapidly presented tones. *Electroencephalography and Clinical Neurophysiology, 79(3),* 170–191.

Wolf, S.S., Jones, D.W., Knable, M.B., Gorey, J.G., Lee, K.S., Hyde, T.M., Coppola, R., & Weinberger, D.R. (1996). Tourette syndrome: Prediction of phenotypic variation in monozygotic twins by caudate nucleus D2 receptor binding. *Science, 273,* 1225–1227.

Woodruff, P.W., Wright, I.C., Shuriquie, N., Russouw, H., Rushe, T., Howard, R.J., Graves, M., Bullmore, E.T., & Murray, R.M. (1997). Structural brain abnormalities in male schizophrenics reflect fronto-temporal dissociation. *Psychological Medicine, 27,* 1257–1266.

Woolsey, T.A., & Wann, J.R. (1976). Areal changes in mouse cortical barrels following vibrissal damage at different postnatal ages. *Journal of Comparative Neurology, 170,* 53–66.

Youdim, M.B.H., & Riederer, P. (1997). Understanding Parkinson's disease. *Scientific American, 276,* 52–59.

Zaidel, E. (1978). Auditory language comprehension in the right hemisphere following cerebral commissurotomy and hemispherectomy: A comparison with child language and aphasia. In A. Caramazza and E.B. Zurif (Eds.), *Language Acquisition and Language Breakdown: Parallels and Divergences* (pp. 229–275). Baltimore: Johns Hopkins University Press.

Zeki, S. (1980). The representation of colours in the cerebral cortex. *Nature, 284,* 412–418.

Zihl, J., VonCramon, D., & Mai, N. (1983). Selective disturbance of movement vision after bilateral brain damage. *Brain, 106,* 313–340.

Zola-Morgan, S., Squire, L.R., & Amaral, D.G. (1986). Human amnesia and the medial temporal region: Enduring memory impairment following a bilateral lesion limited to field CA1 of the hippocampus. *Journal of Neuroscience, 6,* 2950–2967.

Index

ablation 6, 17
accessory structure 57
acetylcholine (ACH) 91, 241
acetylcholine esterase (ACHE) 92
acetylcholine esterase inhibitors (ACHEIs) 92
acetylcholine receptors 91
action plans 83
action potential(s) 241
acupuncture 69
adaptation 55
afferent (sensory) neurons 243
afferent pathways 55
aggregate field 6
aiming/targeting 49
akinesia 94, 96
alcoholism 18
alexia 8, 111
alexia, acquired 169
algogens (pain inducing chemicals) 71
all or none principle 55
Alzheimer's disease 15
Alzheimer's disease, and cell loss 242
amacrine cells, of the retina 237
amnesia 136
amnesia and brain structures 137
amnesia and retrieval failure 141

amnesia, shrinkage of 148
amygdala 139
amyotrophic lateral sclerosis (ALS) 92
analgesia 68, 69
ancient Greeks 3
aneurysm 93
angular gyrus 8, 111
anomia 115
anterior cingulate 14, 88, 120
anterior cingulate, and attention 203
anterior cingulate, and pain 68
anterior cingulate, reciprocal links with the DLPFC 223
anterior commissure 42
anterior hypothalamus 88
anterior superior temporal lobe (on the left), and grammar 118
anterograde amnesia 137, 140, 147
aphasia 6, 49, 97
apperceptive agnosia 159, 161-2
apraxia 34, 52, 89
ARAS, and sleep–wake cycle 192
ARAS, tonic and phasic changes 192
arcuate fasciculus 111, 112
Aristotle 3

arousal and circadian rhythm 183
arousal, and alertness 183
ascending reticular activating system (ARAS) 57, 192
aspiration pneumonia 97
association cortex 80, 249
associative agnosia 160–3, 165
astereognosis 25, 62, 250
astrocyte(s) 237
asymmetry 32, 48
attention, and the brain 189
attention, and brain structures 192
attention, an integrated model 202
attention, LaBerge's 'triangular' model 203
attention, motoric aspects 194
attention, neuropsychological models 195
attention, as a resource 188
attention, to spatial location 186
attention, types of 182
attentional and working memory systems 189
attentional capture 203, 231
attentional resource pools 189
attentional spotlight 182, 193
auditory cortex 37
auditory ERPs to attended and non-attended stimuli 190
auditory hallucination 29
autism 49
auto-immune disease(s) 91, 92
autonomic nervous system (ANS) 243
axon hillock 240
axon(s) 57, 239

balance, sense of 54, 78, 81
Balint's syndrome 199
Balint's syndrome, and damage to the occipital-parietal borders 201
ballistic movements 81
basal ganglia 75, 81, 85, 86, 97, 246
basal ganglia functions 82
basal ganglia, and hemiplegia 93
basal ganglia, and movement 83
basal ganglia, and SMA 89
basal ganglia, regulatory function 98
basic vegetative processes 245
behaviourism 2, 9
bereitshaftpotential 86
bi-lateral symmetry 247
bi-lateral temporal lobectomy 137

bi-manual co-operation 42
binocular disparity 174
biopsy 15
block design test 40, 176
blurred vision, in MS 92
BOLD (blood oxygen level dependent) signal 23, 24
bradykinesia 96
brain damage 48
brain death 245
brain hypothesis 2, 3
brain tumours 242
brainstem 78, 79, 244
breathing 78
Broca 7
Broca's aphasia 107
Broca's area 7, 8, 112, 118, 121

callosal agenesis 41, 46
Capgras syndrome 172
carbon monoxide poisoning 162
carotid artery 17
caudate 81
cell division 242
central executive 132`
central nervous system (CNS) 55, 243, 244
central sulcus 85, 250
cerebellar functions 80
cerebellum 75, 79, 87, 245
cerebellum, and language 120
cerebellum, and PMC 88
cerebellum, intermediate zone 80
cerebellum, lateral regions 80
cerebellum, structure 79
cerebral cortex 4, 17, 69, 78, 79, 236, 244, 246
cerebral cortex, and movement 85
cerebral palsy 94
cerebral palsy, and trauma during foetal development or birth 94
choreform movements 97
choreic stage of Huntington's disease 97
cingulate gyrus 193
cingulotomy 99
clot 93
clumsiness 43
cocktail party phenomenon 183
cocktail party phenomenon, and early/late selection 184

cognitive neuropsychology approach, to language 114
cognitive neuroscience 12
cog-wheel rigidity 96
colour blindness 162
comprehension 49
concept centre 110, 111
concussion amnesia 147
conduction aphasia 7
confabulation in Korsakoff's patients 140
connectionist models 10
connectionist models of language 109
consciousness, in animals 149
consciousness, and attention 230, 231
consciousness, and self-attending 182
consciousness, stream of 131
consolidation 141
constructional skills 175
contention scheduling 221
contralateral control 85
convergence 57
converging inputs 238
coprolalia 98
corpus callosum 4, 17, 35, 41–3, 46, 248
corpus callosum, and myelination 242
Corsi block-tapping test 24, 178
cortical blindness 250
cortical column structure 249
cortical hemispheres 32
cortical maps 64
cortical receptive fields 67
cortico–bulbar pathway 78, 85
cortico–spinal pathway 85
cranial nerve(s) 78
cross-cueing 41
CT (computer tomography) 19
cytoarchitecture 17

D1 dopamine receptors 82
D2 dopamine receptors 82
declarative and non-declarative memory 131
decussation 75
dementia 20
dementia pugilistica 131
dendrite(s) 248
dentate nuclei 80
depth perception 42, 174
derailment 215
Descartes 4

design fluency 33
dichotic listening 43, 48, 184, 188
diencephalic amnesia 139
diffuse (widespread) brain damage 24
digit span 142
direct and indirect basal ganglia pathways 82, 83
disconnection 7, 172
distributed control (networks) 10
distributed control network of language 109
divergence 239
dopamine (DA) 17, 96, 241
dopaminergic 97
dorsal column medial lemniscal system 57
dorsal simultagnosia 201
dorso-lateral pre frontal cortex (DLPFC) and attention 203
dorso-lateral pre-frontal cortex (DLPFC) and the central executive 142, 214, 217
double dissociation 27, 28, 33
double dissociation, of semantic and syntactic processes 114
DSM4 99
dual-task studies 188
dysexecutive syndrome 208
dyslexia 49

echolalia 98, 112
ECT induced amnesia 147
efferent (motor) neurons 244
electroencephalography (EEG) 18
endogenous opioids, and pain 69
end-stage illness 15
engram 143
enriched environment 62
environmental dependency syndrome, and frontal damage 211
epilepsy 17, 18, 41, 172
epilepsy, and hemiplegia 93
epileptic activity 47
episodic-semantic memory distinction 135
equipotentiality 9, 10
ERP studies in attention 189, 190, 223
event-related potential (ERPs) 18, 46, 86
excitatory synapse 241
executive dysfunction, and psychiatric disorders 224
executive dysfunction, and brain mechanisms 216

executive dysfunction, domains of 208
executive dysfunction, inhibition and attention 218
executive functions, and the frontal lobes 208
experiential factors and plasticity 62
explicit-implicit taxonomy in LTM 135
exteroceptive information 56
extinction, as a test of hemineglect 198
extra-cellular fluid 241
extra-pyramidal system 75

face recognition 34, 44
faculty 7
famous faces recognition test 169
fastigial nuclei 80
figure and ground 159
finger mazes 177
Flourens 6
fluency 49
fluent aphasia 7
fMRI studies of memory function 143
focal (localised) brain damage 24
foetal tissue implants 96
forebrain 246
fovea 154
fractionation of executive functions 209
free-will, and anterior cingulate activation 222
frequency coding 240
frontal eye fields 88
frontal eye fields and voluntary gaze 194
frontal impairment in psychiatric patients 225
frontal lobe(s) 83, 86, 194, 249
frontal lobes and memory deficits 217
frontal lobes, and impairments in action control 209
frontal lobes, connections with other brain regions 208
frontal lobes, posterior gyrus of the 75
frontal lobotomy (leucotomy) 224
frozen addicts 94
functional asymmetry 51
functional brain activity 20
functional magnetic resonance imaging (fMRI) 23, 29

Galen 3
Gall 4

gamma amino butyric acid (GABA) 241
ganglia 244
gate control theory (of pain) 68
generative assembly device (GAD) 51
generator potential 55
geographic knowledge, and right-sided damage 177
Gestalt movement 9
gesture 91
glia (glial cells) 237
global aphasia 112
global depth perception 174
globus pallidus 81, 97
glucose 20
glutamate (GLU) 241
goal-oriented behaviour, in frontal patients 213
Gollin picture test 162
graded potential 55
grey matter 244
gyrus 15, 59, 247

haemorrhage 93
hair follicle receptor 56
hallucinations 28
hallucinations, and ACHIEs 92
Halstead-Reitan test battery 24
handedness 47
hard-wired 11, 63, 65
Hayling test 219
heart hypothesis 3
hemineglect 194, 197
hemineglect, and laterality 197
hemineglect, and stroke 197
hemineglect, and the 'disengage' process 197–8
hemiparesis 105
hemiplegia 86, 93
hemisphere(s) 248
hemispheric rivalry 41
herpes simplex encephalitis 115, 138
Heschl's gyrus (primary auditory cortex) 109
hippocampal commissure 42
hippocampus 139
hippocampus, and retrieval 143
hippocampus, and memory 137
Hippocrates 3
histamine 71
HM's amnesia 137

holistic analysis 45
homunculus 60, 67
hormonal factors, and lateralisation 51
horseradish peroxidase (HRP) 15
Huntington's disease 15, 97
Huntington's test, and chromosome 4, 98
hyperactivity 49
hypothalamus 245, 246

ictal focus 35
ideational apraxia 89, 91
image subtraction 22
impulsivity, of frontal patients 211
inferior colliculi 245
inferior colliculi, and orienting to auditory
    stimuli 193
inferior parietal region 174
information processing, without conscious
    awareness 232
inhibition of return 186
inhibition of return, and ERPs 190
inhibitory synapse 241
insight 108
insula 109, 123
integrity (coherence) of brain function 229
intentional tremor 80
inter-hemispheric transfer via the corpus
    callosum 42, 43, 46
interneurons 69, 238, 244
interoceptive information 56
interpositus nuclei 80
in-vivo imaging 14, 19
in-vivo imaging techniques, in language
    research 118
IQ 36, 41
IQ deficit in left handers 49

jigsaw puzzle(s) 40, 42, 44

Korsakoff's syndrome 140

lateral geniculate nucleus 154
lateral inhibition 67
lateralisation 32, 47
laterality and spatial processing 174
L-Dopa 96
left hemisphere 17, 32, 37, 39, 42, 45
left inferior parietal lobe 111
left visual field 37, 39
lesion(s) 6, 9, 17

lexicon 39, 113
lifespan changes, in the nervous system
    242
limbic system 69, 246
line orientation, and geometric relations
    175
line orientation, and right parietal damage
    175
linguistic skills in girls 50
lobectomy 33
lobes of the cortex 236
localisation of function 2, 4, 228
localising points in space 174
longitudinal fissure 248
long-term memory 134–6
Lou Gehrig's disease (ALS) 92
Luria-Nebraska test battery 24

magnetoencephalography (MEG) 19, 65
mamillary bodies 140
mamillo-thalamic tract 140
map reading 50
Marr's model of visual perception 165
mass-action 9, 10
maze learning 49
medulla 57, 245
memory, and consciousness 148
memory, relational nature of 149
meninges 18
menstrual cycle and cognition 51
mental rotation 49, 175
Mesulam's model of attention 196
meta-analysis of in-vivo language studies
    121
microglia 237
midbrain 78, 245
mid-cerebral artery 93
midline 32
mid-superior temporal gyrus 121
modularity 12, 228
modularity, and anomia 228
modulation of pain 68
modules, cortical 11, 157
motion 175
motor apraxia 91
motor cortex 78
motor neuron(s) 55, 74, 86
motor neuron disease (MND) 92
motor planning 80, 86, 87, 88–9
motor strip 85

motor trans-cortical aphasia 112
motor unit 85
MPP 94
MPTP 17, 94
MRI (magnetic resonance imaging) 20
multiple sclerosis (MS) 92
muscarinic ACh receptors 241
muscles 86
myasthenia gravis 91
myasthenia gravis, and muscle weakness 91
myelin sheath 46, 237, 244
myelin, loss in MS 92
myelinated neurons 46, 240
myelination as a developmental process 46

N1 wave 190
naloxone 69
National Adult Reading Test (NART) 25
negative priming 188
neologisms 109, 117, 123
nerve cell(s) 236
nerve impulse(s) 55, 237, 238, 240
nerve(s) 244
nervous system, the 236, 237
neuroglia 237
neurological attentional disorders 197
neurons 15, 237
neuropsychological assessment 24
neurotransmitter (substance) 15, 62, 69, 241
nicotinic ACh receptors 241
nigro–striatal pathway 82
nigro–striatal pathway, and PD 96
noradrenaline (NA) 241
norm referencing 24

object permanence 144
object recognition units 165
object-based selection 187, 188
obsessive-compulsive disorder (OCD) 99
occipital lobe(s) 158, 173, 250
oligodendrocyte 237
open head injuries 6
optic nerve 244
optical aphasia 165
organic amnesia(s) 148
orienting response 183
osmoreceptors 88

P100 wave 190
P300 wave 191, 194
P300 wave and parieto-temporal regions 194
Pacinian corpuscle(s) 55, 57
pain 54, 68
pain and psychological factors 69
pain pathways 69
pain receptors 57
paralysis 3
paraphasias 109
paraplegia 93
parietal damage, and disengagement 196
parietal involvement in movement 75, 85, 89, 91
parietal lobe(s) 59, 61, 87, 173, 250
parietal lobes, and attention 194
parietal lobes, and visuo-spatial processing 250
Parkinsonism 94
Parkinson's disease (PD) 17, 94
Parkinson's disease, and cell loss 243
Parkinson's disease, positive and negative symptoms 95
percept 158, 159, 160, 173
periaqueductal grey area (PAG) 69
peripheral and spinal movement disorders 91
peripheral nervous system (PNS) 243
perseveration 97
perseveration, and frontal damage 210
PET (positron emission tomography) 20, 28–9
PET and memory research 143
PET studies of prosopagnosia 170
phantom limb experiences 54, 65
Phineas Gage 219
phoneme(s) 52, 113
phonological loop 132
phonology 113
phrenology 4, 5, 6
placebo analgesia 69
plasticity 47, 62
Plato 3
poliomyelitis 92
pons 78, 245
Posner's model of visual attention 196
posterior attentional network 196
posterior medial temporal gyrus (Brodmann area 37) 111, 112, 120

posterior parietal cortex 174
post-mortem 7, 15
post-mortem studies, of PD 96
posture 81
pragmatics 113
pre-attentive mechanisms 186
pre-frontal cortex 88, 89
pre-motor cortex (PMC) 80, 86, 87, 88
pre-vocabulary speech 104
primary auditory cortex (Heschl's gyrus) 251
primary motor cortex or motor strip 75, 78, 79, 85, 86–9, 249
primary sensory cortex 249
primary somatosensory cortex (S1) 75, 250
primary visual cortex 17
processing styles 44, 45
prosodic speech 126
prosopagnosia 166
prosopagnosia, and the brain 170
prosopagnosia, and brain damage 172
pseudo-depression 225
pseudo-psychopathy 225
pseudo-psychopathy, and disconnection 220
psychoanalysis 10
psychogenic amnesia 131
psycholinguistics 112
psychological inertia, and frontal damage 209
psychological treatments for OCD 99
psychosurgery for intractable disorders 225
pulvinar region, of the thalamus 193
putamen 81
putamen, in PD 96
pyramidal cell(s) 85, 248
pyramidal system 75

quadriplegia 93

Raederscheidt, Anton 198
Raphe nucleus 69
reafference (in phantom limb syndrome) 68
recency judgements, in frontal patients 214
receptive field(s) 158
receptor potential 55
receptor site(s) 15, 241
recovery of function 93

red nucleus 78, 80
reflex arc 55
regional cerebral blood flow (rCBF) 20, 89
resting tremor 96
retrograde amnesia 137–9, 141, 147
retrograde amnesia, and the 'famous faces' test 140
re-uptake 241
reversed asymmetry 48
Rey-Osterreith complex figure 176
right ear advantage 43
right hemisphere 32, 37, 39, 44, 48
right visual field 37
road map test 177
rods and cones 55
route-finding 40, 50, 177
rubrospinal pathway 78

S1 (in a monkey) 64
S2 61
schizophrenia 18, 172
Schwann cell(s) 237
scotomas 162
secondary memory 131
seizures 35
selective attention 182
selective serotonin re-uptake inhibitors (SSRIs) and OCD 99
self-monitoring, and frontal damage 214
semantic memory 135
semantics 113
sensation versus perception 154
sensory nerves 4
sensory receptors 55
sensory transcortical aphasia 112
sequential planning 213, 214
serotonin (5HT) 69, 71, 241
serotonin, and OCD 99
sex differences 49
shadowing procedure 184
shaking palsy 95
silent synapses 67
silver-staining 15
single dissociation 27
single photon emission computerised tomography (SPECT) 22, 89
skeletal nervous system 243
skilled movements 88
sneezing 78

somatosensation 54
somatosensory cortex 59, 62, 85
somatosensory pathways 57
somatosensory strip (S1) 61
soul, location of 4
spatial attention and spatial working memory 203
spatial functions and the 'where' stream 173
spatial memory 174, 178
spatial orientation 34
spatial processing, and the left hemisphere 178
spatial skills 32
spatial skills, and the right parietal lobe 177
speech apraxia 123
spinal cord 57, 86, 92, 236, 244
spinal cord, segment 55
spinal damage 93
spinal reflexes 93
spino-thalamic tracts 57
spiny interneurons 97
split-brain syndrome 36, 41
Spurzheim 4
stimulus-driven behaviour 211
striatum 17, 81, 97
striatum, and OCD 99, 100
striatum, dopamine and ACH balance 96
strict localisation of function 4, 10
strict localisationist theory of brain-language function 120
stroke 7, 85, 139
Stroop test, and anterior cingulate 194, 218
stutter 49
substance P 71
substantia gelatinosa (and pain) 57, 68, 69
substantia nigra 17, 81, 97
subthalamic nucleus 81
subtraction logic 22, 119
sulcus 15, 47
summation, of influences on a post-synaptic neuron 242
sunburn 68
superior colliculi 192, 245
superior colliculi, and express saccades 192
superior temporal gyrus (on the left) and comprehension 124

superior temporal gyrus 105
superior temporal sulcus and faces 170
supervisory attention system 133, 220
supervisory attentional system and anterior cingulate gyrus 221
supplementary motor area (SMA) 86, 112
supplementary motor area (SMA) 88, 89
supra nuclear palsy 193
supramarginal gyrus 111
synapse(s) 15, 55
synaptic cleft 241
synaptic transmission 91, 237–8, 241,
synaptogenesis 243
syndactyly 64, 65
syntactic 113
syntax 113

Tan 7, 105
tapping test 24
tectum 57
telegraphic speech 107
telemetry 232
temperature sensitivity 54
temporal lobe(s) 7, 250
temporal lobectomy 33
temporal lobes, and object recognition 251
temporal resolution 23, 24
terminal bouton 241
thalamus 81, 193, 245
tics 98
Token Test 39
tool use 52
topographic representation (in mouse brain) 63
topographic representation 18, 59, 60, 64
Tourette's syndrome 98
Tower of London puzzle 214
tract(s) 244
trails test 25
transcutaneous electrical nerve stimulation (TENS) 69
transduction 55, 56, 57
transient aphasia 124
translation skills 49

ultra-sound 47
uni-lateral neurological damage 32
unusual views of objects 163

utilisation behaviour 211
utilisation behaviour, and failure of
  inhibition 219

V2 173
V3 173
V5 (mid-temporal sulcus or MT) 173–4
V7 174
ventral stream 159, 173
ventral tract 78
ventro–medial pathway 78
verbal and non-verbal estimates of IQ
  25
verbal fluency 26, 33
vermis 79–80
vesicle(s) 241
vestibular nuclei 78
vigilance and sustained attention 183
visual agnosia 159
visual attention 185
visual orienting 186
visual search, and conjunctive targets
  185
visual tracking 49
visuo-spatial scratch pad 132
visuo-spatial skills 50

visuo-spatial tasks 40, 49
vocabulary 49
voluntary gaze 88

Wada test 17, 48
Warrington's facial recognition memory
  test 167
Wechsler Adult Intelligence Scale revised
  (WAISR) 25
Wernicke 7
Wernicke's aphasia 107, 109, 123–4
Wernicke's area 8, 111, 123–4
'what' and 'where' streams 155
whisker barrel 63
white matter 244
Wisconsin card sort test (WCST) 25
Wisconsin card sort test (WCST), and
  frontal damage 211
Wisconsin card sort test, modified version
  213
working memory 23, 27, 131, 132
working memory and executive control
  203
working memory processes and language
  125
working memory, imaging studies 144